Number Forty-nine
Number Fifty
Number Fifty-one
Number Fifty-two

Edited by
Wayne Rice
and
Tim McLaughlin
Illustrations by
Robert Suggs

ISBN 0-910125-37-6 (Ideas Combo 49–52)
ISBN 0-910125-00-7 (Ideas Complete Library, Volumes 1–52)

1224 Greenfield Drive, El Cajon, Ca 92021
619/440-2333

Ideas in this book have been voluntarily submitted by individuals and groups who claim to have used them in one form or another with their youth groups. Before you use an idea, evaluate it for its suitability to your own groups, for any potential risks, for safety precautions that must be taken, and for advance preparation that may be required. Youth Specialties, Inc., is not responsible for, nor has it any control over, the use or misuse of any of the ideas published in this book.

There are lots more ideas where these came from.

This book is only one of an entire library of ***Ideas*** volumes that are available from Youth Specialties. Each volume is completely different and contains tons of tried and tested programming ideas submitted by the world's most creative youth workers. Order the others by using the form below.

Combo Books

52 volumes of ***Ideas*** have been updated and republished in four-volume combinations. For example, our combo book ***Ideas 1-4*** is actually four books in one—volumes 1 through 4. These combos are a bargain at $19.95 each (that's 50% off!).

The Entire Library

The ***Ideas*** Library includes every volume and an index to volumes 1-52. See the form below for the current price, or call the Youth Specialties Order Center at 800/776-8008.

SAVE UP TO 50%!

IDEAS ORDER FORM (or call 800/776-8008)

COMBOS
($19.95 each)

- ❑ Ideas 1-4
- ❑ Ideas 5-8
- ❑ Ideas 9-12
- ❑ Ideas 13-16
- ❑ Ideas 17-20
- ❑ Ideas 21-24
- ❑ Ideas 25-28
- ❑ Ideas 29-32
- ❑ Ideas 33-36
- ❑ Ideas 37-40
- ❑ Ideas 41-44
- ❑ Ideas 45-48
- ❑ Ideas 49-52

SINGLES
($9.95 each)

- ❑ Ideas 53
- ❑ Ideas 54
- ❑ Index to volumes 1-52

❑ **Entire Ideas Library**—54 volumes and Index (volumes 1-52) for only $199.95 (regularly $289—save over 30%!)

SHIPPING CHARGES	
ORDER SUBTOTAL	ADD
$ 1.00- 9.99	$3
$ 10.00- 24.99	$4
$ 25.00- 49.99	$6
$ 50.00- 74.99	$7
$ 75.00- 99.99	$9
$ 100.00 AND UP	$10

PAYMENT METHOD:

❑ Check or money order enclosed. (Calif. residents add 7% sales tax; S.C. residents add 5% sales tax)

❑ Credit card: ❑ Visa ❑ MasterCard Acct. # ______________________

Name on card: ______________________ Exp. __________

❑ Please bill me. (Shipping charges plus a 5% billing fee will be added to the total)

NAME ______________________________________

CHURCH OR ORG. (if applicable) ______________________________________

STREET ADDRESS ______________________________________

CITY ____________________ STATE ________ ZIP ____________

DAYTIME PHONE (______) ______________________________________

Clip and mail to Youth Specialties, P.O. Box 4406, Spartanburg, SC 29305-4406
or call 800/776-8008

Prices subject to change

Your Idea May Be Worth $100

It's worth at least $25 if we publish it in a future volume of ***Ideas***. And it's worth $100 if it's chosen as the outstanding idea of the book it appears in.

It's not really a contest, though—just our way of saying thanks for sharing your creativity with us. If you have a good idea that worked well with your group, send it in. We'll look it over and decide whether or not we can include it in a future ***Ideas*** book. If we do, we'll send you at least 25 bucks!

In addition to that, the ***Ideas*** editor will select one especially creative idea from each new book as the outstanding idea of that particular book—and send a check for $100 to its contributor.

So don't let your good ideas go to waste. Write them down and send them to us, accompanied by this form. Explain your ideas completely (without getting ridiculous) and include illustrations, diagrams, photos, samples, or any other materials you think are helpful.

Fill out below

Name ______________________________

Address ______________________________

City ______________ State __ Zip ________

Phone (_____) ______________________

Write or type your idea(s) (one idea per sheet) and attach it to this form or to a copy of this form. Include your name and address with each idea you send. Mail to Ideas, 1224 Greenfield Drive, El Cajon, CA 92021. Ideas submitted to Youth Specialties cannot be returned.

Ideas Combo 49–52

CONTENTS

Best Comic of the Week

Ask the kids to read the newspaper's comics in the coming week and bring the ones they think are the funniest. At the beginning of the next meeting, allow them to read aloud the comics they've brought. Then ask the group to vote for the best comic strip and post it on the bulletin board.

To add an element of competition, explain that the way you will decide which comic strip to post is by how many kids bring in that particular comic strip. If more kids bring in the "Peanuts" strip from Tuesday than any other comic, for instance, those kids and that comic win. The fun, however, is in reading each strip and laughing (or groaning) together. (Contributed by Mark A. Simone, Ravenna, Ohio)

Chain Reaction

Give each person an 8½ x 11-inch sheet of paper, each sheet with a different question at the top. The question—marked with the number 1—may come either from the following list or from your own collection.

- What is the most enjoyable part of the day for you?
- What would you consider to be your greatest accomplishment?
- What is it about you that your mother or father brags about the most?
- Which TV show do you watch the most?
- Have you ever played a musical instrument?
- Do you know any good jokes? Tell me one.
- What do you like about school?
- Where have you been that no one else in the room has been?
- What is the most beautiful thing you have?
- What is your favorite seasonal activity?
- Where were you born?
- What were you for Halloween this year?

- What is your favorite book?
- Where is your favorite place to eat?
- What percentage of the Bible would you say you have read?
- What is your motto for your life?

Now follow these steps to create your own chain reaction:

• Everyone mingles and pairs up. Each pair asks each other their question 1 from their own sheets. They needn't write down the answer—just listen.

• Then the partners copy each other's question 1 to their own sheets and number it 2.

• Now everyone mingles again and finds new partners. They ask their new partners **the question they just copied onto their sheet from the latest partner.** They all listen to each others' answers, then copy their new partner's question 1 to their own sheets and label it 3.

• Rule of thumb: **Always ask the last question on the list, and always copy the first question.** (Contributed by John Morgan, Caldwell, N.J.)

Connect-a-Name

This get-acquainted activity uses only a large piece of paper and a magic marker. Form teams of four to six people each. For round one, at a signal each team attempts to connect every team member's first name in one crossword puzzle (see diagram) in the shortest amount of time. For round two combine two teams and play it again. Continue playing rounds until all are in one big team and making a crossword puzzle of all the names. Display the final crossword during a Bible study on 1 Corinthians 12 to illustrate that all Christians are part of the same body. (Contributed by Michael W. Capps, East Flat Rock, N.C.)

```
   KYLE
   E
  EVA
   I   J
   NELLIE
         L
         LANCE
```

Football Frenzy

To break the ice at a fall meeting or during the Super Bowl season, or as a preliminary to "Teddy Bear Football" (see page 58), hand out to each player a game sheet on page 9 listing various activities. The object is to be the first person to complete in front of a witness each activity on the game sheet and get the signature of the witness beside the activity entry. Each of the 15 tasks must be signed by a different witness. (Contributed by Steve Smoker, Raleigh, N.C.)

FOOTBALL FRENZY

RECRUITING YOUR TEAM

_________ 1. Recruit three people to join you in yelling one of the following: "We love the Dallas Cowboys" or "We hate the Dallas Cowboys." Request each person in your group to sign your game sheet.

SPRING TRAINING

_________ 2. Enlist someone to time you while you run in place for ten seconds.

_________ 3. Recruit two people to perform four jumping jacks with you, counting out loud.

_________ 4. If you are a guy, find a girl with blue eyes and ask her, "Will you cheer for me today in the big game?" If you are a girl, find a guy with brown eyes and ask him, "Can I cheer for you in the big game today?" Get both the signature and telephone number of the person you talk to.

THE BIG GAME

_________ 5. In a huddle with two other people, stack your hands on top of each other's and yell, "Go team!"

_________ 6. Persuade someone to gently tackle you.

_________ 7. Run up to someone you do not know well and say, "Put me in the game, Coach!" Be sure to get your "coach's" signature.

HALF TIME

_________ 8. You are in the band performing at half time. Persuade someone to watch you pretend to play the trombone as you march from the back of the room to the front. Hum your school song as you march. Don't forget to ask your fan to sign your game sheet.

_________ 9. Lead another player in any cheer you know. If you can't think of a cheer, try this one: "Two, four, six, eight. Who do we appreciate?" Then yell the name of your youth pastor.

_________ 10. Run up to a person of the opposite sex and say, "Please put me in, Coach!"

_________ 11. Wad this paper into a ball. Ask someone to hike it to you and then run out to receive your pass. Throw the wad to the person. If either of you drops the wad of paper, you must repeat the activity. Then smooth out your paper for your receiver to sign.

_________ 12. Wow! You just scored the winning touchdown. Find a leader and give the leader ten (slap hands with the leader) while yelling, "I scored the winning touchdown!"

BIG GAME WRAP-UP

_________ 13. Greet a friend and say, "I'm famous now! Can I give you my autograph?" Sign your friend's game sheet.

_________ 14. It's time to go to the locker room to change from your cleats to your shoes. Persuade another player to watch you take off your shoes and then put them on the wrong feet.

_________ 15. Report to the person conducting this game. If you are the first, second, or third person to complete the sheet, prepare yourself to win a prize!

Mangled Maxims

On page 11 is a list of verbose maxims. Supply directions that fit your own event and group (for example, "In groups of five, figure out the common version of each of the following sayings"), photocopy the page for everyone, and have fun with them! (Contributed by John E. Morgan, Caldwell, N.J.)

Nose Names

Here's a variation of Who Am I?, in which celebrities' names are pinned to the backs of players; players must guess who "they" are by asking yes or no questions of other players. In "Nose Names," the celebrity name is written on a file-folder label and stuck to the player's nose. (Contributed by Rob Marin, Whittier, Calif.)

Swinging Marshmallow

Pair up the kids (player A and player B) and give each pair a four-foot-long piece of string and two marshmallows. At a signal the pairs tie one marshmallow on each end of the string. Player A in each pair holds one marshmallow in her mouth while standing and facing the front of the room. Player B stands to the side of player A at an arm's length, looking toward player A.

Moving only her head, player A begins to swing the string back and forth like a pendulum while player B attempts to catch the swinging marshmallow in his mouth. Player B may move only his head. The winner is the first pair in which player B catches the marshmallow. (Contributed by Greg Miller, Knoxville, Tenn.)

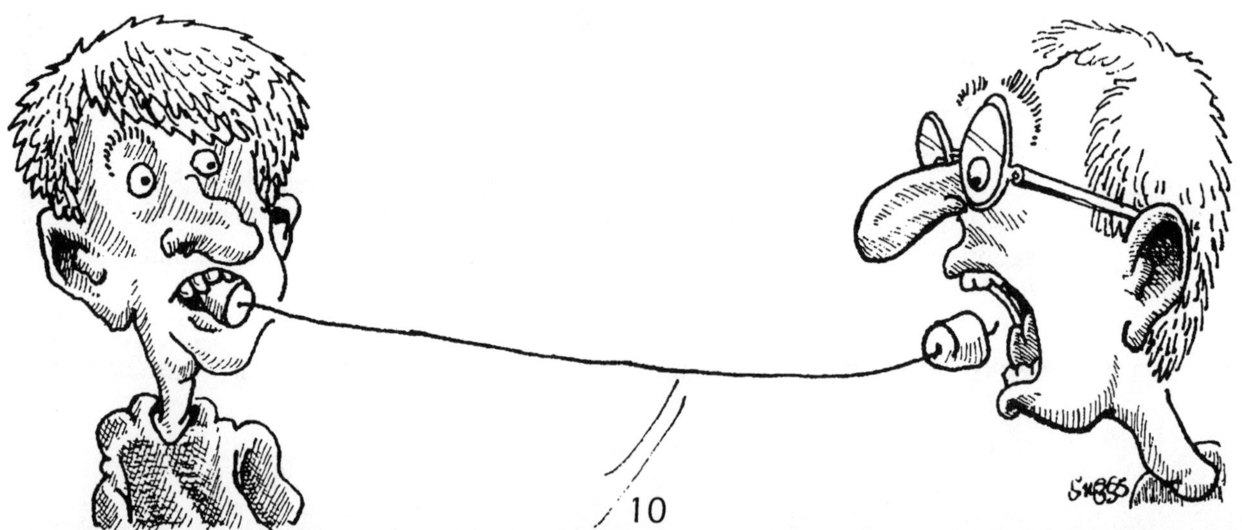

Mangled Maxims

1. Splintered wood and mineral chunks can rupture my skeletal system, but nomenclatures do not impair me.
2. Swab your dentures tri-daily.
3. A needle-and-thread mark in hours passed hoards eight plus one.
4. Do not traverse the gantry until you approach it.
5. Offspring should be endowed with visibility but not oral facilities.
6. Hemoglobin is more viscous in consistency than H_2O.
7. Pulchritude pertains solely to the epidermis.
8. If primary failure is imminent, new attempts should be made repetitiously.
9. The most prompt feathered biped seizes the annelid.
10. Perambulate in moccasins and shoulder a gargantuan wooden rail.
11. Focus your optical apparatus on the spheroid.
12. A maximum of toil and a minimum of disport and dalliance causes Jack to become a dim-witted, stagnant dunce of the young male species.
13. That which is acquired without difficulty is dispersed with equal facility.
14. A red fruit of the Malus genus absorbed into the digestive system every 1440 minutes keeps a medical practitioner from entering the ridge pole of home sweet home.
15. Individuals continuing daily functions surrounded by fused sand structures should be forbidden to hurl missiles.
16. Refrain from enumerating your poultry prior to their emergence from calcified enclosures.
17. A moving and twirling rock picks up no green matter.
18. Departure causes the blood-pumping organ to become more loveable and liked.
19. Distant meadows are inevitably more verdant.
20. Dissipate not needlessly, and impoverishment will not be your destiny.
21. Do not shed tears over a white liquid that has become earthbound.
22. Everything is justified in intense liking and in combat or battle.
23. It is not possible to both retain your Angel Food or Devil's Food and consume it.
24. Grab and obtain it, or set it down and release it.
25. View with your optical organs prior to jumping with great steps.
26. A pan under constant scrutiny will never reach 212 degrees F.

Twenty Trifles

Pair kids up with those they don't know well, distribute copies of page 13, and then instruct them to discover from each other the obscure facts asked for on the sheet. Players write down their partners' responses. (Contributed by Keith Curran, Titusville, Fla.)

Which of Us Am I?

Create a questionnaire that pulls out of kids little-known facts about themselves: favorite food, birth month and day, birth city, color of eyes, favorite vacation spot, favorite character in the Bible, favorite TV show, someone admired, favorite color, color of hair, favorite season of the year, one thing valued in life, hobby or interest (one that most of the group doesn't know about), favorite song, a world problem they consider significant.

As kids arrive, hand out the questionnaires on page 14 for them to fill out—**but without including their names**. When all the sheets are completed, shuffle them and then tape them at random on the backs of the players. During this part of the crowd breaker, players attempt to guess their new identities by asking other players yes-and-no questions about the information on their backs.

When players believe they know their "Guess Who?" identities, they remove the sheet from their backs, write their own names at the top and their new identities at the bottom, and turn them in. Number the sheets in the order they are received, since winners are the **first** three or four who correctly guess who they were. When all the sheets are collected, read through them one by one, allowing the entire group to guess whom the sheet is describing. Then ask the person it actually describes to stand. Award prizes to the three or four winners. (Contributed by Tommy Baker, Florence, Ky.)

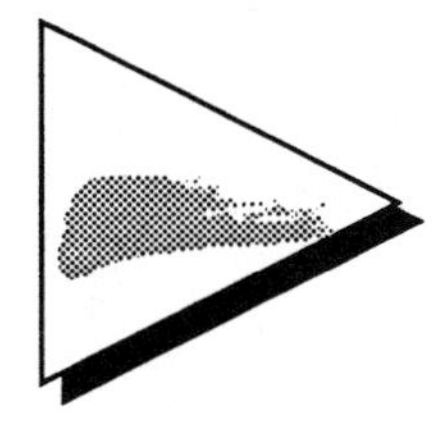

Twenty Trifles

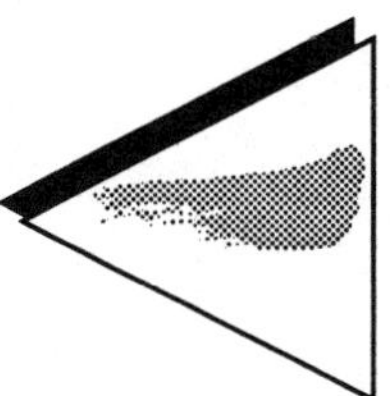

_______________ Favorite month of the year

_______________ The worst radio station, in your opinion

_______________ Your shoe size

_______________ Grandparents' first names

_______________ The longest time you ever went steady

_______________ Have you ever driven a car?

_______________ Do you like scavenger hunts?

_______________ What you like most about Jesus

_______________ What food you'd most likely order at McDonald's

_______________ Your mother's maiden name

_______________ Favorite place to sit in church

_______________ Favorite biblical character

_______________ Name of P.E. teacher

_______________ Place of your birth

_______________ Color of socks you're wearing

_______________ Favorite flavor of ice cream

_______________ Favorite drink

_______________ Have you ever hit a home run?

_______________ Do you like veggies?

_______________ Show me, if you can, a scar. (Write down its location.)

Which of Us Am I?

Directions: If you're the one describing yourself by writing answers to these questions, do not sign your name. Sign your own name here when you've guessed your "Guess Who?" identity.

Birth month and day

Your city (address)

Color of eyes

Favorite vacation spot

Favorite character in the Bible

Favorite TV show

One person who has had a great influence on you (other than family member)

Favorite color

One thing you really value in life

Color of hair

Favorite season of the year

Hobby/interest (one that most don't know)

Favorite song

One thing you really value in life

A world problem that concerns you

Sign your "Guess Who?" identity here when you've guessed it.

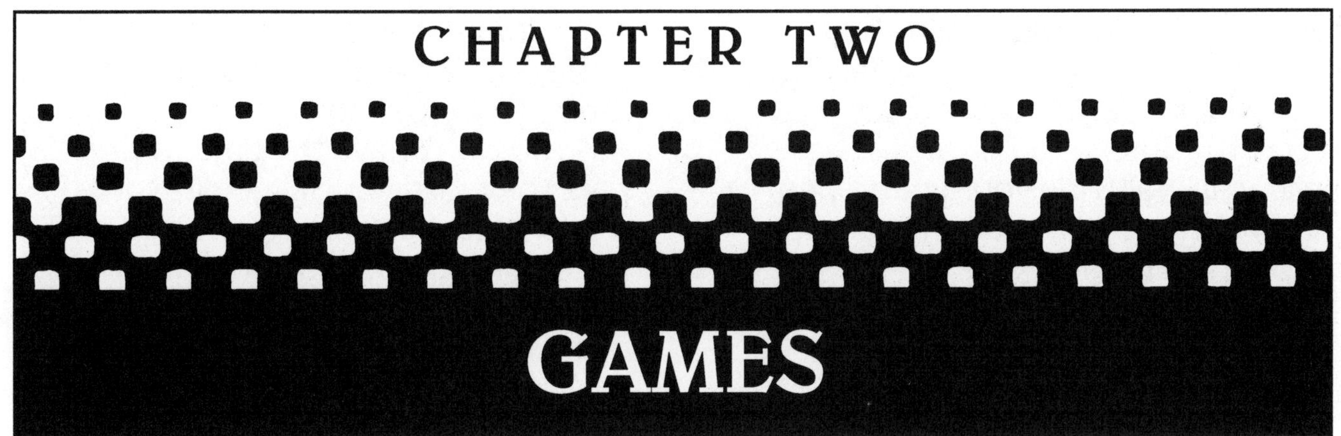

Balloon Balance Relay

Form teams and give each team **one** baseball cap or painter's cap. The first player from each team dons the cap and balances an inflated balloon on the bill (bouncing on the bill is permitted). The players then walk to a point 10 feet away and back again while balancing the balloon on their hats. Then, using their hands, they pass the balloon and hat to the next players in line, who do the same thing.

A player whose balloon falls to the floor or is held up by any part of the body has to start over. (No fair blowing on the balloon to keep it in place.) The first team whose players all complete the circuit are declared the uncontested balloon balance relay champions of the world. (Contributed by Michael Frisbie, Hobbs, N. Mex.)

Beef Jerky Chew

Place a package of beef jerky on a table 10 feet in front of three volunteers. On a signal the volunteers race to the table, grab a piece of jerky, and eat it as quickly as possible. The one whose mouth is completely empty first is the winner. (Contributed by Amy Zuberbuhler, Pittsburgh, Pa.)

Box Maze

A good substitute for a haunted house, this maze makes an exciting event around Halloween—but it works for any "A-Maze-ing Nite" on your calendar.

Solicit donations of refrigerator boxes from a box company, appliance and furniture stores, or your kids' neighborhoods. After you've collected at least 40 boxes, start plotting your maze. Remove all staples from the boxes to avoid injuring the kids or ruining their clothing. Insert the end of one box into another, and tape the seams well. A series of four-way intersections, T intersections, and dead ends will challenge your young people as they crawl through the maze on their hands and knees.

Before the kids come into the room containing the maze, turn out the lights so they can't picture how the maze goes. Station volunteers inside the maze with a flashlight in case any problems occur. Send kids through in groups of three or four, and assure them that there's someone inside the maze with a flashlight ready to assist them if they call out.

If you don't have the time to prepare the maze yourself, enlist some students to create the maze and staff it. Seniors, for example, delight in subjecting younger unfortunates to rigors of any kind. Or you can use the maze as a springboard for discussing God's guidance, decision making, fear, or walking in darkness. (Contributed by Elliott Cooke, Nanuet, N.Y.)

Buckle Up Relay

You'll need one bench seat per team for this game (the van variety, with seat belts attached); the removable seats from mini-vans work fine. Place the bench seats at a starting line. At a designated distance mark a finish line. Divide the kids into two (or more) groups. Place half of each team at the starting line and the other half at the finish line.

Instruct the first three at the starting line on each team to belt themselves into the van seats. On "Go!" the three belted-in players of each team stand to their feet and lumber toward the finish line, lugging the bench seat with them. When they arrive at the far line, they set the seat down, release the seat belts, and the second set of three strap themselves in and race back. Play continues until one team wins by releasing the belts of the final three racing members of the team. (Contributed by Jerry Meadows, Palmyra, Pa.)

Bunny Buster

Play this relay with small party balloons and teams of ten—five girls and five guys. The guys on each team line up on one side of the room, and the girls about 35 feet away on the other side of the room. The first guy in each team is handed a balloon, which he must inflate as quickly as possible without stretching it first. Once he's blown it up, he carries it in his mouth, without using his hands, to the girl opposite him. She removes it from his mouth with her hands, not letting any air out, and holds it on the floor without tying it. The guy must sit on the balloon and break it. Once he breaks it, he runs back and tags the next guy in line, and the cycle starts over.

Not only is it hilarious watching the guys try to blow up the balloons without stretching them, but sometimes the balloon escapes as they race to the girls or the now slobbery end of the balloon slips out of the girls' fingers or the guy smashes the girl's hand when he tries to pop the balloon or...well, you try it! (Contributed by Keith King, Whittier, Calif.)

Candy Quiz

Hand out the quiz on page 18 as an individual challenge or a small-group project. Each phrase is a clue to the name of a candy bar. (Contributed by Roger Haas, Grand Prairie, Tex.)

Candy Quiz Answers:
1. Musketeers
2. Twix
3. Mounds
4. Milky Way
5. Red Hots
6. Mars
7. Hollywood
8. O'Henry
9. Snickers
10. Butterfinger
11. M & M's
12. Clark Bar
13. Baby Ruth
14. 5th Avenue
15. Kiss
16. Payday
17. Slow Poke
18. Black Cow
19. Junior Mints
20. Milk Duds
21. Bit-o-Honey
22. Almond Joy
23. Reese's Pieces
24. Sweet Tarts
25. Rolos

Carnival Concentration

For this variation of the TV game show "Concentration," ask one of the kids with artistic flair to create a Concentration-style puzzle to put on a bulletin board. The puzzle could be a common expression, a line from a popular song, the title from a TV show or movie, or a verse of Scripture. Then tape inflated balloons over the entire puzzle using clear tape.

When it's time to play, break the group into two or three teams. Teams take turns throwing darts at the balloons. When a player pops a balloon, that player's team gets fifteen seconds to try to solve the puzzle. A team can only guess the puzzle when one of its members has popped a balloon. The winning team is the first to successfully solve the puzzle. (Contributed by Jim Bell, Hamilton, Ohio)

Candy Quiz

1. A famous swashbuckling trio of old ____________________
2. Elmer Fudd's slight-of-hand or magical maneuvers ____________________
3. Places of interring enemies of those who tend and drive cattle and who are usually mounted on domesticated, large solid-hoofed, herbivorous mammals ____________________
4. A broad, luminous, irregular band of astral lights that encompasses the stellar sphere ____________________
5. Crimson-colored libidinous cravings ____________________
6. A celestial body fourth in order from the sun, conspicuous for the redness of its light; its planetary symbol is ♂ ____________________
7. The hard fibrous xylem substance produced by the Aquifoliaceae family of shrubs and trees, characterized by their thick, glossy, spiny-margined leaves and usually bright red berries ____________________
8. Author William Sidney Porter's pseudonym ____________________
9. Multiple expressions of mirth, joy, or scorn in a covert or suppressed manner ____________________
10. An idiom, used here singularly, employed to describe one whose dexterous deficiency denies proficiency in getting a grip on goods ____________________
11. Possessive clone alphabetical characters ____________________
12. A saloon named after the newspaper-reporter alias of a superhero ____________________
13. Childhood name of a former renowned baseball player whose strike-out record is recondite ____________________
14. Celebrated street in the Big Apple ____________________
15. Labial massage ____________________
16. The 24-hour part of the week set aside to compensate for labor or toil ____________________
17. A sluggish jab ____________________
18. Ebony-colored country critter ____________________
19. Subordinate spices or seasonings ____________________
20. Lactic flops ____________________
21. A morsel of regurgitated sweet viscid material from the social and colonial hymenopterous insect ____________________
22. The jubilant sensation of an ellipsoidal and edible nut ____________________
23. Label on the body bag containing the remains collected after a cat named "Reese" was run over by a mower ____________________
24. Dissonant confectionery mixture of dulcet and piquant seasonings ____________________
25. To rotate several members of the cylindrical-shaped component of the vowel family ____________________

Centipede Relay

Form equal teams of six to eight kids each and line up, alternating boy-girl. Instruct teams to back up to the wall at one end of the room, leaving three to four feet between the last person and the wall.

On a signal each team must take three short steps forward. As soon as the team has moved forward the last step, the first players in the lines break away to the right and run around their team three times as fast as possible, finally taking their place at the back of their team's line. Once in place, the runner yells, "Go!" and the process repeats with three more steps and new front runners.

The relay continues until the line itself arrives at the youth leader standing at the other end of the room, or crosses a line drawn on the floor.

(The room need not be large, since teams don't need that much room to move forward. They mainly need room on the sides of the lines to run around their teams without bumping into the competition. For every three steps forward, the team loses one body-space backwards as the runner takes his place at the end of the line.)

As a true test of speed and skill, each person tries to run around the team faster and faster. The key to winning this relay, however, is for everyone to press as close as possible to the people in front and behind them. To make each line tighter, instruct players to grasp hold of the waist of the ones standing directly in front of them. (The kids may feel awkward doing this at first, but they'll comply as soon as they see their team losing the race.)

Be sure to point out that each person on the team may have to run several times in order for the entire team to reach the marker at the other end of the room. Also point out that the three short steps must be **short**. Demonstrate how they can move forward by simply placing one foot directly in front of the other and moving. (Contributed by Michael Capps, East Flat Rock, N.C.)

Church Scavenger Hunt

Besides getting to run all over the church facilities, the kids on this hunt learn about their church by searching for answers to questions in order to win the game. Groups of two to three kids (who cannot split up to speed their investigation) must search out answers to questions like the following:

- What translation of the Bible is in the pews?
- What does the first window on the left of the pulpit show?
- What is the office phone number?
- Who is the custodian?
- What kind of piano is in the Sunday school?
- What date is on the cornerstone?
- How many choir robes are hanging up?

The winning team is the first to fill in their sheet with correct answers within the time limit. (Contributed by Lyn Wargny, Palmyra, N.J.)

Closet Caper

Here's a twist on "Dressing in the Dark" (**Ideas 49**). Fill two boxes with the same number of similar articles of clothing such as loud boxer shorts, wigs, suspenders, huge nightgowns, crazy hats, sunglasses, jewelry, and maybe some unmentionables.

Blindfold two contestants, who will compete to be the first to correctly put on all the items in the boxes in front of them. When the winner is declared, remove the blindfolds and provide a long mirror for participants to view their startling fashion statements. Be sure to take lots of pictures of the process and the end results. (Contributed by Sondra Edwards, Boone, N.C.)

Community Bowl

Next time your group goes bowling, turn it into a community-building event. The team objective is not only to bowl a high score, but to find out 10 new or interesting things about each person in the group.

Randomly assign four people to a lane, with no more than one adult per lane. Ask the teams to list their names not only on the front of the score sheet, but across the top of the back of the score sheet as well. Beneath each name on the back, number from 1 to 10 to record the answers to questions.

During the line of bowling, team members take turns asking each other questions about small but significant details in their histories, tastes, habits, etc. Once a question has been asked, that question cannot be asked again within that group. Teams receive one point for each answer with a maximum of 40 bonus points possible. Larger teams may simply ask fewer questions per person to receive their 40 bonus points.

When the teams have finished a round, they combine their bowling scores with their bonus points. The team with the highest combined score wins. Your group will get so caught up in finding out things about each other that they may forget who is next to bowl. (Contributed by Tommy Baker, Florence, Ky.)

Crazy Baseball

Create teams of five or more players. With a Nerf Ball and bat, play like regular baseball. Here's the crazy part: after a hit, batters can run to **any** base—but they cannot run through the pitcher's circle. Base runners score not by touching home plate, but by touching all three bases—first, second, and third—though in any order. Teams get six outs. (Contributed by David Killinger and Chris Moore, Aurora, Colo.)

Connect Four

For this intimate relay either divide a large group into teams of five or six pairs, or ask the entire group to pair up and form a line of pairs. The first pair places a rubber playground ball between them at stomach level. To help keep the ball from falling and to help maintain balance, the two players place their hands on each others' shoulders. At a signal the next pair in line, in the same stance, tries to get the rubber ball from the first pair not

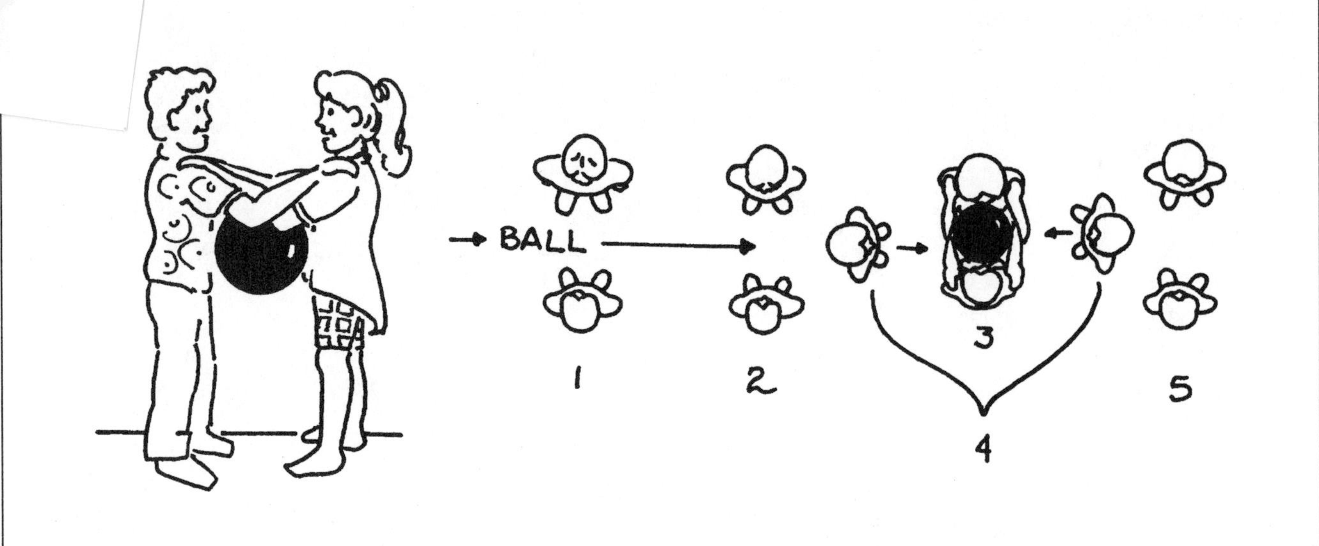

with their hands, but by securing the ball between them at the stomach (see diagram). The object is to pass the ball as quickly as possible from one set of people to the next without letting it fall. (Contributed by Michael W. Capps, East Flat Rock, N.C.)

Double Body Surfing

Ask the kids to take off their shoes, and then form a circle or an oval in the middle of the floor. Have everyone lie down on their backs, side by side with their feet to the center of the circle. Enlist two volunteers—one guy and one girl—to serve as "surfers." Let the group lying on the floor practice rolling to the left and right, all moving in the **same direction**. Then have the two volunteers lie down across several of the participants with their arms outstretched as if they are about to ride on a really big wave.

On the signal, everyone on the floor begins rolling to the right. At the same time the two volunteers crawl across the rolling players in the same direction. If the group is rolling to the right, for instance, then the two surfers will crawl to the right. The first surfer to make it back to the starting point by crawling across everyone wins. (Contributed by Michael Capps, East Flat Rock, N.C.)

Drawing in the Dark

In a dark room or with tightly closed eyes, participants must make a pencil drawing of a scene you describe to them.

Give every student a sheet of paper and a pencil. The idea is to direct them to draw portions of the entire picture in the dark so they can only guess at the accurate position to place an object. Turn out the lights, then tell them to draw, say, a house in the middle of the paper. Then ask them to place a tree to the left of the house. Then add a snowman to the right. Now put a chimney on the roof of the house. Draw a mailbox by the door. Draw a boy by the snowman. Put a scarf on the boy. Put smoke coming out of the chimney. Draw a dog by the tree. Put curtains in the window, a hat on the snowman, a nest in the tree, a flag on the mailbox, and so on. Post the masterpieces at the end of the game. (Contributed by Lyn Wargny, Palmyra, N.J.)

Dressing in the Dark

To play this game you need piles of activity-specific clothing and blindfolds. Each pile must contain the same type of clothing. On 3 x 5 cards write instructions for which activity players are to dress for, followed by a list of specific clothing to put on. For example, the card reads, "You are going to play tennis. Put on: sweatshirt, socks, tennis shoes, T-shirt." Another card might read, "You are going skiing. Put on: ski jacket, gloves, socks, overalls."

Divide your group into teams of seven or eight, and give the index cards describing the first outfit to one player from each team. After the players have memorized the clothing they are to put on, blindfold them and guide them to their team's pile of clothing. The blindfolded players have three minutes to pull from the pile the correct articles of clothing and dress themselves correctly and neatly—buttons in the correct buttonholes, shirts on inside in, and pants on correctly. The only help the blindfolded players have is their sense of touch and shouted clues from their teammates. At the end of three minutes, if no one is completely dressed, the leader decides who is the best dressed. Otherwise, the team whose player finishes correctly dressing first gets the point. (Contributed by Fay Wong, El Monte, Calif.)

Driving Range

After a rousing game of Goofy Golf (**Ideas 30**), what could be more natural than a trip to the driving range? Or, say, your homemade version of a driving range? Find a room with a high ceiling and try this low-budget thriller.

The advanced preparation is simple. Hang on a wall a large piece of butcher paper that goes from ceiling to floor. Draw a series of greens and a water hazard, each with designated points (see diagram at the top of the following page). Try to hit a marshmallow onto one of the greens with a golf club; if you succeed, you get the number of points marked on the green. If you land outside of the green, you get the number of points marked in that particular area. If you hit the water hazard, you lose 10,000 points. The person with the highest number of points wins. (Contributed by Michael Frisbie, Hobbs, N. Mex.)

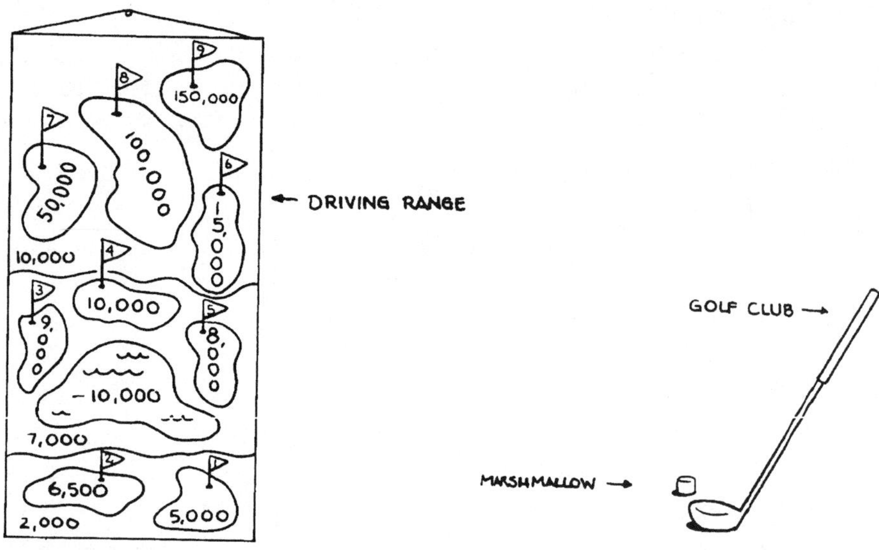

Find the Mailman

Tell the kids that it's April 15 and your tax forms need to get to the post office. Hold up a fat envelope and tell them you have the tax forms, but they have to figure out who the mailman is.

Ask everyone to sit in a circle. Give one player your envelope of tax forms and ask her to wait outside of the room. Now choose another person to be the mailman, and assign him a mannerism like one of these:

Blinks a lot
Answers questions by saying "Awesome!"
Sits with legs crossed
Arms are always folded
Taps his foot
Name is Mr. Mailman
Sleepy, yawns
Ends each sentence with "...you know?"
Scratches head a lot
Laughs a lot
A Bible is on his lap
Always says "I don't know"
Hands are in a praying position
Coughs a lot
Wears someone else's jacket
Always asks if you need some stamps
Twiddles his thumbs
Licks his lips a lot
Can't talk
Shifts in his chair a lot
Puts his arm on his neighbor's chair
Smiles a lot
Ends each sentence with "Have a nice day!"
Hands have both index fingers pointing at you
Winks at you

Set a time limit (one or two or three minutes, depending on the size of your group) and a limit on how many questions the tax-envelope holder ("It") can ask each student in the circle—say, three questions per player—by which time "It" must put the envelope in the Mailman's hand. When "It" returns to the room, suggest to her that she pay attention to body language as well as peculiarities in how kids answer her questions. Players must respond honestly to "Its" questions. (Contributed by Mark Schwartz, Kasson, Minn.)

Four-Team Crab Soccer

This outdoor game for groups of all sizes is fun to watch as well as play.

Place four cones 25 yards apart (see diagram). The field can be made larger or smaller to accommodate your group size. Evenly divide players among four teams. Teams line themselves up between the cones. All players assume the crab-walk position and, at the sound of the whistle, advance toward the four-foot beach ball in the center of the playing field. The object of the game is to kick the ball across the field through the markers of the team opposite them.

Because of the size and weight of the ball, players are allowed to use their hands to shield themselves from the ball, but they may not advance the ball with their hands. (Contributed by Tom Lytle, Marion, Ohio)

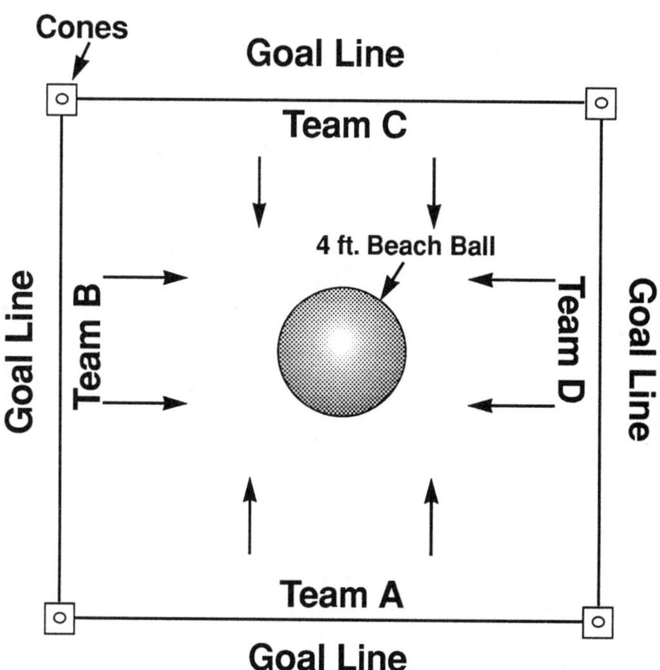

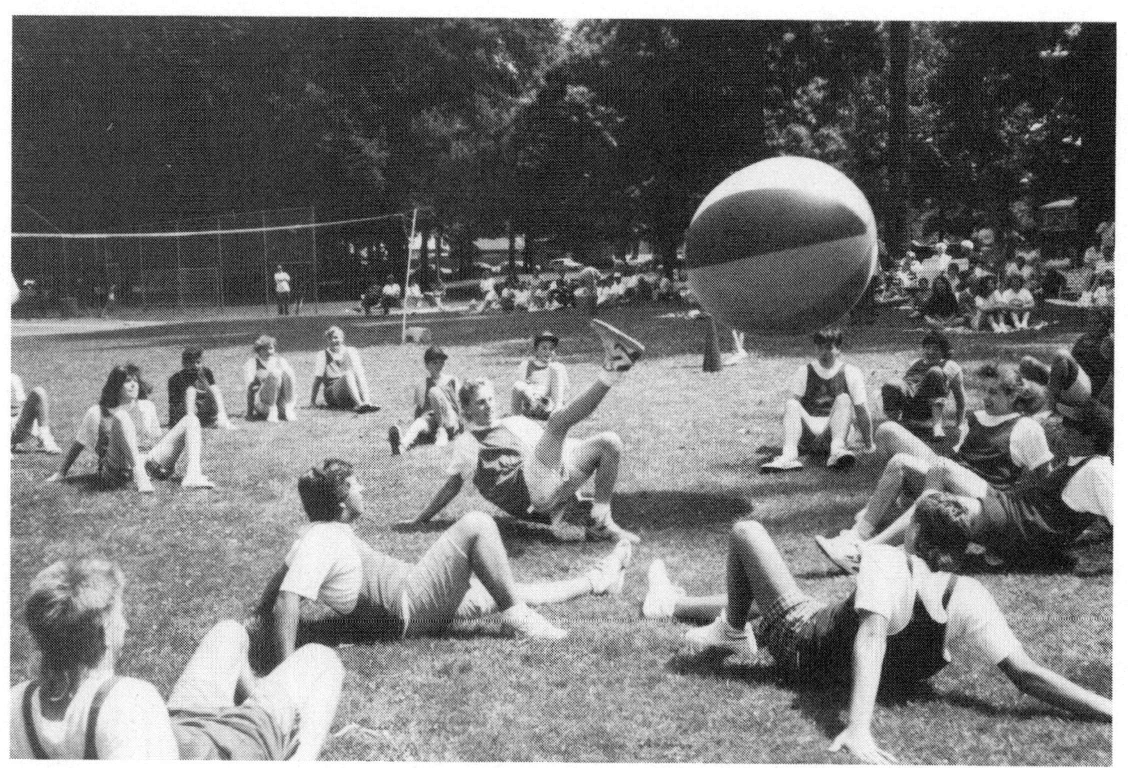

Frisbee Swat

What you'll need for this indoor/outdoor active game are two (or more)

Frisbees, two chairs, two cones (or liter bottles), two teams, and a pillow polo stick or rolled up newspaper for each player. At each end of the playing area place a chair with a cone on its seat. The purpose is for each team to knock the other team's cone off the chair with a Frisbee. Points are awarded for each knockdown.

Team members pass the Frisbees to each other as they work their way down the field. No one is allowed to run with the Frisbee—they can only pass it. Team members hold a pillow polo stick or newspaper in one hand, which is used for knocking down the opponent's Frisbee, and use their other hand to catch and throw their team's Frisbee. To play the game teams must attempt to score on offense and at the same time maneuver around on defense to "swat" the opponent's Frisbee out of the air. (Contributed by Ed Martinez, Long Beach, Calif.)

Gargle a Tune

Give everyone a small paper cup full of water and instruct them to gargle several different tunes on command ("Mary Had a Little Lamb," "Jingle Bells," "Row, Row, Row Your Boat," and so on). Make a contest to see who can guess what tune a person (or small group of people) is gargling. Have plenty of towels handy to clean up the mess that is sure to be made on this one. (Contributed by Michael Capps, East Flat Rock, N.C.)

Go Fly a Kite!

For a March fling any time of year, bring a window fan and some yarn, and ask the kids to bring materials to make kites—paper, straws, Popsicle sticks, glue, Scotch tape. Announce a kite-flying contest, but tell everyone to bring what they need to **make** a kite. (Don't let them bring already-made kites.) The ones the group will fly must be several times smaller than regular kites because they'll be flown with the help of the yarn and the window fan.

Give the kids a set time to create small kites, using whatever materials they wish, just so long as the kite can stay up whenever the fan is blown at full blast (see diagram). The best kites

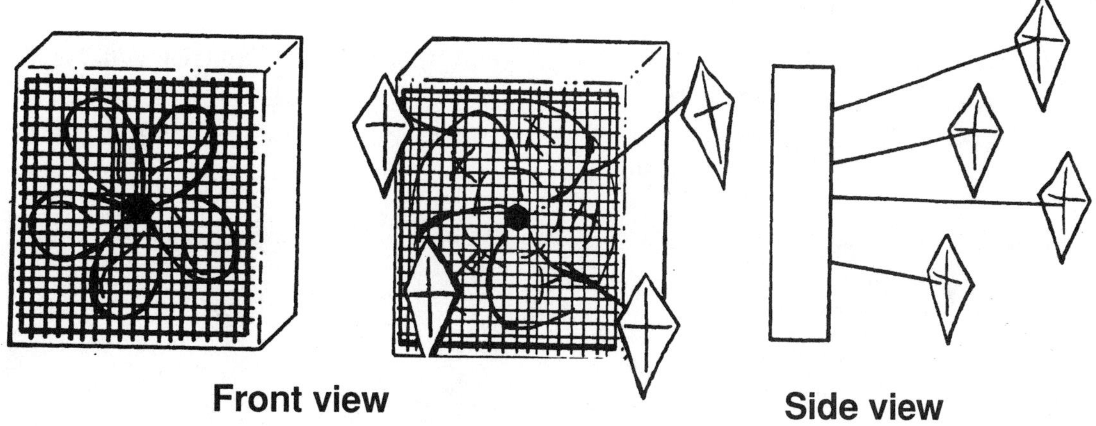

are those made in the traditional diamond shape. After everyone has made a kite, begin tying them to the fan one at a time with about three to four feet of yarn (shorter lengths if the yarn is heavy), and turn the fan on full blast, facing away from the house or into the center of the room. Add more kites and see how many you can fly without tangling them up together. This activity works well with a small youth group or study group. (Contributed by Michael Capps, East Flat Rock, N.C.)

Golf Ball and Plunger Cap Relay

Have the camera ready for this game! Make two teams and give a plunger (a plumber's helper) and a golf ball to each team. Ask the first player on each team to unscrew the wooden stick from the plunger and place the golf ball where the stick screwed in.

Players in this relay now must walk a prescribed course with the plunger cap on their heads, and the golf ball balanced on the plunger cap. (The course can be simple—out 10 or 20 feet, around a chair, and back, for example.) Players who drop the ball return to their line and start over. For more of a challenge, place obstacles in the course, make the kids walk it backward, etc. (Contributed by Rob Marin, Whittier, Calif.)

The Great Giveaway

Buy some play $1000 bills or make youth-group dollars for this game. Photocopy "The Great Giveaway" on page 29, one per person. Give each player as many $1000 bills as there are players in the game. (Contributed by Bradley Bergfalk, Bedford, N.H.)

Guess the Object

Whether your group's large or small, this living-room game is fun. Tell the group that five volunteers will leave the room while the remainder of the group chooses an object for them to guess when they return. However, once the volunteers are out of the room, give the **real** rules of the game.

Rather than choosing an object, tell the large group a set of conditions like the following: If a volunteer guesses anything whose name **ends** with F, the large group will say "More specific." If the name of a guess **begins** with F, the group responds in unison, "Yes!" If the guess neither begins nor ends with F, the group response is "No."

When the conditions for that round have been explained, one of the five people comes back into the room and is told to guess what the object is. The group responds in unison according to the conditions. The volunteer continues guessing until the group responds, "Yes!" At this point, the game is explained to the volunteer and a new set of conditions is announced for the next volunteer. (Contributed by Laurie Delgatto, Carlsbad, Calif.)

Head Hacky Sack

To each 7-to-10-person team, give a punch-ball-type balloon. The teams form circles and try to keep the punch ball in the air using only their heads. Play by the same rules as hacky sack,

Continued on page 30

THE GREAT GIVEAWAY

Instructions: You have been given $1000 for every person in the group. Your objective is to multiply your money as quickly as possible by approaching every member of the group and challenging each of them to one of the following activities. After you compete with those in your group, ask them to write their initials in the space at the left.

Some of these activities are based on elements entirely outside of your control; others demand a certain level of expertise (albeit not very much). You have a limited time to play The Great Giveaway, so play your hand wisely.

Oh, one other thing. You cannot approach the same person more than once for the same numbered challenge.

__________ 1. Find another person whose birthday is the in the same month as yours. The person whose birthday is closest to the first of the month earns $1000.

__________ 2. Play Rock, Paper, Scissors (up to three times). Winner takes $1000 per time.

__________ 3. Bubble gum blow—the largest bubble wins $1000.

__________ 4. The person with the most pocket change between the two of you wins $1000.

__________ 5. The person who can recite John 3:16 from memory wins $2000. If there is a tie, the person who can recite an additional Bible verse from memory wins.

__________ 6. Say "ahhh" together until one person runs out of breath. Whoever can say "ahhh" the longest wins $1000.

__________ 7. The one who can curl his tongue takes $1000. In case of a tie, the one who can curl her tongue and flare her nostrils at the same time wins.

__________ 8. The one who can name the most Christian rock artists wins $2000.

__________ 9. Thumb wrestling—the winner takes $1000 (play up to three times).

__________ 10. The person with the longest fingernails wins $1000. In the case of a tie, the longest toenails.

__________ 11. The person who can stand on her head and hum the national anthem at the same time wins $3000.

__________ 12. The person who has the longest eyelashes without mascara wins $1000.

__________ 13. The person who can ask "Where's the bathroom" in another language takes $1000.

__________ 14. Add up the letters of your first, middle, and last name. The competitor with the longest name wins $1000.

except that the head is the only part of the body with which players can legally hit the ball. If the punch ball falls to the floor, pick it up and start over. The team with the most **consecutive** hits is the winner. (Contributed by Michael Frisbie, Hobbs, N. Mex.)

Headbangers Volleyball

This is played like regular volleyball, except that boys can use only their heads to hit the ball. (If your girls feel slighted by the supposed sexism in this game, just tell them that the guys need a hit on the head to get their brains going). The rules are as follows:

- Guys can use only their heads to hit the ball.
- Girls can hit the ball according to standard volleyball rules.
- A guy must hit the ball at least once every time the ball comes over the net, or that team loses the point.
- Each team can hit the ball five times to get it over.
- The ball can bounce once each time it comes over.

Otherwise, the game is played by the normal volleyball rules. This game is as much fun to watch as play. (Contributed by Jack Hawkins, Sierra Madre, Calif.)

Hidden in Plain Sight

In a relatively cluttered room, hide about 20 small items where they can be seen without having to open drawers or move other items. A shoelace can be wrapped around a chair leg, a dollar bill can be folded up and wrapped around a book spine, a pen can be placed atop a door frame with only the end showing, a button can be taped to a doorknob. Write out and photocopy a list of the things you've hidden—a pen, a bobby pin, a clothespin, a match—and then place a duplicate of each hidden item on a tray beside the lists.

When the kids are ready to play, give them each a copy of the list of hidden items, and leave the tray of duplicate items out for comparison. Set a time limit for the players to search the room to find each of the listed items. They are not to remove the items; they are only to note the location of each item. The winner is the player who finds the most items within the time limit. (Contributed by Lyn Wargny, Palmyra, N.J.)

Indoor Baseball

In a large room tape off three bases and home plate. With a foam ball and the batter's arm, play regular baseball. Everything ahead of home base is a fair ball—even off the walls. Players can put batters out only by tagging them with the ball, however—batters cannot fly out or be thrown out. (Contributed by Len Cuthbert, Hamilton, Ont., Canada)

Indoor Frisbee Golf

In an appropriate section of the church building (nowhere near stained glass), set up an indoor course, labeling as "holes" trash cans, teachers' podiums, chairs, doors, and so on. On page 32 is a master score-card with rules and a blank list of the 18 holes. On the master, fill in the holes. For example:

Hole 1—Trash can by phone
Hole 2—Music, Room 201
Hole 3—Library, Room 2
Hole 4—Second grade, Room 3
Hole 5—Nursery, Room 4
Hole 6—Fifth/sixth grade, Room 5

Then photocopy enough scorecards for all your Frisbee golfers.

Now for the "Frisbees": Gather 30 or more lids from five-pound cottage-cheese containers, or find similar six-inch disks. The lids are small enough to be unable to break anything, but large enough to be thrown with at least some accuracy. Number the lids so the kids can tell them apart. Explain the rules that are printed on the scorecard, then start each team in a different location, theoretically so that they can all start and finish at the same time.

Once you collect the parts for this game, keep cards and lids on hand for that moment when the VCR eats your evening's tape. It's a great spur-of-the-moment lifesaver. (Contributed by Kevin Bueltmann, Normal, Ill.)

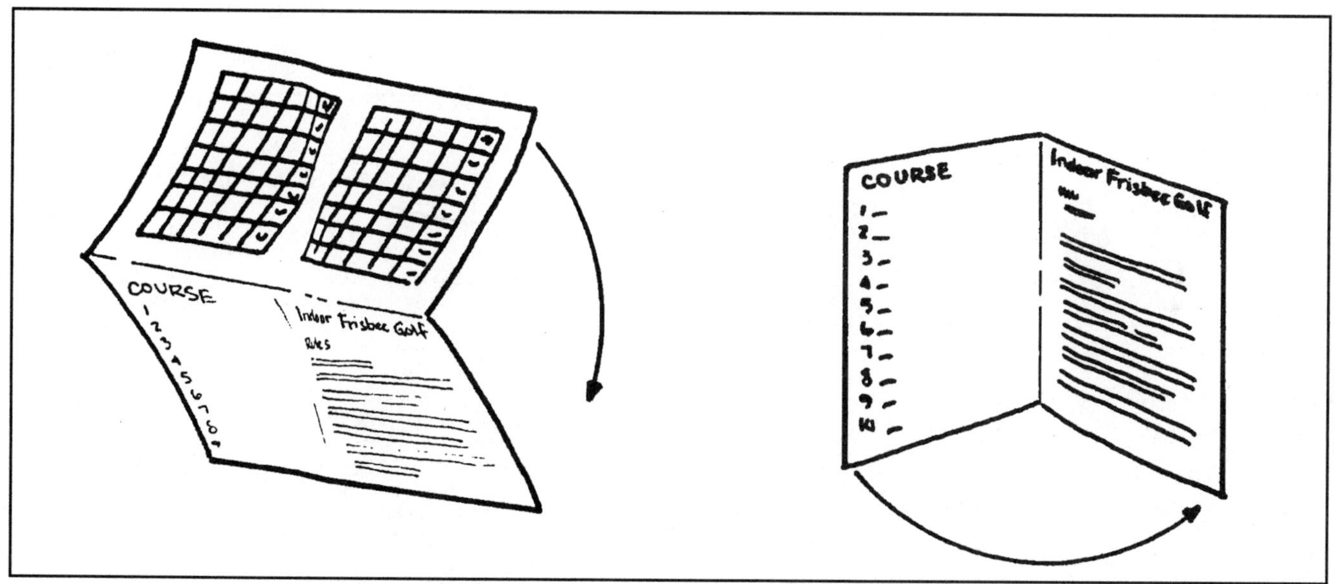

King Pong

If you have ever felt that the ping-pong table was just too short for your style of play, then this game could revitalize ping-pong for your group. Set **two** ping-pong tables end to end, and place the net as close to the middle as possible. Play regular rules or invent twists like relay-round-robin, multiple hits per side, or teams of four or more. The results are as fun to watch as they are to play. (Contributed by Kevin Turner and the Camp McCullough staff, Tacoma, Wash.)

PLAYER \ HOLE	1	2	3	4	5	6	7	8	9	TOTAL

PLAYER \ HOLE	10	11	12	13	14	15	16	17	18	10–18	1–9	GRAND TOTAL

Course

1—
2—
3—
4—
5—
6—
7—
8—
9—
10—
11—
12—
13—
14—
15—
16—
17—
18—

Indoor Frisbee Golf

Rules

1. Golf teams are 2-4 players.
2. Stay with your group, and don't run around wildly.
3. At each hole take turns throwing your first putt. The player closest to the hole finishes his turn, followed by the player next closest to the hole, and so on.
4. Keep (honest) track of how many throws it takes to make your putt. Record that score in the appropriate box. (Lowest score wins.)
5. You must be **within three feet** of the previous hole when you start throwing to the next.
6. You may not stop a Frisbee that is moving or rolling.
7. Except for when you "tee off," one foot must touch the spot where the Frisbee lands when you throw it.
8. Each team decides at the beginning if it will use Pro Rules (the Frisbee must land inside the trash can) or Beginner Rules (the Frisbee need only hit the can).
9. It is polite for a slower team to allow a faster team to pass it. It is not polite for a faster team to interfere with a slower team's game.
10. All holes are trash cans, except where noted otherwise.
11. For simplicity, par is four on all holes (72 total).
12. Have fun, but don't destroy the building in the process.

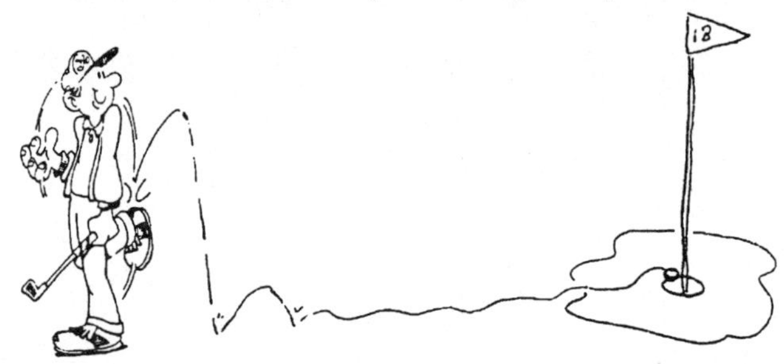

Kool-Aid Taste-Off

Ask three volunteers to sit in chairs facing the rest of the group. On a signal they each open a different flavored packet of Kool-Aid. Volunteers then lick just one finger and dip it into the packet. The person who in that manner can eat all of the Kool-Aid in the packet first wins. It's hilarious because they do not anticipate it being so sour, and they usually end up with it all over their lips. (Contributed by Amy Zuberbuhler, Pittsburgh, Pa.)

Laser Squirt

To get the same effect produced by expensive laser-tag guns, try this version of tag. Use water-color markers to color a three-inch circle on a 4 X 6 card for each participant. Ask kids to bring their squirt guns and wear old shirts; you provide buckets for refilling. Tape a card to the chest of each player—and have at it! When the colored circle is hit with water, the color runs—and that player is dead and out of the game.

Form five-person color-coded teams and allow a few minutes of pregame planning before signaling hostilities to commence. The team with the most unsquirted members at the end of the time period wins. (Contributed by Mark Adams, Derwood, Md.)

Lego Olympics

Buy several small Lego sets—race car, airplane, spaceship—(or ask your students' younger brothers if you can borrow them) and create races that require the students to assemble the sets under some limitation. You'll discover that youths of all ages love putting Lego sets together. Create your own Lego Olympic events. Some suggestions:

- **Blindfold Sprint.** Two players work together. One player can do nothing but read the instructions. The other player is blindfolded and must construct the item solely from verbal directions from the teammate.
- **100 Yard Dash.** A pure speed contest—who can assemble a Lego figure the fastest?
- **Relays.** Teams take turns adding pieces to build the item.
- **Hurdles.** Place pieces of the Lego set around the room. The player must move around the room to find the pieces needed to finish the item in the fastest time.

- **Awards ceremony.** At an awards ceremony following the event, give Lego sets to the team or individual with the most wins. Play a tape recording of you or some students singing each winner's high school alma mater or fight song.

(Contributed by Mark Schwartz, Kasson, Minn.)

Marshmallow Driving Range

Divide your group in half, into the "drivers" and the "flags."

- **The Drivers.** Give all drivers a golf club, a tee, and several marshmallows, then line them up in a straight line about 10 feet apart from each other (enough distance to swing without hitting each other).
- **The "Flags."** Place the "flags" at varying distances from the line of drivers. Arm each with three or four marshmallows.
- **The Game.** Drivers tee up their marshmallows, aim at the flags, and hit their marshmallows with the clubs. Flags may retaliate by throwing their supplies of marshmallows at the drivers.
- **The Point of It All.** The game soon degenerates into an all-out marshmallow war.

(Contributed by Brian Cheek, Richmond, Ind.)

Medical Mix-up

Everyone knows teens love to play word games to make a point or get their way with parents and peers. Let your teens have fun with this play on medical words. You can make up your own with any jargon or terminology.

Here are the answers to the game on page 35:

1. H
2. S
3. O
4. I
5. T
6. D
7. M
8. U
9. C
10. J
11. Q
12. F
13. V
14. X
15. G
16. B
17. R
18. N
19. E
20. K
21. A
22. P
23. L
24. W

(Contributed by Rob Marin, Whittier, Calif.)

℞ ℞ ℞ ℞ ℞ ℞ ℞ ℞ ℞ ℞ ℞ ℞ ℞ ℞ ℞ ℞ ℞ ℞

MEDICAL MIX-UP

Instructions: Match the terms at left with their definitions at right. Be careful—some of the definitions may be a little mixed up. Example: Serology—the study of English knighthood.

1.______ artery
2.______ barium
3.______ colic
4.______ coma
5.______ congenital
6.______ dilate
7.______ fester
8.______ G.I. series
9.______ grippe
10.______ hangnail
11.______ medical staff
12.______ minor operation
13.______ morbid
14.______ nitrate
15.______ node
16.______ organic
17.______ outpatient
18.______ post-operative
19.______ protein
20.______ secretion
21.______ tablet
22.______ tumor
23.______ urine
24.______ varicose veins

A. small table
B. musical
C. a suitcase
D. to live long
E. in favor of young people
F. coal digging
G. was aware of
H. the study of fine paintings
I. a punctuation mark
J. a coat hook
K. hiding anything
L. the opposite of "you're out"
M. quicker
N. a letter carrier
O. a sheep dog
P. an extra pair
Q. a doctor's cane
R. a person who has fainted
S. what you do when CPR fails
T. friendly
U. a baseball game with teams of soldiers
V. a higher offer
W. veins that are close together
X. lower than the day rate

℞ ℞ ℞ ℞ ℞ ℞ ℞ ℞ ℞ ℞ ℞ ℞ ℞ ℞ ℞ ℞ ℞ ℞

Missile Mania

For a massive-strike water-balloon fight, purchase a water-balloon slingshot and mark off a playing field (see diagram). At each end of the field is a launching pad where several designated players work the slingshot. In between the pads is a hand-to-hand open combat zone (the OCZ) where individuals may hand-throw water balloons at opponents. A player hit with a water balloon must go to the opposition's prison, located near the launching pad. There's also a safety zone at each end in which a player is immune from being taken prisoner and into which no opposition players may enter.

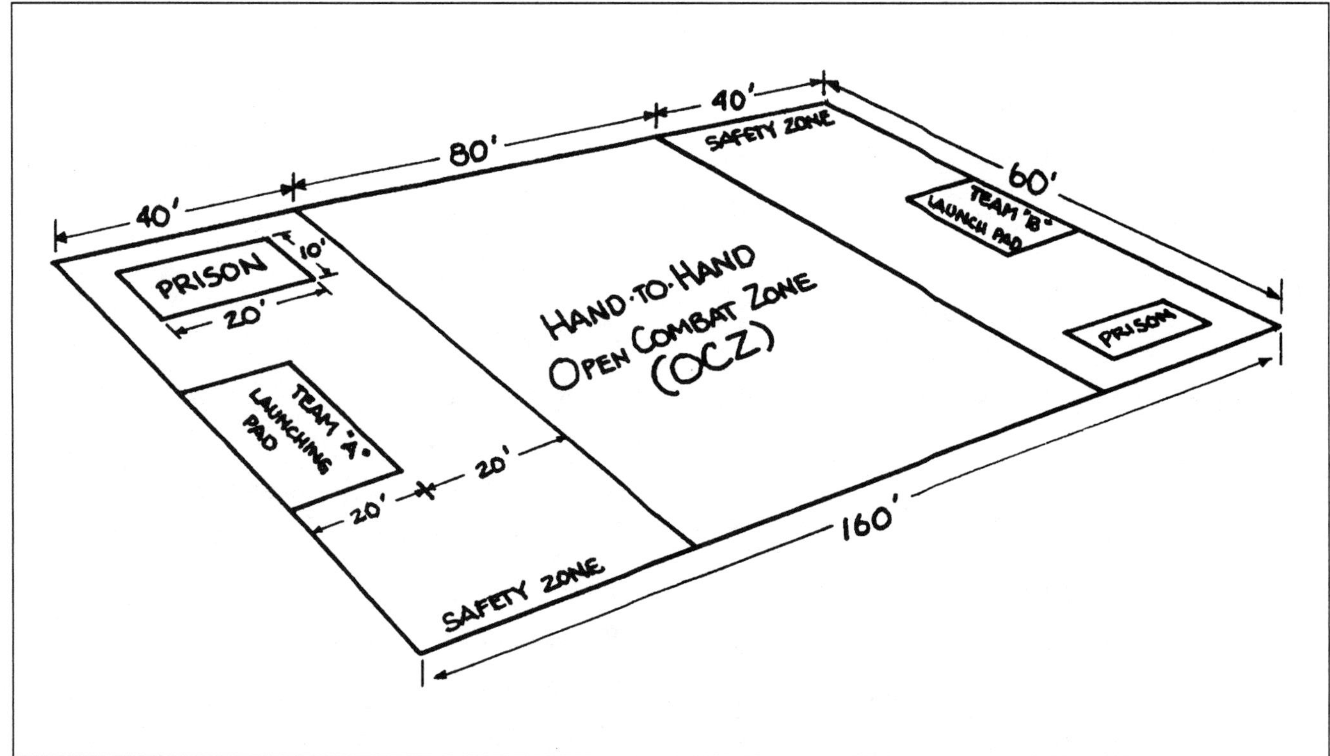

The object of the game is to hit a launcher on the opposition with a water balloon, thereby "knocking out" their launching pad.

After you divide the group into two teams, each team designates players who must remain at all times in their team's launching pad and use the water-balloon launcher to fire balloons over the OCZ in an attempt to hit any of the enemy launchers inside the opposition's launching pad. Once a launcher is hit by a balloon, the pad is considered "knocked out," and the opposing team scores a point.

Other players engage in hand-to-hand balloon combat in the OCZ as they try to knock out a launching pad by throwing the balloons. In addition, they try to take enemy prisoners by hitting them in the OCZ. Those hit in the OCZ must remain in the opposition's prison until a knockout point is scored by their own team, at which time they are freed and may join the war again.

The first team to score 10 knockout points wins. (Contributed by Gene Stabe, Newhall, Calif.)

Murder Mystery

Directions

In this game the kids are detectives questioning suspects in an effort to find the killer of Mr. John Stone. The five suspects (Mr. Mun, janitor; Steve Stone, John's brother; Sam Swade, lawyer; Mrs. Stone, John's wife; and Ms. Wright, secretary) are prepared ahead of time to act their part using the scripts provided. They should come costumed for their parts—the secretary looking seductive, the lawyer shady, the janitor in overalls, and so on. The players are divided into groups of five or six and will attempt to solve the mystery by working within their groups.

The game begins with everyone seeing the scene of the murder (see "Setting Up the Murder Scene") and hearing the scripted opening comments given by the host. After the opening, each suspect leaves for a separate room, and the groups of detectives move from room to room questioning the suspects (one group in a room at a time, with a time limit of 5 or 10 minutes per visit). Groups may visit any suspect as many times as they like.

At the conclusion of the game, all groups return to the scene of the murder and write on a piece of paper who they think killed John Stone and how and why they think the murder took place. The game leader then reads all the solutions offered by the kids as well as the solution provided (see "Solution to the Mystery").

The success of this game lies with the actors playing the five suspects. Skillful youths may play these parts, but it usually works out better with adults. Before the game is played, the suspects meet to listen to each others' scripts and hear the solution to the mystery, for during the game itself the detectives will ask many questions not covered by the scripts, and although the suspects may say, "The question you asked is not relevant," suspects may also ad-lib on the story line as long as it does not conflict with or give away the solution. This can only be done if they already know each others' material.

Each suspect's script is divided into two or three parts: an alibi and confessions. Suspects tell their alibi to every group, but they only offer their confession if the detectives can prove by quoting evidence from other suspects that the suspect being questioned is lying. For example, many suspects will claim that they were not at the office that night, but the janitor will place them all at the scene. When the detectives tell the suspects that the janitor testifies to seeing them at the office, the suspects spill their guts, giving the second part of their script.

The suspects must use discretion in their answers. If they are stingy with information, the game will go on too long; if they too readily tell all, the detectives will catch on too quickly. The janitor's first part is rather simple, but the key phrase is when he says that he found the body while checking to see if John and his friends had left. The janitor gives his second part only when the detectives ask if he saw others there.

Setting Up the Murder Scene

The scene is a business office containing a desk and a table (or bookshelf) holding an aquarium. The office is topsy-turvy from an apparent struggle. Papers and file folders are strewn about the room and on the desk. Clearly visible among the papers on the floor is a broken picture frame containing a photo of the actress who plays the part of Mrs. Stone. On the desk is an agenda showing meeting times as follows: secretary 8:00 p.m., Steve Stone 8:30 p.m., Sam Swade 9:15 p.m. The aquarium is tipped over with the gravel falling off the edge of the table. Add some broken glass around it, and on the floor beneath it place some dead fish (from a local pet store's casualties) or cutouts of fish. Also below the aquarium trace the outline of a person with either chalk or masking tape to indicate where the body was found. Add some ketchup, broken glass, and water around the outline of the head.

Solution to the Mystery

The solution to the Murder Mystery is on page 65. (Contributed by John McLendon, Pasadena, Calif.)

Opening Comments to Players

This is the office of John Stone, who was murdered last night. The janitor found him on the floor at 10:00 p.m. The cause of death was a blow to the back of his head, and the time of death was between 8:00 and 10:00 p.m. From the agenda on the desk, we know that he was working late and was to see his secretary at 8:00 p.m., his brother Steve Stone (who was his business partner) at 8:30 p.m., and his lawyer Sam Swade at 9:15 p.m. We have all three of these people here for you to question. We also have Mr. Stone's wife here as well as the janitor who found his body.

Your job is to find out who killed John Stone and how and why they did it. That is, by evidence at the scene and from what you learn from the suspects, you must prove who the murderer is, the motive for the murder, and the method of the murder. Once you know this information, write it on a paper. We will read all your conclusions at **[insert the time you will conclude the game]**, then I will tell you who is right.

Some suggestions: You are investigators. When you get some evidence, use it to get more information. One or more of these people will be lying, but if you confront them with evidence, they will come clean. For instance, if you find out that one of the suspects made a death threat, do not say to that person, "Did you say you would kill John Stone?" Say instead, "I have a witness who will testify that you said you were going to kill John Stone."

The suspects are working from a script and will not have answers to all your questions. If they seem to be making up answers to some of your questions, it is not **always a clue that they are lying**. They may be trying to give an appropriate answer that will not at the same time lead you off track. They may also decline to answer saying that your question is not relevant to the case.

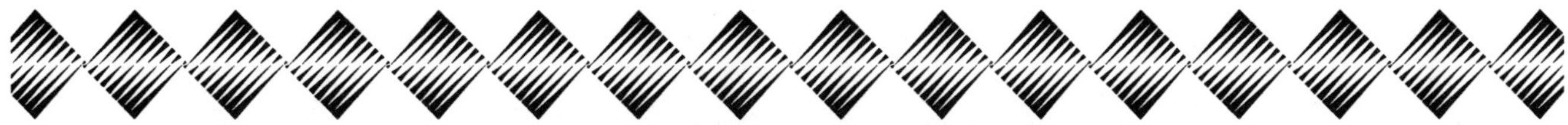

MRS. STONE, JOHN'S WIFE

Alibi: All I know is my husband was a good man, and I don't know why anyone would want to kill him. I was home all night long until 10 o'clock when the police called and (she begins to cry) told me John had been killed.

Confession: I had a phone call from someone. He would not give his name, but he said my husband was having an affair with his secretary. I had suspected it for a long time and had told several of my friends that if I found out it was true I would kill him. When I got the call I went to his office. I was very angry, but I was not going to kill him. When I got there, the place was a mess. Papers were everywhere, my picture was smashed, and the carpet was soaked from the broken aquarium. It looked like there had been a terrible fight. John was **(attempting to retain emotional control of herself)** lying there—blood all over the back of his head. I can still see him in my mind—his blank expression and all those fish wiggling around him. I couldn't have killed him. I loved him.

MR. SAM SWADE, LAWYER

Alibi: I was scheduled to meet with John Stone at 9:15 to finalize the signing of some business papers that he and his brother were working on. But my paging service left a message with me that someone had called and cancelled the appointment. She didn't say who called—I just assumed it was John. The message said the meeting would be rescheduled for the next day sometime, so I never went to John's office. The first thing I heard was when the police called me at home around 10 o'clock.

Confession: Yes, I did go to John's office at 9:15. When I walked in, John was lying on the floor. Things were messed up—papers all over the floor, some pictures were broken. I went around to look at John closer. There was a little blood on the floor, which seemed to come from the back of his head. I could tell by looking at him he was dead.

I was going to call the police, but first I had to check on some records. Steve Stone had been having some power struggles with his brother, and I had helped him falsify some records so he could gain more power in the company. When I looked, though, the records were gone. Steve was the only one who knew about them, so I knew he had to be the one who took them. I knew he was hungry for power. In fact, although I can't prove it, I think he was also blackmailing John.

Two days before his death John told me somebody was blackmailing him. He had been having an affair with his secretary Sandy Wright and told me someone was getting him for big bucks to keep it from his wife. He asked me for advice on how to get out without legal problems. I told him the first step was to break the relationship with Ms. Wright and get her as far away from him as possible. In fact, he was going to do that when she brought the papers by the night of his murder. I'm innocent. I didn't kill John Stone. He was dead when I got there. The more I think about it, the more the finger points straight at Steve Stone.

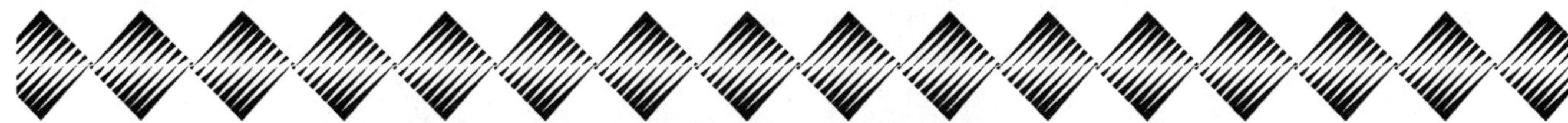

MR. STEVE STONE, BROTHER TO JOHN

Alibi: I had a meeting set up with my brother to finalize some papers on an account we had been working on. I was to meet him at his office at 8:30, but I had an emergency come up and was not going to be able to make the meeting. I called several times to tell John I wasn't coming and that he should make whatever decisions had to be made and that I'd back whatever he thought was best, but I never got an answer at his office. I never left my office. In fact, I was still there when the police called to tell me John had been murdered.

Confesssion: Yes, I was at John's office at 8:30 for our meeting. When I walked in he was on the floor. There were signs of a struggle—some pictures were broken, some papers were scattered on the floor. I went to look at John, and there was a small pool of blood from a blow to the back of his head. I would have called the police, but my brother and I had been having some problems.

You see, John was greedy for power and money. **(getting angry now)** He was trying to cut me out of the business. I had been working with our lawyer Sam Swade to steal the control of the company from John. There were some papers in John's office we had falsified, and I thought it would be best if I got them out of the office before I called the police. But I couldn't find them. That's when I knew Sam Swade must have killed John. He was a crook to begin with, and there's no telling what kind of deals he's been pulling. I didn't know what to do, so I left and went back to my office as if I'd never left there and waited until the police called.

I didn't kill him. He was already dead when I got there. I couldn't kill him. He was my brother! But I'd bet my life Sam Swade is behind this.

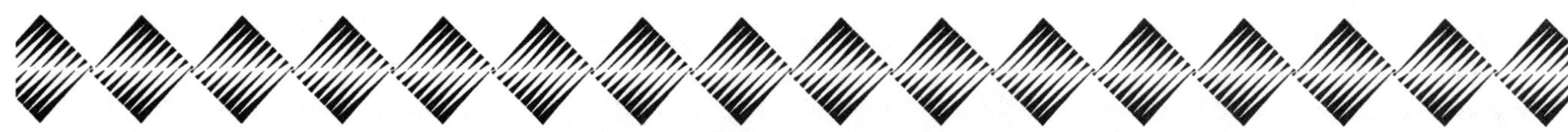

MR. MUN, JANITOR

Alibi: I had been working in the building like I always did. Mr. Stone told me he had some late meetings, which was not uncommon. So about 9:55 I went by to make sure he and his friends were gone before I locked up. When I walked in, it was a pitiful sight. Someone had torn the place to bits, and Mr. Stone was dead on the floor. As soon as I saw him, I called the police.

Confession A: [Use the following speech only if the detectives ask who you saw come in.] Well, his secretary came by to drop off some papers. I was cleaning the hall. She went in and came right back out. Then a while later I saw Mr. Stone's brother going through the main lobby. I'm not sure how long he was there because I didn't see him leave. A little later I saw Mr. Stone's lawyer Sam Swade getting out of his car in the parking lot, but I didn't see him leave, either. Mrs. Stone's wife must have also been there because her coat was on the rack when I went to lock up around 9:50. But it wasn't there when I had cleaned the hall at 8 o'clock.

Confession B: Okay, I was cleaning the hall when Ms. Wright came by with the papers. She went into the office. After a little while I heard glass break and some yelling. I came down the hall and walked into the office. As I did I saw Mr. Stone coming around the desk toward Ms. Wright. As he got to her she pushed him away and he tripped and fell backwards. His head hit the aquarium and it busted everywhere. Then he fell to the floor. I checked him for his pulse, but he was dead.

I knew it was an accident, so I told Sandy—ah, Ms. Wright—to go home, that it was an accident, and that I would make it look like someone had robbed the place. She left, but before I could do anything, Mr. Stone's brother showed up. He saw his brother, then snooped around the place looking for something. He finally left. When I was sure he had gone, I started again to make the place look like a robbery. But then Mr. Swade came down the hall. He looked all over the room also, but didn't leave with anything. Not long after that Mr. Stone's wife came and then ran out. After that I just messed the place up a little and called the police. I was only trying to help Ms. Wright.

MS. SANDY WRIGHT, SECRETARY

Alibi: I came by the office at 8 o'clock to drop off some papers for Mr. Stone. He needed them for some meetings he was having that evening. I was only there for a minute. He was on the phone, so I left them on his desk. He said thanks, and I left. That's all I knew until the police called me at my home around 10 o'clock to tell me Mr. Stone was dead.

Confession: Yes, I was having an affair with Mr. Stone. When I came in to drop off the papers, he told me it was all over—I was being let go Monday and he told me not to ever set foot in the place again. He treated me like some undesirable business deal. I was hurt and angry. I pulled his wife's pictures off the wall and broke them. Then I started yelling at him. He started toward me from around the desk. I didn't even want him to touch me, so I pushed him away and he tripped over the lamp cord and hit his head.

Then he just laid there and didn't move at all. I didn't mean to kill him. It was an accident. **(starts crying)** You can ask the janitor. He heard the pictures breaking and heard the yelling and came into the office just as John fell and hit his head. He told me he knew it was an accident. He said for me to go home and he would make it look like a break in and robbery. I did it because I looked so guilty and was afraid. I swear I did not mean to kill him.

Music Video Pillow Wars

Similar to musical chairs, this game uses pillows—but not to sit on. Turn out the lights and load a music video into the VCR. Scatter pillows around the room, using one less pillow than there are players. A remote control makes the game easier for you to conduct.

When the music starts, the kids walk around in the dark. When you stop the music (with the pause button, for example), the kids pick up a pillow and fight until you resume the video. Players are eliminated when they're hit with a pillow. Eliminate players until only two or three kids are left, then start over. (Contributed by Jim Ramos, San Luis Obispo, Calif.)

Neckloose

Here's a contest suitable for almost any thematic event, be it a Hawaiian luau, western round-up, or sweetheart banquet. The only item used in this event is a necklace (of sorts), which can be either a plastic lei (for a luau) or an old necktie (for a hobo party) or a string of candy hearts (for a sweetheart banquet).

Begin by having everyone make a loose circle, alternating boy-girl-boy-girl. Place the "necklace" around one neck and instruct that on the signal the necklace is to be passed around the circle in the following way: the person beside the one wearing the necklace places his head inside the necklace—which is still around the first player's neck—and, without using hands, carefully removes it from the original wearer without breaking or tearing it in any way.

The necklace should be large enough to make the game comfortable, but small enough to make it a challenge. For added fun, start two necklaces in opposite directions and see what happens when they meet in the middle. (Contributed by Michael Capps, East Flat Rock, N.C.)

Nonstop Cricket

I say, how 'bout a game of English nonstop cricket? Using the diagram on page 42 to guide you, make a bat (or use a similar wooden paddle), make wickets from old broom sticks and a base block, and buy a foam ball. Form two teams of 6 to 11 participants—the fielders and the players. Choose a wicket keeper from the fielders and a score keeper from among nonplayers (or have a batter record the runs).

To play:

- The batter attempts to hit the ball and on a hit must run and touch the scoring line and return to his crease, so scoring a run.
- Meanwhile, the fielders (the field surrounds the wicket instead of spreading out only in front of the wicket) return the ball to the bowler, who immediately bowls (pitches) to the batter, aiming to hit the wicket, whether or not the batter has returned to the crease.
- The batter must run on the third

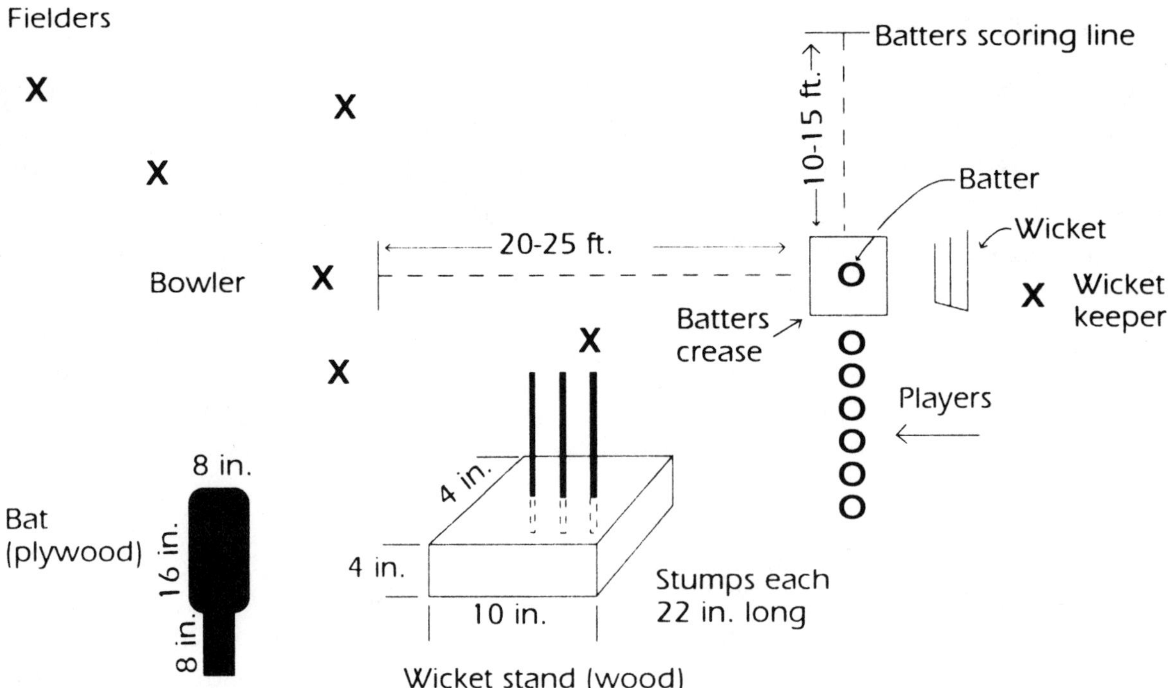

bowl or forfeit a turn.

• The whole of the batting side is out if a fielder takes a full catch.

• The batter is out if the wicket is hit by the bowler, a bowl hits the leg of the batter in front of the wicket, the ball is returned by a fielder and hits the wicket before the batter returns to the crease, or the wicket keeper hits the wicket with the ball while the batter is out of the crease.

• The batters keep playing until the last batter is out. The batters then become the fielders, and the fielders the batters. Play for a set time or until an agreed score is reached. After a trial run, adjust boundaries or rules. Bowler bowls underarm. (Contributed by Fred Swallow, Auckland, New Zealand)

Nose Knockers

Ever watch a game end in chaos as students who were supposed to move an object using their noses began to use anything they could to win? Nose Knockers are simply nose extensions that will restrain cheating by making the games easier to perform while providing some great camera shots.

Purchase some paper cups and poke a hole on two sides of the cups. Attach a large rubber band to the holes to allow students to place the cups over their noses like masks (see diagram at the top of the following page). Use Nose Knockers in relay games with golf balls, ping-pong balls—even dead roaches. (Contributed by Rob Marin, Whittier, Calif.)

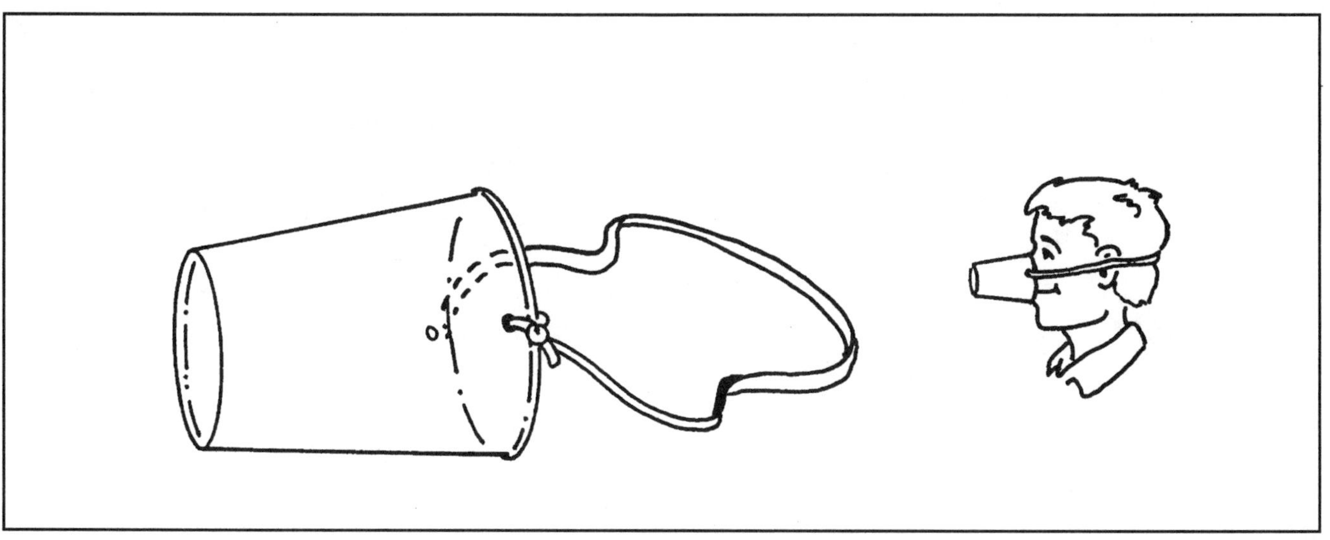

Oddball Crawl

Begin this relay by creating two or more teams of 8 to 10 players wearing their grubbies. At one end of a long room, line the teams up alternating boy-girl-boy-girl on each team. In each line players get on their hands and knees side by side on the floor. On the signal, the players at the end of each team's line closest to the wall begin crawling over and under their teammates as fast as possible. The stationary players alternately drop to the floor or arch up their backs (still keeping hands and feet on the floor) to make passage quicker for their traveling team member (see photograph) .

As soon as possible after the first players have crossed the second players, the second players may begin their trip over and under the stationary teammates. When traveling players reach the end of the line, they either lie flat or rise to allow other players to pass over or under them. The relay continues until everyone on the team has successfully crawled over and under the rest of the team. The team that completes the relay first is the winner.

If your group is too small for two teams, form one team and play several rounds to go for the fastest team time. Have a camera handy to catch some of the action.

Awkward personal contact is rare, for the youths are sufficiently caught up in the race that they don't take time for mischief. (Contributed by Michael Capps, East Flat Rock, N.C.)

Off the Wall

Here's a high-energy competition that blends dodgeball with capture the flag.

Create a playing court in your gym (or large room, provided the walls are very sturdy) by assigning each wall a color and taping 50 inflated balloons of that color to the wall. Create a territory for each color that extends out 20 feet from the wall, leaving a large "free zone" in the center of the gym (see diagram). In the center of each of the four territories, set a "safe" (a large box). At the edge of each territory, mark off an area to be the team's "jail."

Now divide your group into teams—one team for each territory. Each team designates certain players as Invaders, Defenders, and one Jailkeeper.

- **Invaders.** Invaders try to hit opposing teams' balloons off the wall with soccer balls or playground balls thrown only from the central free zone. An Invader cannot throw a ball unless he or she remains in the free zone. Invaders may also steal balloons from an enemy's wall by invading their territory. Stolen balloons are taken back to the Invader's own team's safe. Invaders may not, however, steal balloons from an opponent's "safe."
- **Defenders.** Defenders defend their

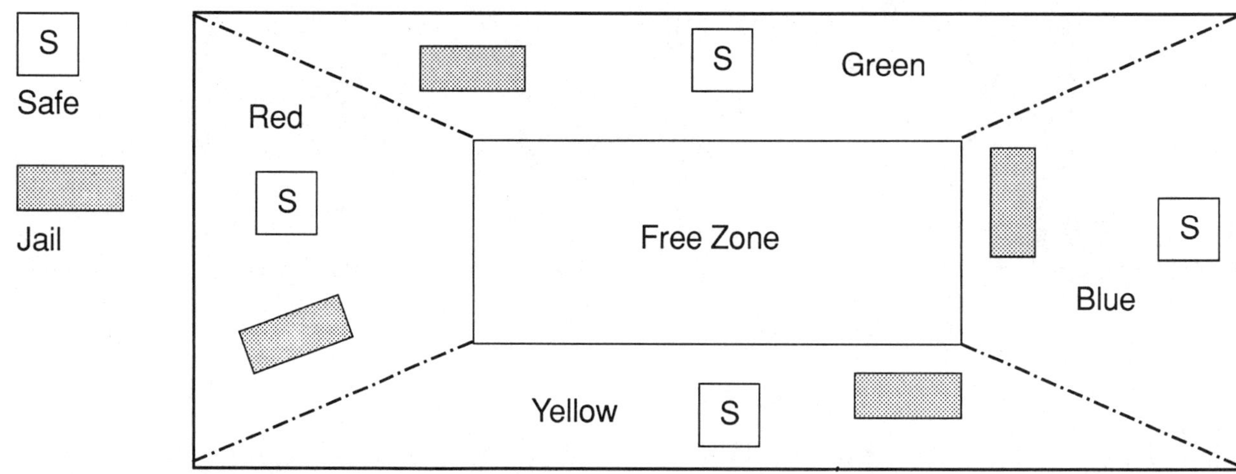

wall by catching or deflecting balls. They may capture Invaders by tagging them within the Defender's territory. Captured Invaders are taken to the jail. Defenders may not return to the wall balloons that were hit off.

• **Jail rules.** A team may ransom its Invaders who are in jail by exchanging three balloons from its safe for its incarcerated Invader. The team holding the Invader in jail may then return these recovered balloons to its wall.

Assign a time limit for the game to be played out. At the end of the game, each team earns 5 points for every balloon remaining on its wall and 10 points for every captured balloon still in its safe. (Contributed by James Bell, Hamilton, Ohio)

Pew Crawl

Play this game in your church sanctuary—if you can get away with it. Divide into two teams (more if you have a large sanctuary with several sections of pews). Each team begins the game by standing behind the pew farthest from the front of the auditorium. Their team captain and a team referee is at the front of the auditorium.

On "Go!" each team captain randomly opens a hymnbook. The captains yell out the last digit on the right hand page, and all the team members hit the floor to crawl under that many pews before standing up again. Let's say a team captain opens to page 352 in the hymnal—he yells "Two!" and teammates must crawl under two pews, then stand up in front of the second pew (counting, remember, from the back). Moving toward the front of the sanctuary this way, the first team to reach the front wins the game.

A captain cannot yell out the next number until his or her entire team is standing up again in front of the correct pew. (No need to wait for the other team, however—this is a race!) As soon as the last member of a team is up, their captain yells out a new number, and the team hits the floor again, crawling as fast as they can.

The referees ensure that everyone abides by only two rules: The hymnbook must be opened **randomly**, and the entire team must be standing before the next number is called. (Contributed by Larry Stoess, Crestwood, Ky.)

Pictionary Charades

You'll want to play this game often. Divide your group into two teams and, using the cards and timer from a Pictionary game, play charades.

One member of Team One chooses a Pictionary card and scans the words listed. When the timer is started, that player must act out for her teammates each of the words or phrases on the chosen card in any order. (Hint: Do the easy ones first.) Teammates try to guess the word or phrase being acted out. Once a word is guessed, the acting player can go on to another word on the chosen card, acting out as many words as possible within the time limit.

The team receives one point for every correct guess within the time limit. If a team guesses all five words or phrases on the chosen card, it receives two bonus points. Team Two then chooses a card and repeats the process. (Contributed Sheridan Lehman, Ephrata, Pa.)

Pillow Hockey

This game is played in a long court like Broom Hockey (**Ideas Combo 1-4**) (or can be amended some to play like Circle Soccer, **Ideas Combo 13-16**).

The object: to use pillowcases stuffed loosely with crumpled newspapers and tied off to hit, hockey fashion, a playground ball into a goal.

Lay the available pillows out on the court (an equal number on both sides of the court), then call for teams to select players, who run out to the

court and immediately begin playing. When one side scores, call for new players from each team.

What makes this game fun is that it's difficult to hit the ball with much force, or even be too sure you hit it at all. Also, unlike broom hockey, players don't get smacked accidentally by wooden handles. (Contributed by Keith King, Whittier, Calif.)

Ping Bag

Several early-bird students in a youth group came up with this idea for passing time while waiting for slower groups to finish a discussion question. Every player has a Ping Pong paddle to toss and catch a small bean bag. You can toss the bag to anyone in the circle—it's every man for himself. If players miss the bean bag, they're out. If the toss is determined by group consensus to be uncatchable, the tosser is out. The trick is toss the bag so that it's difficult but still possible to catch by an aggressive player. When only one player is left in the circle, everyone joins the circle and round two begins. (Contributed by Doug Partin, Lubbock, Tex.)

Ping-pong Soccer

From 6 to 16 people can enjoy this indoor version of soccer. The rules are the same as regular soccer—except you play with a ping-pong ball, there are no out of bounds, and you should make the goals a lot smaller.

Although the size of the "field" is small, the game plays amazingly like soccer because a well kicked ping-pong ball travels only 15 to 20 feet. Have plenty of ping-pong balls—they tend to get squashed on a blocked shot. Penalize a ball-squashing team by awarding the opposing team a free kick at the goal. (Contributed by Elliott Cooke, Nanuet, N.Y.)

Play in the Dark

Attach a Cyalume glow stick to a Frisbee to play Frisbee in the dark. For nighttime football, make a hole in a Nerf ball and push a glow stick into the end of the ball. Point the lighted end toward the receiver for passing downs. (Contributed by Larry Smith, Carrollton, Tex.)

Pucks and Pigskins

Time to put all your sports-spectating prowess to work. The object of the two quizzes on page 49 ("Touchdown!" and "On Ice") is to identify the football teams and the hockey teams from the clues. Photocopy the quizzes and pass them out to your group for some fun during the half-time of a TV game they're watching.

The answers are on the following page.

TOUCHDOWN!

1. Dallas Cowboys
2. Washington Redskins
3. Philadelphia Eagles
4. Phoenix Cardinals
5. New York Giants
6. Minnesota Vikings
7. Chicago Bears
8. Green Bay Packers
9. Detroit Lions
10. Tampa Bay Buccaneers
11. San Francisco 49ers
12. New Orleans Saints
13. Atlanta Falcons
14. Los Angeles Rams
15. Miami Dolphins
16. Indianapolis Colts
17. New England Patriots
18. New York Jets
19. Buffalo Bills
20. Pittsburgh Steelers
21. Houston Oilers
22. Cleveland Browns
23. Cincinnati Bengals
24. Los Angeles Raiders
25. Denver Broncos
26. Seattle Seahawks
27. Kansas City Chiefs
28. San Diego Chargers

ON ICE

1. Pittsburgh Penguins
2. Hartford Whalers
3. Buffalo Sabres
4. Minnesota North Stars
5. Winnipeg Jets
6. Philadelphia Flyers
7. Montreal Canadiens
8. Detroit Red Wings
9. Calgary Flames
10. St. Louis Blues
11. New York Islanders
12. New York Rangers
13. Toronto Maple Leafs
14. Edmonton Oilers
15. Boston Bruins
16. Quebec Nordiques
17. Los Angeles Kings
18. Washington Capitals
19. Vancouver Canucks
20. Chicago Black Hawks
21. New Jersey Devils

(Contributed by Phil Rankin, Upland, Calif., and Terry H. Erwin, Monroeville, Pa.)

Puzzle Relay

You'll need five sponsors, a large gymnasium or field, and two new 25-piece children's jigsaw puzzles.

- Mark one box with an X, and mark the back of each piece from that puzzle with an X as well.
- Mark the other box with a Z, and mark each of the corresponding pieces with a Z.
- Mark 16 small envelopes with an X, place one piece from the X puzzle in each envelope, and seal it. Put the nine remaining pieces back in their box.
- Do likewise for the 16 pieces from the Z puzzle.
- Set up a big table at home base, then designate five checkpoints about 30 to 40 yards away from home.
- Of the 32 envelopes, give to each of four sponsors four X envelopes and four Z envelopes.
- To the fifth sponsor give the two puzzle boxes.
- Assign one sponsor to each checkpoint; the sponsor with the boxes goes to checkpoint five.

Now divide all the kids into an X team and a Z team. Choose a team captain for each team, then divide both teams into four equal subteams. While the two team captains stay at home base, each subteam makes the round of the checkpoints in a different order:

Group A:	1-2-3-4-5
Group B:	4-1-2-3-5
Group C:	3-4-1-2-5
Group D:	2-3-4-1-5

The entire subteam must travel to and from each checkpoint together. The sponsor at each checkpoint gives each subteam a task to perform; upon

Continued on page 50

FOOTBALL

TOUCHDOWN!

CAN YOU RECALL WHICH NFL TEAMS GO WITH THE FOLLOWING CLUES?

__________ 1. Ranch hands

__________ 2. Cherokee, Navajo, Blackfoot, etc.

__________ 3. Bald birds

__________ 4. Catholic officials

__________ 5. Goliaths

__________ 6. Eric the Red's crew

__________ 7. Koala, grizzly, panda, etc.

__________ 8. Suitcase stuffers

__________ 9. Kings of the beasts

__________ 10. Pirates

__________ 11. Gold diggers

__________ 12. Holy ones

__________ 13. Swift birds of prey

__________ 14. Head bashers

__________ 15. Small whales

__________ 16. Young horses

__________ 17. Minutemen

__________ 18. F-15s

__________ 19. William Cody namesakes

__________ 20. Ironmen

__________ 21. Fossil drillers

__________ 22. Earth colors

__________ 23. India's cats

__________ 24. Vandals

__________ 25. Rodeo mounts

__________ 26. Aquatic fliers

__________ 27. Indian leaders

__________ 28. The electric company

ON ICE

HOCKEY

COME ON, ALL YOU HOCKEY JOCKS. SEE HOW MANY NHL TEAMS YOU CAN NAME FROM THESE CLUES. AND REMEMBER— NO HIGH-STICKING!

__________ 1. Birds in tuxedos

__________ 2. These big ones available at Burger King

__________ 3. These are "lite" swords

__________ 4. The compass always points to these satellites

__________ 5. Fast airplanes

__________ 6. Frequent ones receive bonus mileage

__________ 7. These guys are from the Great White North

__________ 8. Embarrassed parts of a bird

__________ 9. On fire and all ablaze

__________ 10. "You got me singing the —"

__________ 11. Remote inhabitants, much like Gilligan

__________ 12. Forest police

__________ 13. Falling from a syrupy tree

__________ 14. Well-drilled wells, not for water

__________ 15. Name of the bear in Reynard the Fox

__________ 16. A native of northern Europe

__________ 17. Ten, jack, queen, —

__________ 18. This is a great kind of idea

__________ 19. French Canadian or Canadian French

__________ 20. A dark bird of prey

__________ 21. The fallen angel

completion of the task, the sponsor gives the group one envelope for their team's puzzle. Here are sample tasks; create tasks appropriate for your own group:

Checkpoint 1: Sing one verse of "Pharaoh Pharaoh"
Checkpoint 2: Recite John 3:16 backwards
Checkpoint 3: Sing "Deep and Wide" with hand motions while running in place
Checkpoint 4: Form a six-person pyramid and recite the Pledge of Allegiance
Checkpoint 5: (captain only) Do an impersonation of Elvis

Each subgroup must return to home base after each checkpoint and hand the envelope to their captain. The captain will put the **unopened** envelopes on the table. When all the envelopes are in and the entire team—that is, all four subteams—has returned to home base, the team captain must then go to checkpoint five, complete the task given, and return to home base with the box containing the remaining pieces to the team's puzzle. The envelopes are then torn open and the puzzle is completed by the team. The first team to complete its puzzle wins. (Contributed by Gary Tapley, Monahans, Tex.)

Pudding Fling

For this sloppy relay race, form teams of four boys and four girls each. Give each team a five-pound can of chocolate pudding, a large spoon, and a toilet seat. Teams choose one member to sit on a chair about eight feet from the rest of the members and, holding up the toilet seat, put his face in its circle. The teams line up in columns.

On a signal players one at a time scoop up a spoonful of pudding, fling it at the face of the person with the toilet seat, and run to the back of the line. Team members continue taking turns flinging pudding until their can is empty.

You decide what constitutes a win. The winning team may be the team whose pudding is gone first, the team who got the most pudding on the toilet seat and the face of their teammate, or a combination of both. Equip the team member holding the toilet seat with a plastic garbage bag to wear as a poncho to keep the pudding off her clothes. (Contributed by Jerry Meadows, Hershey, Penn.)

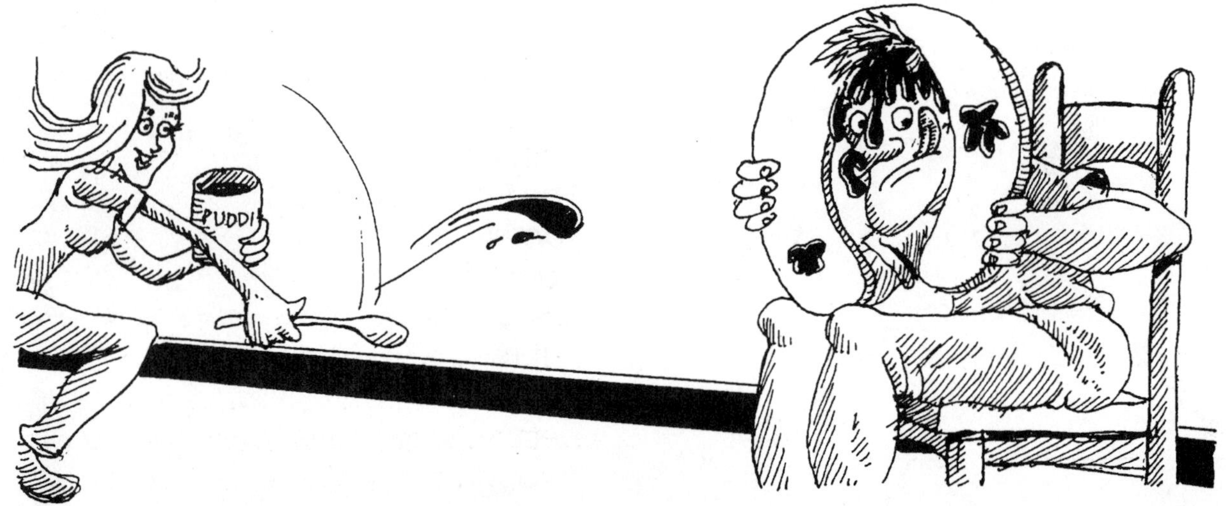

Q-Tip Shuffle

This game may leave the taste of cotton in kids' mouths, but it's fun!

Form teams of 10 or less. Place one person from each team about 30 feet ahead of the rest of the team. The first players on each team place up to 10 Q-Tips in various parts of their body (ears, nose, mouth, hair, crook of arms, pockets, shoes). They cannot carry any Q-Tips with their hands.

Then they shuffle ahead to their teammates, trying not to drop any Q-Tips. Their teammates must then dislodge the Q-Tips **with their teeth** and drop them into their team's pile. The "biter" then runs back to the rest of the team and tags the next person in line, who already has their Q-Tips placed and is ready to do the shuffle. The first carrier stays at the Q-Tip pile and becomes the next "biter."

The relay continues until all the members of one team have completed the relay, shuffling their team to victory. (Contributed by Michael Anderson, Englewood, Colo.)

Quiz Crisscross

Mark off a square playing area. Label the four corners with A, B, C, and D. Divide the group into four teams and assign each team a corner of the square. The object of the game is for each team to begin at its point of the square and move to the opposite corner.

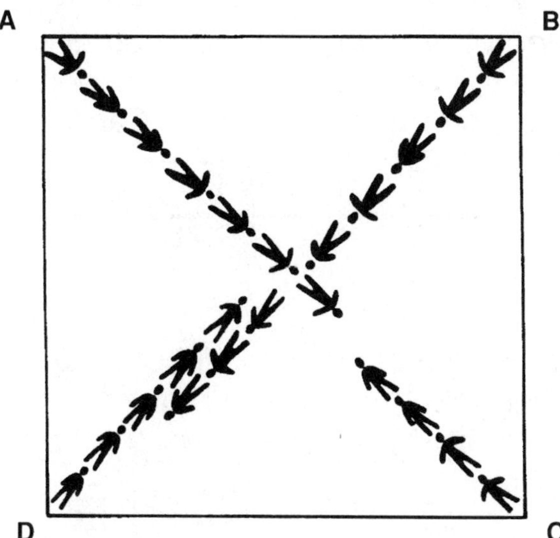

Teams move by correctly answering a Bible question. Players who answer correctly move their team toward the opposite corner by lying down on the floor with their feet toward their **home** corner and their head toward the **opposite** corner—their destination. As other players correctly answer questions, they lie down feet-to-head with the players already lying down. The idea is to make a human, horizontal "ladder" that reaches from their home corner to the opposite destination corner.

If the first person on team A cannot correctly answer the question, team B gets a chance to answer, and so on through teams C and D if necessary.

The first team to reach their opposite corner is the winner. To make it easier let the whole team have a shot at answering the question before moving on to another team. However, no one who is already lying down may answer a question. (Contributed by Mary Legner, Flushing, N.Y.)

Reverse Garbage Bag Soccer

Fill a garbage bag with inflated balloons and twist-tie it. Wrap the bag with masking tape to reinforce the bag, and use it for a soccer ball. Set up the field like regular soccer, but reverse the rules of play as follows: The fielders cannot kick the soccer ball, but must use their hands to hit or throw the ball to other players. Fielders incur a penalty for kicking the ball.

The goalie, on the other hand, is not allowed to use his hands—he blocks goals by using his body and feet. Keep an extra garbage-bag soccer ball on hand in case you bust one. (Contributed by Bert L. Jones, Opp, Ala.)

Rollerball

When you discuss 1 Corinthians 12 or the need for teamwork in your group, use this idea.

All players lie down on the floor in two lines, side by side with teammates and toe to toe with the other team. Ask players in one line to scoot towards players in the other line until the back sides of the legs are almost touching. On the signal, the pair at one end of the line passes a Nerf ball to the next pair using only their feet. The object is to pass the ball from one end of the line to the other and back again, using only the feet. Play several rounds so the players can get the hang of working with each other to keep the ball from hitting the floor or falling off the line. (Michael Capps, East Flat Rock, N.C.)

Scared Stiff

For this hair raiser, choose several long-haired guys as contestants. Each guy chooses two girls to be on his team. Give the girls a full bottle of super-hold hair spray, a blow dryer, and a brush, then tell them the objec-

tive: to style the guys' hair in five minutes. The winner is the guy whose hair is sticking up and out the farthest. Award consolation prizes for "do's" that are especially funky. (Contributed by Stephen Troglio, Palo Heights, Ill.)

Scripture Scattergories

Here's a version of the popular game Scattergories. Print up a Scattergories-type game sheet listing the categories below and distribute to individual players or to teams. For each round of the game, randomly choose a letter of the alphabet (you can use the letter selector in the Scattergories game or write letters of the alphabet on slips of paper to be drawn from a hat). The object of the game is to see which player or team can come up with the most answers that begin with the letter of the alphabet selected. For example, if the letter is B, then the answers could be **Bartholomew**, **Battle Hymn of the Republic**, **Bible**, **beautiful**, and so on. Play several rounds using a different letter each time.

Points are scored for every word that was not chosen by another player or team. In other words, if more than one player writes "Bartholomew," then no one gets any points for it. To earn points players must write down words or phrases that no one else has written down.

A character in the Bible
The title of a hymn or Christian song
A Christian book
A word that describes the Christian life
Something to pray for
A well-known preacher
A book of the Bible
A place in the Bible
The name of a church or denomination
Something you do in a worship service
Another word for **sin**
A member of our church (or youth group)
A Christian musician or recording artist
Where people go after church
First word of a Bible verse you can quote from memory
Something you find in a Sunday-school classroom
Another name or descriptive word for **Jesus**
An excuse people give for not going to church

Search and Destroy

It's the last day of camp, the kids need an outdoor free-for-all, and—if you've been keeping track of team points all week—you need a final contest by which even the last-place team could conceivably catch up and win the entire week's competition.

So here's a combination scavenger hunt/water-balloon fight. First hide water balloons throughout the playing area (the more colors of balloons, the better). Begin the game itself by dividing players into teams and telling them the rules:

• After players find balloons, they must run, crawl, walk, sneak, or bluff their way back to "headquarters," where a sponsor tallies the balloons and records the score for the appropriate teams.

• Here's the twist: the point values of different balloon colors are not told to the players until the end of the game. (For example, yellow ones are 20 points each; blue, 15 points; red, 5 points; white, –5 points; pink, –10 points; three orange brought in on one trip by a player, 30 points; etc.)

• After the sponsor records players' points, the players are free to dispose of the balloons any way they want—and here's where the water-balloon fight begins.

• Players continue the process of finding, recording, and destroying until time runs out.

To keep the scorekeeper's skin dry, deduct big points for lobbing balloons at them. And when the melee is over, conduct a brief but crucial game to see which team can pick up the most balloon pieces. (Contributed by David Holton, Elyria, Ohio)

Shaving Cream Piñatas

At your next slop-fest (or whatever you call messy-game night), fill several large balloons with shaving cream and let some burly hunks take turns bashing the balloons. The game doesn't have to have a point—it's just fun. You could also fill the balloons with whipped cream or anything that comes in a pressurized can. All you need is patience to fill the balloons. (Contributed by Michael Frisbie, Hobbs, N. Mex.)

Spell My Feet

The object of this hilarious game is for players to form words as quickly as they can. Two teams of five members each sit facing the audience. Using a large black marker, the leaders inscribe letters on the soles of the feet of the players. The first player on each team gets an A on one foot and an N on the other; the second receives an E and a T; the third G and R; the fourth O and M; the fifth S and P.

The leader then calls out a word, and the group that is able to line up their feet to spell that word in the shortest amount of time wins that particular round.

Easy words, worth 5 points each: **master**, **roast**, **smear**, **togas**,

snore.

More difficult phrases, worth 10 points each: **ten proms**, **get Spam**, **great son**, **more naps**.

The last series, worth 20 points per word, requires teams to compose their own words: the team using the most letters to form a word or combination of words wins the round. (Contributed by Jim Johnson, Longview, Tex.)

Sticky-Buns Balloon Burst Relay

For this takeoff on "Tapehead" (**Ideas 46**), ask the kids to line up in pairs behind a line on one side of the room. On the other side of the room spread inflated balloons across the floor. Give each team of two a roll of masking tape, and tell the kids that on "Go!" they are to apply the tape around the midsection of the person whose birthday is closest to today. The pair must use the whole roll of tape and it must be put on sticky-side out.

When the tape is used up, the taped players must crab-walk to the balloons and bring back to their partners waiting at the starting line as many balloons as they can carry without using their hands. The waiting partner must then burst the balloons and save the ring part of the balloon (where you blow it up) to verify the number of balloons retrieved. Balloons popped by the sticky-bunned teammate don't count. The pair with the most rings wins.

This is a game to videotape. The kids are so dizzy from spinning around to get the tape on that they have a hard time doing the rest of the relay. (Contributed by Keith Posehn, Folsom, Calif.)

A Strobe Situation

Can you imagine charades illuminated with a strobe light? Then you begin to get the idea of this game. Be careful, though—it can be as thought-provoking as it is hilarious.

Before the meeting, write on slips of paper situations that the group can role play—a family confrontation, spectators at a sports event, a dance, impressions of the congregation on Sunday morning, the choir and director, a church conference.

Form groups of four or five kids, then hand out your prewritten situations. Allow five minutes for the groups to plan their presentations. They can use actions only—no words. Each group performs for the other groups, who try to guess the situation being acted out.

The surprise element is that when the acting starts, the lights go out and the strobe goes on until the performance is concluded. Customize the situations to your own group. Discussion following the "strobe situation" may be appropriate. (Contributed by Sondra Edwards, Boone, N.C.)

Sword Search by the Numbers

Here's a twist on the old Sword Drill. If your group uses the same translation of the Bible, create a question they must decipher by using your clues.

To code the question "Who kissed Jesus?" for users of the New International Version, for instance, you'd write on an overhead projector the numbers 40-1-16-16, 10-14-33-35, and 54-6-3-17.

Here what the first set of numbers indicates: the 40th book in the Bible (Matthew), chapter 1, verse 16, and the 16th word in the verse ("who"). The second set of numbers indicates 2 Samuel 14:33, the word "kissed"; and the third set, 1 Timothy 6:3, the word "Jesus." The first student to stand, state the decoded question, and answer it gets the point. (Contributed by Richard Crisco, Milton, Fla.)

Tarzan Kickball

Jazz up traditional kickball by setting up a portable sound system and playing background music of prerecorded bits of fast-moving, motion-picture soundtracks. You can also throw in some lively old stuff like "Oklahoma!" Your local library is a good resource for music. As you're making the tape, every once in a while dub in a Tarzan yell (also from the library). The cassette should run about 35 minutes, with 10 to 15 Tarzan yells interspersed throughout the recording.

With the music playing in the background, play regulation kickball, only with the following addition: When players hear the Tarzan yell, they must immediately stop playing, no matter what the action is. The kicking team must run to their team base in center field and squat down, while the fielding team runs to their team base behind home plate and squats down. Making the teams run through each other to get to their base adds to the excitement of the game. The first team all together and squatting down receives 10 points.

Once the winner is determined for that yell, normal play resumes exactly where it left off. Runners return to their positions on the bases, and the ball is returned to whomever had it at the time of the yell. Runs are scored as usual. The team with the most runs at the end of the time period wins.

To play longer than the tape's 35 minutes, just rewind the tape. Assign a judge to say which team is first to be all together and squatting after the yell.

A variation: Rather than using the three-out system, let each team bat once through the lineup, then switch to outfield. (Contributed by Rich Cooper and Tim Maughan, St. Charles, Ill.)

Team Nintendo

Borrow or rent a big screen TV and the latest Nintendo offering for two teams of kids to battle for the video-game championship.

Start the game with one person from each team at the controls and the rest of the team standing 10 feet behind the players. Players have 30 seconds at the controls—you manage the stopwatch—while their teams cheer them on. After 30 seconds the next two players run up to the controls and take over, hopefully without missing a shot. When all members of the teams have taken their turn playing, round one is over and the score is recorded.

Play as long as enthusiasm lasts and promise a stupendous prize to the team with the most points. (Contributed by Jeff Koch, Elk Grove, Calif.)

Team Volleybasket

Divide the group into two teams on opposite sides of a volleyball net that is set in a basketball court. The serving team lines up along the sideline facing the server (see diagram), who does a normal volleyball serve from the normal serving position. After serving the ball, the server runs to the first person in line and gives that player a **high** five. That player in turn gives a **low** five to the next person, who gives a **high** five to the next, and so on to the end of the line. That last person then runs to the first person in the line and starts the process all over. Each time they complete the line (called the "slap-happy wave") they get one point.

Meanwhile, on the other side of the net, the volleyball is volleyed among the team members until it gets to the stationary shooter. It doesn't matter if the ball hits the ground during the volley. Players just pick it up and continue to volley to the shooter, who grabs the volleyball and shoots it, basketball-like, through the hoop. The shooter keeps at it until a basket is made, which also stops the action on the serving side of the net.

At that point the volleying team lines up facing the former shooter, who is now the server. The server makes a legal volleyball serve and starts the "slap-happy wave" while the receiving team volleys the ball back to **their** shooter. The serve alternates each time after the basket is made.

There are no points given for the basket—only for completing a slap-happy wave. The first team to 21 points wins. (Contributed by Brad Edgbert, Fremont, Calif.)

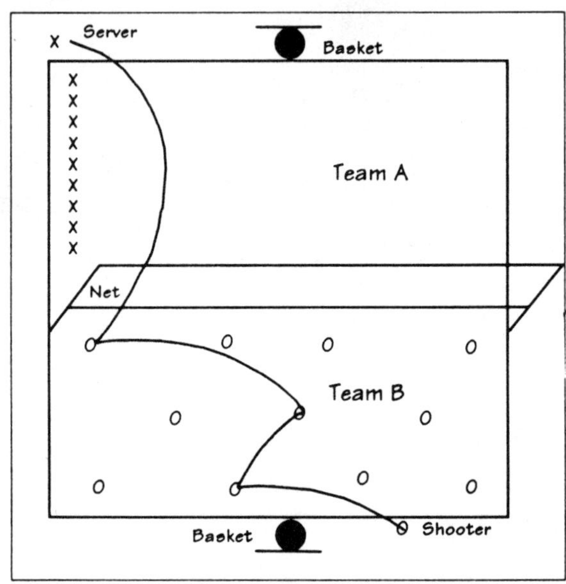

Teddy Bear Football

Although this game sounds corny, bear with us—a little hype and the right mix of humor makes this flag-football perversion more than bearable. In fact, it's actually become an annual event at one church, drawing players and spectators alike.

It's traditional flag football, though played in a gym or fellowship hall—and with a teddy bear instead of a football.

In a gym roomy enough for running, passing, and—yes—kicking a teddy bear, erect goalposts from two-by-fours, or use crepe paper taped to the walls for field-goal markers. In a short gym, for instance, allow only five downs. If the team does not score, it must punt the bear to the other team or try for a field goal on the fifth down. (Be sure to use traditional punting and kicking formations.) You may want to include a girls-only quarter, followed by a boys-only quarter. During the remaining quarters, keep the girls active by requiring that a girl touch the ball once during each possession. In co-ed teams, of course, limit the physical contact involved in blocking or running over people.

A 15-inch bear is just the right size; it will work well for kickoffs, passes, punts, and field goals. (The smaller stuffed bears just don't provide the same level of sadistic pleasure.) KIPP in

Indianapolis sells reasonably priced carnival bears (800/428-1153 or 317/634-5507). You may be able to borrow a bear, but the likelihood of returning it the way you received it is slim. In fact, you'll probably need a replacement bear to finish off the game—so get two.

Cue the referee to use creative calls like "Roughing the teddy!" Then play traditional flag football, modifying the rules to fit your situation.

Halftime? Offer a refreshment stand (free snacks), a kazoo marching band, and the crowning of a queen (a guy dressed up like a girl). (Contributed by Steve Smoker, Raleigh, N.C.)

Toilet Tag

This version of tag brings a new flush to that time-worn game. Mark off the playing area suitable for your size group. Designate one or more players to be "It"—who run around attempting to tag other players, who are then "dead" and must kneel down on one knee with one arm out and to the side. Dead players can reenter the game only when a free player sits on their knee and pulls down their hand—"flushes the toilet." The game ends when all the players except "It" are kneeling. (Contributed by Randy Hausler, Iowa City, Ia.)

Trac-Ball Tourney

Here are two games—an outdoor field game and an indoor gym game—that use Trac-Ball scoops—something like the Mexican jai alai. You can pick up a Wham-O Trac-Ball set (two scoops and a ball or two) for around $15 from most department, toy, or sporting-goods stores. (Contributed by Dik LaPine, Auburn Hills, Mich.)

Trac Football

Remember the variation of football called "Speedball" or "Razzle Dazzle Touch Football"—where the quarterback must pass, and then receivers themselves can pass anywhere on the field in order to move the ball toward the goal? Now play with Trac-Ball scoops and a Trac-Ball ball—and you've got Trac Football.

Only three rules:

1. Play is dead not by touching or tackling the ball carrier, but when the ball touches the ground. Defensive strategy, then, calls for interfering with a throw or a reception, and trying to knock the ball from a carrier's scoop. A team gets four downs in which to score (see rule 3 about first downs).

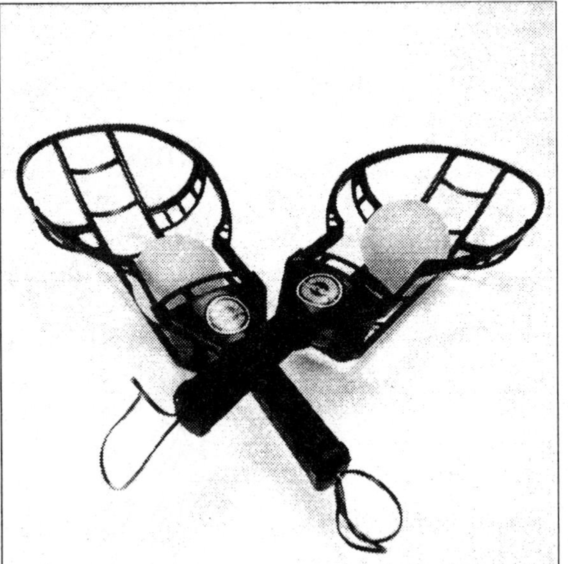

2. The ball is advanced only by throwing it, not by running it. A player may scramble behind the line of scrimmage (i.e., the point at which the play begins, or the point at which he catches the ball), but a ball carrier may not run beyond the line of scrimmage until he hurls the ball. Teammates (potential receivers) may run anywhere, of course.

3. Two complete passes earn a first down. Those passes may come within a single play; or one may occur in the first down, the other during the third down. Any time during the four downs that a team completes its second pass, it earns a first down. (If your group gets good at Trac Football, increase the difficulty of earning first downs: require three completes for a first, award two consecutive first downs if a team completes three passes within a single play, etc.)

Interceptions, kickoffs, hikes, punts—they're all done similarly to regular touch football, but within the limitations imposed by these three rules.

Six scoops may be a minimum to start out with. Some Trac Football players don't think a maximum exists. "The more rackets, the better!" they say.

Macho Trac-Ball

This lacrosse-like game will become a favorite of the rough-and-tough guys in your group. Situate two equal teams of any size on opposite sides of a center line. Now supply indoor hockey nets at either end (or draw or tape an area on the two opposite baseline walls, or simply use the closed gym doors as goals if they are at the proper ends of the gym).

Equip players with two balls and at least six Trac-Ball scoops. The object of the contest is to hurl a ball into the opponent's goal—but at no time can players cross the center line into their opponents' side. Teams may defend their goals by putting as many of their players as they want in front of the goals. In so doing, they'll get stung a bit by balls flung at their goal, but they'll also be thwarting attempts on their goal by the opposition across the center line.

The twist to this dodging game is the spin that Trac-Ball scoops put on the ball. It's hard to judge curves coming at you 60 to 80 miles per hour.

Turnover

Form two teams of six players each (more are okay, but no fewer than four players on a team). Using a volleyball and regulation net and court, play volleyball, but with this difference: The player whose mistake gives the other team the serve or a point will be turned over to play on the opposing team's side.

It gets heroic as one team dwindles to two or even one player who must stand 10 or 11 opponents. (Contributed by Greg Miller, Knoxville, Tenn.)

Turns and Trades

Form two concentric circles of equal numbers of kids facing each other. Tell the kids to trade one thing they have on for one thing the person facing them has on—jewelry, shoes, socks, belts, hats, etc. The players must then put on the items they traded for.

Now ask the inner circle to move three people to their right so that each player has a new partner. Partners must make another trade; **but they cannot trade anything they've received in a trade**. Next ask the outer circle to move two people to their right and repeat the trading process. Call for one more turn and trade.

Kids will now have run out of jewelry, shoes, etc., and may be getting embarrassed about another impending trade. So have some fun with them: tell the outer circle to move two people to the right again. You'll hear moans, but when they move, tell them to trade something that has already been traded. Repeat this twice.

Now tell them they have two minutes to retrieve all of their items. Offer a prize to the first one to bring all of the items up to you, or you can time the group to see how quickly they can all retrieve their things and then sit down. (Contributed by Terry Linhart, Fort Wayne, Ind.)

Ultimate Water Balloons

Remember Ultimate Football (**Ideas 45**)? Played with a Frisbee, that game combines teamwork with athletic prowess as the Frisbee is moved down the field in nonstop, continuous play with any one of a number of various twists to the game.

A favorite warm-weather variation is to substitute water balloons for the Frisbee. The referee should be supplied with 36 water balloons in advance (for an approximately 30-minute game), which are stored up and down along the sidelines (this allows for quick replacement of the two balloons that the ref always carries in his hands). The referee must hustle to get a balloon to the other team when one breaks as soon as possible so that play is not unduly interrupted. (Contributed by Kevin Turner, Tacoma, Wash.)

Velcro War

For this textile tag game, go to a craft store and purchase golf-ball-size plastic balls and Velcro strips. Use a hot-glue gun to attach the strips to the balls. (The more balls you have, the better the game.)

Then declare a Velcro war among the kids. All combatants must wear a fluffy wool sweater to qualify them to carry "weapons" (the prepared plastic balls). They should also wear some kind of eye protection. In the church or at a school, identify a playing area that includes lots of hiding places accessible by more than one route.

The following rules will get you started. Once it's all-out war, make up the rules as you go along.

- Once a Velcro ball sticks to your sweater, you're not allowed to take it off—it's a wound. Three wounds equal a kill.
- You can play the game as teams, like a lethal version of Capture the Flag. The smaller the group, however, the better it is to play every man for himself.
- You may expand the target area by requiring all players to wear wool caps.
- The harder you throw the balls, the less likely they are to stick and the more likely they are to injure, so attack with lobs and crafty tosses.

(Contributed by Dik LaPine, Auburn Hills, Mich.)

Wacky Balloon

Place a ball of Silly Putty inside a seven-inch balloon and partially blow up the balloon. Clip the knot off as close as possible and you've got a durable balloon that moves in swirls. Now play "volley-pong" on a ping-pong table, using hands instead of paddles to hit the balloon. Except when players serve or return the serve, they must make the balloon bounce off the opponents' side before it can be returned. Place teams of two on either end of the table. Play to five, and then trade teams so everyone gets to play.

You can also use the wacky balloon to play indoor baseball. The pitchers can get the Silly Putty whirling around the inside of the balloon before they pitch the ball. Or during the teaching time, toss the balloon to indicate who must answer one of the questions. (Contributed by Doug Partin, Lubbock, Tex.)

Water-Balloon Soccer

On the next hot day when you're outside, divide the group into as many teams of 10 to 15 as you can. Before the game fill a minimum of three water balloons per team member. Also prepare one hat (or helmet) per team: with duct tape, affix tacks, point out, to a helmet or ball cap. The hat is then placed on an X on the ground about 20 feet from the starting line.

On a signal, the first person in line for each team runs to the hat and puts it on. The second person in the line lobs a balloon in the air in the general direction of the first player, who attempts to break the balloon with the hat. If the hat-wearing teammate misses, a second and third balloon are thrown. If he **still** doesn't puncture a balloon with his hat (and drench himself in the process), he puts the hat down and goes to the end of his line—and the next teammate in line tries her luck. The first team that cycles the entire team through wins the event. (Contributed by Brad Edgbert, Fremont, Calif.)

Water Joust

Play this active game in the shallow end of a swimming pool or lake. You need two large truck or tractor inner tubes, two boards large enough to cover the inner tubes, two plungers, and two six-foot broom handles. Tie a board on each inner tube to make a fighting platform, and replace the plunger handles with the broom handles to extend the reach of the "lance."

You're ready to joust.

Divide your group into two teams. Each team sends two people into the water for each round. The "squire" maneuvers the inner tube, while the "knight" kneels on the board and wields the "lance." The object is to push the opposing knight off the inner tube with the soft end of the plunger. (No swinging of lances to hit opponents!) The team winning the most rounds wins the event.

WARNING: Leaders who use this idea must consider safety precautions appropriate to their groups and the circumstances in which they play—spotters to guard falling jousters from striking the pool edge, safety guards to separate jousters if the game gets too rough or the action moves out too far into the lake, life jackets, and so on. (Contributed by Barry W. Perkins, Paducah, Ky.)

Waterball Samurai

The object of this wet warfare is to hit the other team's samurai with a water-soaked foam ball as many times as possible in one minute.

Materials needed: Wiffle bat, foam balls (at least six), water buckets (at least three), step stool (from the water fountain), time keeper and point counter, chalk or tape.

Make boundaries for the game by drawing or marking with tape a six-foot-diameter circle. Place the low stool in the center of the circle. Fifteen feet outside the circle's edge, place three buckets on a line.

Divide the groups into teams of five or six players each, and ask each team to select one player to be the samurai. The samurai from the defending team stands on the stool in the center of the circle and may not step off the stool during the round. The remaining defending-team members position themselves on the perimeter of the circle to defend their samurai from the waterballs. They can move neither into the circle nor beyond its perimeter. They must confine their movements to the edge of the circle. Their samurai, meanwhile, defends himself with a Wiffle bat to divert waterballs.

From behind the water-bucket line, the opposing team throws water-soaked foam balls at the samurai in the circle, attempting to hit him. If a thrown ball falls short of the circle, an offensive team member may run up

to retrieve it and either carry it back to the line to throw it again or else toss it to one of the other team members already behind the line, who may then throw the ball at the samurai. Offensive players may not, however, enter the defending team's circle to retrieve any balls.

The round ends when one minute is up or all the waterballs are inside the circle. The offensive team gets one point each time they hit the samurai with a waterball, or for each time the samurai steps off the step stool.

If you have more than three or four teams, you may want to get more foam balls and mark out more water-ball courts so you can have several games going on simultaneously. Winners from each court can play one another in a championship game. (Contributed by Doug Partin, Lubbock, Tex.)

Whisper the Flavor Relay

Using a package of assorted Lifesavers or any other type of hard candy or flavored jelly beans, play this relay in which team members guess the flavor candy they are tasting.

Divide the group into teams of five to eight players. Each team chooses one member to be the distributor, to whom you give plastic sandwich bags of candies that are identified by flavor. The teams line up in columns, with their distributors standing about 10 feet away from the head of the line. On the signal the first person on each team (the "runner") races to the team's distributor, receives a piece of candy, and races back to the team. The runner puts the candy in the mouth of the second person in line (the "eater"), who should not see the color of the candy. As soon as the eater recognizes the flavor, he or she whispers the name of the flavor to the runner, who returns to the distributor and whispers the flavor guessed.

If the guess is correct, the runner races to the end of the line, and the eater then becomes the new runner. Play continues as before.

If the eater's guess is incorrect, the runner returns to the eater to ask for another guess, then returns to the distributor to repeat the guess in a whisper. (If all distributors give out the same flavors of candy at the same time, one team could hear the guess of another team if the guessing is not done in whispers.) A team must repeat this until the correct flavor is guessed.

The team that is first to return its initial runner to the front of the line is the winner. (Contributed by Greg Miller, Knoxville, Tenn.)

You Look Great Tonight!

This revealing games goes over most effectively at a dressy event that the kids attend with their dates. Select several male "volunteers" to leave the room for a few moments. They return one at a time, blindfolded, and each one hears this:

> Thank you for taking part, [name]. You were recommended to be one of our contestants on the basis of your highly developed ability of observing girls' styles. Don't you agree that our girls always come out nicely dressed? Great. I'm sure you'll have no trouble giving us a full description of the style and colors of the clothes your date is wearing tonight.

After a few moments of vague mumbling, detached observation, or sometimes brilliant improv, bring the next guy in. (Contributed by Fred Swallow, Auckland, New Zealand)

Solution to Murder Mystery (from page 38)
John Stone was in his office at 8 o'clock when his secretary Ms. Wright (with whom he had been having an affair) came in. On the counsel of his lawyer, John broke off the relationship with her and let her go as his secretary to avoid being blackmailed. She reacted violently, smashing the picture of John's wife. John came around the desk to try and restrain her, but she pushed him away. He tripped, fell backwards, and hit his head on the aquarium stand. He fell unconscious on the floor, but not dead. The janitor came in just as John hit his head and fell to the floor. He saw it was an accident and told Ms. Wright to go home and he would make it look like a robbery.

Before he was able to do this, however, Steve Stone came in. Seeing the mess and his brother on the floor, he went to the file and took out some papers he had falsified so that he could steal the company from his brother. He felt that if they were found it would make him look guilty of killing John. He was sure that the lawyer had killed his brother and was going to pin it on him. He then went back to his office and waited there as if he had never left.

Again the janitor was unable to finish making the place look like a robbery because the lawyer came in. He also looked for the papers that Steve had taken. When he could not find them, he figured that Steve was the murderer and that he was going to use the papers to frame him. So he also left and created an alibi.

Soon after this John's wife received a call telling her that he was having an affair. When she came down she was out for blood, but it had already been shed. When she saw the mess she was afraid that it would look like she had indeed killed her husband in a fit of rage. She also left, but what she saw was the main piece of evidence. She said that the fish were alive ("wiggling around him") at 9:50, which meant that the aquarium could not have been broken by the secretary at 7 o'clock. However, no one else had mentioned the aquarium being broken—except the janitor. Mr. Mun said Ms. Wright pushed John, and his head hit the aquarium busting it.

When Sam Swade left John's office, the janitor again tried to mess up the room. His intent was not simply to make it look like a robbery, but to really rob John Stone. Since he believed his blackmail scheme was already destroyed (Mr. Mun thought John was dead), he decided to remove the safe keys from John's body, clean the place out, and pin the murder and robbery on Ms. Wright, Steve Stone, or Sam Swade. But as he searched John's pockets for the keys, John began to wake up. Mr. Mun picked John up enough to strike his head again, this time truly killing John Stone.

To cover his tracks, he called John's wife and told her John was having an affair. He knew she suspected it and had overheard her threatening John in the office. He did not anticipate that it would be her testimony that would put him away.

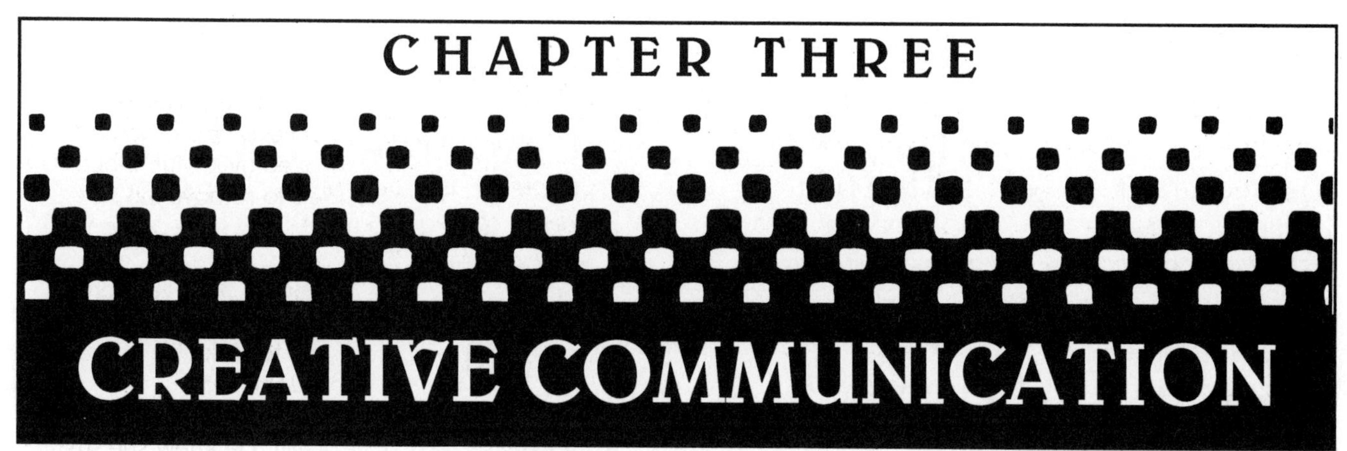

CHAPTER THREE

CREATIVE COMMUNICATION

ABC Christianity

Your kids have doubtlessly noticed that there are different types of Christians. Here's a small-group activity that allows students to creatively examine the types—and in the process, maybe take a hard look at what kind they are.

Divide into groups and assign a letter of the alphabet to each group. Using their assigned letter, the groups then come up with as many words as they can that describe different types of Christians or Christianity. To avoid irrelevant words, require groups to write a short explanation or description of vague words. Some examples are given on this page. (Contributed by Tom Daniel, Little Rock, Ark.)

boring
bashful
billboard
(showy, like to attract attention)
baby

faithful
frontier
(bold leaders away from church "frontier area")
financial
(try to buy their Christianity)
future
(party now, live the Christian life later)

dull
dedicated
dependent
(depend on others for their Christianity)
deceiving

Amazing Discoveries

Using a TV talk-show format, offer a youth night of Amazing Discoveries that features kids who act the part of biblical characters who observed or experienced some miracles of Jesus. Prepare one student to be the host and several others to tell about the miracles they witnessed or experienced. (Contributed by Bert Jones, Opp, Ala.)

Baseball Card Devotional

Have the kids in your group bring their baseball-card collections to the meeting and share information about their favorite cards, most valuable cards, unusual trades, and so on. You might invite a professional collector or dealer to the meeting to explain why some cards are more valuable than others, how to collect cards as an investment, and so on.

With that introduction, the stage is set for a devotional using sports cards as an object lesson. Ask the group to imagine that they are on a Christian card—a card with their picture on the front and biography and stats on the back. Here are some questions to pose for your group:

- The front of a sports card always captures the individual in a flattering, complimentary pose. If you were pictured on a Christian card, what would your card catch you doing—singing, marching, debating, cheerleading, sports, or—?
- What would the stats on the back of your card reveal about you? Most cards' stats begin with the year a player first entered the league; if the first year listed on your card was the year you accepted Christ or began your spiritual journey, what would the following years say about you, statistically?
- What makes some cards unusually valuable is the fact that they are "error cards"—that is, the publishers made a mistake on the card. Some detail on them is wrong. What mistake, failure, shortcoming, handicap, or lapse in your faith has given you opportunity to grow stronger and to become more valuable to the kingdom?
- When a player autographs his own card, its value increases. How have you put your signature on people and places around you? What kind of mark are you making on the world?

Wrap up with a discussion of 2 Timothy 4:7-8. (Contributed by Kevin Wieser, Hobbs, N.M.)

Bowling Tourney Devotional

Use the sample on the following page to create a do-it-yourself Bible study for kids to take home and complete after a youth bowling tournament. Or you could adapt it for your wrap-up devotional talk immediately after the event. (Contributed by Mark Adams, Derwood, Md.)

STRIKES, SPARES, SPLITS, AND GUTTER BALLS

Ever notice how bowling is a lot like the Christian life?

• **STRIKES** occur in a Christian's life during times of great spiritual highs (like retreats and youth rallies). Because of those times, we follow through in our determination to put God first in our lives. Life actually becomes abundant! (Read **Matthew 6:33** for more about this.)

• **SPARES** usually follow shortly after the strikes. You leave a mountain-top experience committed to daily Bible study and prayer, and you keep rolling those strikes—at least for a week or so. Then you let yourself slip into old habits, and pretty soon your abundant life starts becoming meager again. If you realize your mistake and put God first again—start spending time with him again—abundant life can resume, kind of like picking up a spare. (Read **John 10:10** to see the kind of life God wants us to have.)

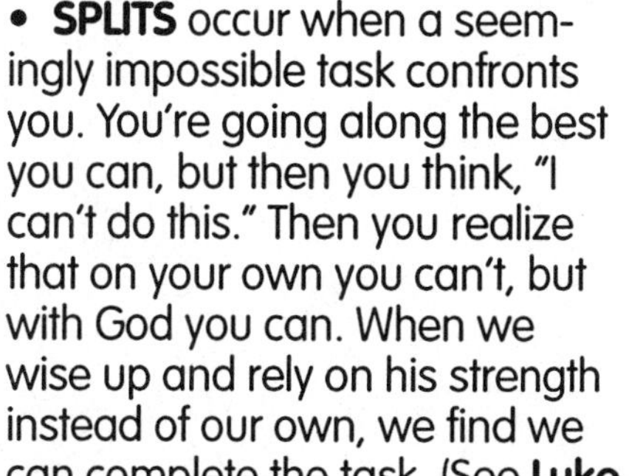

• **SPLITS** occur when a seemingly impossible task confronts you. You're going along the best you can, but then you think, "I can't do this." Then you realize that on your own you can't, but with God you can. When we wise up and rely on his strength instead of our own, we find we can complete the task. (See **Luke 1:37**.)

• **GUTTER BALLS** are what you get when you're too close to the edge and your momentum carries you into the gutter. Sometimes we Christians push God farther and farther from the center of our lives. We reserve him for Sundays alone. We wander from his will during the week, and sooner or later the inevitable happens—we tumble over the edge of association with the wrong crowd into participation with what they do. We've conformed to the standards of the world. (Paul warns about this in **Romans 12:1-2**.)

Well, fellow holy roller, it's my prayer that your Christian life will be full of strikes and spares—but mostly strikes!

Can You Hold, Please?

Assigned to a student or sponsor ahead of time so it can be practiced, this monologue suits a lesson or discussion about priorities and time with God. (Contributed by Brad Fulton, Millville, Calif.)

A man or woman is seated at an office desk covered with paperwork, which obviously consumes the worker's time. A telephone and calculator are on the desk; a wall calen-

dar hangs conspicuously within arm's reach. The phone rings.

Hello, Nancy speaking...Jesus? Jesus who?...uh huh...*(phone rings)* Can you hold please? *(switches lines)* Hello, Nancy speaking...Oh, hi honey...Sure, what do you need?...uh huh...yeah, I'll pick it up. White or whole wheat?...Okay...right, and four rolls of pastel blue two-ply...Sure, I'll run by there...oh, I forgot about that...yes, I'll meet you at the restaurant at, oh, say eight tonight...okay, see you then...*(crosses Monday off calendar)*...bye-bye, sweetheart. *(returns to the original call)* Thanks for holding. Okay, how can I help you?...Are you looking for a donation?...What's the cause? *(phone rings)* Sorry, can you hold again? *(switches lines)* Hello...yes sir...yes sir...of course, Mr. Jones...Thursday?...Sure, I don't see why not. How late do you think it will run?...uh huh...okay, Thursday it is. *(crosses Thursday off the calendar and returns to first caller)* Thanks for waiting. Now what did you say you wanted?...*(cradles the receiver on her shoulder, occupies herself with paperwork as she listens, obviously apathetic about the call)*...uh huh...and this is for which cause? *(phone rings)* I'm sorry, can you hold please? *(switches lines)* Hello, Nancy here. How are you, Sue?...Really? Great! So you're joining the health club, too?...Yeah, gotta take some pounds off, as usual...I'd love to give you a ride on Tuesday...okay... *(crosses Tuesday off)*...Bye. *(returns to original call)* All right now, what is it you're wanting?...*(writes memos and notes obviously unrelated to her conversation, punches calculator keys)*...Gee, I don't know...yeah...well, I'd rather not get involved right now...*(phone rings)*...Can you hold please? *(switches lines)* Hello?...Hi, Tom...yeah, I thought the kids responded well to my lesson last Sunday...sure, we'd better get down to planning that retreat...*(glancing at calendar)*... Friday night's open...Okay, Tom, see you Friday *(returns to first call)* Hello? You know, I just don't think I...yes, I know, but...That's true, but...of course...I understand, but I still don't want...*(phone rings)* I'm sorry, can you hold please? *(switches lines)* Hello, Nancy speaking...Hi, Miriam...it is?...where is it showing?...all right, I'll get the tickets for...let's see...*(studies calendar and crosses off Wednesday)*...for Wednesday...okay, bye. *(returns to first call)* Yeah, I'm back...yes I know it doesn't require much time, but I...I know that...look, I'd rather...no, you're not asking too much, it's just that I...*(phone rings)* Can you hold please? *(switches lines)* Hello, Nancy here...hi, honey...oh, no, I forgot all about it...yes, I remember now... Brian's weekend soccer tournament...*(crosses off Saturday and Sunday on the calendar)*...yeah...make sure he finishes his homework as soon as he gets home from practice tonight...okay...bye bye, honey. *(returns to original call)* Look, I've—*(aloud but to herself)* Funny, he hung up...*(looking at calendar)*...oh well, I was too busy anyway. *(hangs up phone, puts on coat, and walks out, briefcase in hand)*

Cheat Sheets

Want your students to take time during the coming week reviewing the lesson you just delivered? Promise a quiz next week over the same material, with tantalizing rewards for high scores—and then give them legitimate crib sheets to study from. You may even want to give them copies of the actual quizzes. Add Scripture references to the questions to allow them to find the answers for themselves in the Scripture. In short, do anything you can to help them do well on the upcoming quiz.

On Q day, however, they can't use notes during the quiz. (Contributed by Len Cuthbert, Hamilton, Ontario, Canada)

Chutes and Ladders

Life is full of ups and downs. Using a Chutes and Ladders game board and rules, play with the following additions: When players land on a ladder, they describe a good experience; when landing on a chute, they describe a bad experience. If players have trouble thinking of specific experiences, use the following questions to prompt them:

- What was the experience?
- Has the experience left a lasting impression on you?
- Describe the lesson you learned, whether it was a reward or a reprimand.
- How have you grown from this experience?

Conclude the play by discussing the kinds of experiences that individuals apparently have little control over—like the roll of the die. Ask the group how they think God fits into these kinds of experiences. Ask how God is a part of the good and the bad in our lives. (Contributed by Laurie Delgatto, Carlsbad, Calif.)

The C.O.N.D.O.M.

To assist your kids to take action against the lure of becoming sexually active, try this brand of C.O.N.D.O.M.

Ahead of time make up a set of cards the size of business cards like the sample below. Bring them to a meeting in a small, unlabeled box. At the meeting explain the following to the group:

> Since many schools have decided that the best method to assure safe sex is to distribute condoms, it's time for the church to take action and engage in the battle for the lives of America's youths. After much prayer I have decided that I will distribute condoms to this youth group.
>
> Unlike the condoms that schools distribute, however, my brand of condom has unique features. It is 100 percent effective, it's reusable, it has no clumsy wrapper to mess with, it doesn't need a government-paid social worker to demonstrate how it is used, it doesn't need to be hidden from nosy parents (in fact, I encourage you to give one to your parents), it fits easily in a wallet or a purse, and it's the only condom that promotes truly safe sex. It's even endorsed by God. With features like these, it just makes good sense that every teenager use the C.O.N.D.O.M. every day.

(Contributed by Mark Lehman, Grandview, Wash.)

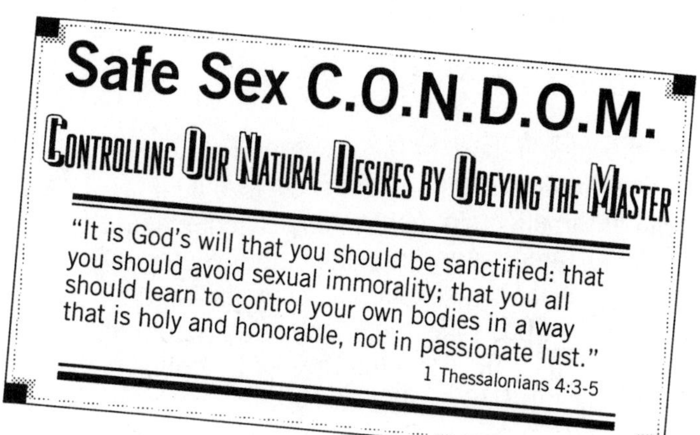

Safe Sex C.O.N.D.O.M.
Controlling Our Natural Desires by Obeying the Master
"It is God's will that you should be sanctified: that you should avoid sexual immorality; that you all should learn to control your own bodies in a way that is holy and honorable, not in passionate lust."
1 Thessalonians 4:3-5

Dare Box

In this adaptation of the game Truth or Dare, your kids may find creative ways to put their faith into action. Make a master list of activities (dares), including challenges that get your youths outside of their comfort zones (see the list on page 73 for ideas). Then put each dare in a numbered envelope and seal it.

Put all the envelopes in a box and ask each student to pick one. (Keep track of which dare each person has so that you can offer encouragement if needed.) The students read their dares, but they must keep them secret from the rest of the group until they've completed theirs. When a dare is completed, encourage the student to tell the rest of the group about the experience. If a dare is too intimidating to a student, allow that student to trade for a different one. (Contributed by Leslie Riley, Wright, Kans.)

Dear Believer

The handout on the page 74 is the partial text of a pamphlet published by the Freedom From Religion Foundation in Madison, Wisconsin.

Hand it out to your group, then set the students off on a mission to answer the articulate and potent arguments in this pamphlet. Direct them to get answers to the objections in this pamphlet from wherever they want—the Bible, their parents, other adults in the church, wherever. Then have them use their research to write a response to the "nontract."

Dedication Service

Adapt this script to suit your own needs when you plan a service devoted to recognizing Sunday school teachers, department superintendents, youth sponsors, etc. (Contributed by Denny Finnegan, Lancaster, N.Y.)

ADDRESS

This morning in both of these worship services we want to do more than just recognize and applaud the efforts of our Sunday school teachers, department superintendents, and youth advisors—we want to dedicate and commission their efforts to the Lord. As the apostle Paul wrote in 1 Corinthians 3:6, "I planted the seed, Apollos watered it, but God made it grow."

CHARGE TO THE TEACHERS AND YOUTH ADVISORS

To the teachers and youth advisors, here is your charge:

- James 3:1 says, "Not many of you should presume to be teachers, my brothers, because you know that we who teach will be judged more strictly." James wants us to take seriously our role and our responsibility. If you will take your role and responsibility seriously, say "I will."
- Philippians 3:14 says, "I press on toward the goal to win the prize for which God has called me heavenward in Christ Jesus." The apostle Paul knew how important it was for us to personally keep growing in Christ. You can't give what you don't have. If you will seek to keep growing in

Continued on page 75

SUGGESTED DARES

Photocopy this page, then cut out the slips you want to use for your own Dare Box. Or make up your own!

1. Ask for a salvation testimony from one of the elders of our church. Be prepared to share parts of it with the class.
2. Read Philippians chapter 1. Write a letter to your parents expressing your thankfulness for their support in your life.
3. Memorize the first chapter of James. Recite it for the class.
4. Select a secret pal from the youth group and do something special for that person every day for one week.
5. Ask for a missions testimony from someone on the missions committee. Share it with the class.
6. Offer to work in the nursery next Sunday in someone's place.
7. Bake a batch of brownies or cookies for one of the leaders in our church, with a note that simply says "Thanks!"
8. Wash your parent's car. Accept no money for doing it.
9. Empty all the trash cans in your house and scrub them all with soap and water.
10. Make a phone call to someone who is not in Sunday school this week but should be.
11. Send a funny card to someone who needs encouraging.
12. Go with the group to the rest home services.
13. Give one of your parents a back rub.
14. Choose a favorite Scripture passage and share it with the class. What does it mean to you?
15. Interview our pianist:
    • When did you join our church? • What was your most moving experience at our church? • What do you think have been the three greatest events in the history of this church? • What is the funniest thing that ever happened in our church? • When you were my age, what was your Sunday school group like?
16. Interview the chairman of the deacon board:
    • When did you join our church? • What was your most moving experience at our church? • What do you think have been the three greatest events in the history of this church? • What is the funniest thing that ever happened in our church? • When you were my age, what was your Sunday school group like?
17. Interview the oldest member of our church:
    • When did you join our church? • What was your most moving experience at our church? • What do you think have been the three greatest events in the history of this church? • What is the funniest thing that ever happened in our church? • When you were my age, what was your Sunday school group like?
18. Watch a movie and answer the following questions:
    • Who do you think is the hero of this movie? Who is the villain? Why? • What is the bad or evil thing that could or does happen? How is the evil dealt with? • What do you think the producer and director are trying to teach us through this movie? • Do you agree with what they are saying? • Do you feel this movie will help build up your relationship to God, your family, or your friends? • Read Philippians 4:8-9.
19. Watch a music video and answer the following questions:
    • Name the music video and the artist. • Did you like this video? Why or why not? • Did the visuals have anything to do with the song? • What was the song about? • What did the person singing the song want to happen? Is this a good thing? Why? • Do you think that this is a video a Christian could recommend as good for someone to watch or listen to? Why? • Does it fit the qualifications that Paul wrote about in Philippians 4:8-9? How?

DEAR BELIEVER

Dear Believer,

You ask me to consider Christianity as the answer for my life. I have done that. I consider it untrue, repugnant, and harmful.

I find it incredible that you ask me to believe that: The earth was created in six literal days; women come from a man's rib; a snake, a donkey, and a burning bush spoke human language; all animal species, millions of them, rode on one boat; a detached hand floated in the air and wrote on a wall; Jesus walked on water unaided; fish and bread magically multiplied to feed the hungry; water instantly turned into wine; a fiery lake of eternal torment awaits unbelievers under the earth while there is life after death in a city that is 1,500 miles cubed, with mansions and food, for Christians only.

If you believe these stories, then you are the one with the problem, not me. These myths violate natural law, contradict science, and fail to correspond to reality or logic. If you can't see that, then you can't separate truth from fantasy. It doesn't matter how many people accept the delusions inflicted by "holy" men; a widely held lie is still a lie.

If Christianity were simply untrue, I would not be too concerned. Santa is untrue, but it is a harmless myth that people outgrow. But Christianity, beside being false, is also abhorrent. It amazes me that you claim to love the God of the Bible, a hateful, arrogant, sexist, cruel being who can't tolerate criticism. I would not want to live in the same neighborhood as such a creature!

The biblical God is a macho male warrior. Though he said "Thou shalt not kill," he ordered death for all opposition. He punishes offspring to the fourth generation; ordered pregnant women and children to be ripped up; is partial to one race of people; judges women inferior to men, is a sadist who created a hell to torture unbelievers; created evil; spread dung on people's faces; sent bears to devour forty-two children who teased a prophet; punishes people with snakes, dogs, dragons, swords, axes, fire, famine, and infanticide; and said fathers should eat their sons. Is that nice? Would you want to live next door to such a person?

And Jesus is a chip off the old block. He said, "I and my father are one," and he upheld "every jot and tittle" of the Old Testament law. He preached the same old judgment: vengeance and death, wrath and distress, hell and torture for all nonconformists. He never denounced the subjugation of slaves or women. He irrationally cursed and withered a fig tree for being barren out of season. He mandated burning unbelievers. (The Church has complied with relish.) He stole a horse. You want me to accept Jesus, but I think I'll pick my own friends, thank you.

I also find Christianity to be morally repugnant. The concepts of original sin, depravity, substitutionary forgiveness, intolerance, eternal punishments, and humble worship are all beneath the dignity of intelligent human beings. They are barbaric ideas for primitive cultures cowering in fear and ignorance.

Do you see why I do not respect the biblical message? It is an insulting bag of nonsense. You have every right to torment yourself with such insanity but leave me out of it. I have better things to do with my life.

your relationship with Jesus Christ, say "I will."

• John 10:12-13 says, "The hired hand is not the shepherd who owns the sheep. So when he sees the wolf coming, he abandons the sheep and runs away. Then the wolf attacks the flock and scatters it. The man runs away because he is a hired hand and cares nothing for the sheep." Jesus calls us to be his shepherds, not his hired hands. If you will take care of and love these sheep entrusted to you, say, "I will."

CHARGE TO THE CONGREGATION

To you who are under the care of these shepherds, here is your charge:

• Hebrews 13:17 says, "Obey your leaders and submit to their authority. They keep watch over you as men who must give an account. Obey them so that their work will be a joy, not a burden, for that would be of no advantage to you." *Submit* is an unpopular word today. But unless the sheep submit to the love and care of the shepherd, the sheep can easily be harmed. If you will seek as best you can in God's grace and power to submit to these leaders, say "I will."

• Ephesians 4:13 says that teachers are given to the body of Christ so that it may be built up "until we all reach unity in the faith and in the knowledge of the Son of God and become mature, attaining to the whole measure of the fullness of Christ." As the teachers and youth advisors are to seek their growth, so are you to seek your growth. If you will seek to become mature in Christ Jesus, by God's grace and God's power, say, "I will."

CHARGE TO ALL

The final charge is to us who recognize that it truly is God who causes the growth.

Ephesians 6:18 says, "Pray in the spirit on all occasions with all kinds of prayers and requests. With this in mind, be alert and always keep on praying for all the saints." It is vital that we continually and earnestly lift one another up before God in prayer. No one's prayer is unimportant. And so my charge to each one of us is: If you will seek to pray regularly and sincerely for each other—teachers and advisors for their students, the students for their teachers and advisors—say, "I will."

PRAYER OF THE COMMISSIONING AND DEDICATION

It is God who causes the growth. Let us pray...

Dressed for Defense

Divide your youth group into three equal groups. Group one dresses a teammate as a defensive player of **football** (linebacker); group two, as a defensive player of **baseball** (catcher); group three, as a defensive player of **hockey** (goalie). Groups dress players with construction paper, scissors, clear tape, and any other creative materials you want to provide. Groups dress their defensive players with helmets, masks, pads, gloves, etc., appropriate to each player's sport. Encourage your athletic fashion designers to be creative!

Now discuss these questions:

1. What is the purpose of each item of protection?
2. What areas of the body are protected?
3. What is **defense**?
4. Why are the players covering only the front of their body?

After discussing the homemade costumes, read to your group Ephesians 6:10-20 (about the armor of God) and discuss the following questions:

1. What is the purpose of each item of protection (girdle, breastplate,

shoes, shield, helmet, sword)?
2. What areas of the body are protected?
3. Why isn't the back of the body protected?

Conclude your discussion by calling attention to the weaknesses in the Christian armor (the rear, the back, Achilles tendon, back of neck—the same weaknesses of the protective gear of the defensive players). These areas of our body are susceptible to injury if exposed to an external force and subject to severe pain when injured.

Reread verse 11—we wear God's armor to "stand against the devil's schemes." To do this we must face the enemy, not retreat; use our defenses, not run; use our weapons, not surrender. Our armor protects as long as we face our enemy, but our unprotected areas are easy targets if we turn and run.

We are in a daily battle with Satan. If we let down our defenses or expose our backsides, we are more likely to fall instead of standing our ground when the evil comes. (Contributed by Rick Sanders, Oneonta, Ala.)

Elevator

Need a jump-start for a discussion about worry? Try this skit—two girls and two boys can do a good job of this with a minimum of rehearsal, script in hand if necessary. Following the skit on page 77 use these discussion questions and Scripture references for a Bible study on worry.

To begin the discussion after the skit, ask your group questions like these:

- What do you worry about?
- What is your worst fear?
- What causes fear?
- Should Christians worry? About what?
- Should Christians fear the future?

Then ask students to read several of the following verses aloud; ask the group if anything in those verses changes their opinions about Christians worrying.

Luke 10:38-42
Jeremiah 17:7-8
Matthew 13:22 (or read the whole parable and its explanation in 13:1-23)
Mark 4:19; Luke 8:14 (parallel passages for the parable of the sower in Matthew)
Matthew 6:25-34 (cf Luke 12:22-34)
Matthew 10:17-20 (cf Mark 13:9-11; Luke 12:11-12; 21:12-15)
Philippians 2:25-30
1 Peter 5:7
Deuteronomy 28:58,64-68
Psalm 139:23-24
Proverbs 12:25
Ecclesiastes 2:21-22
Philippians 4:6-9

(Contributed by Becky Ross, Westminster, Colo.)

Elevator

Cast:
Woman 1
Woman 2
Man 1
Man 2

*(**Woman 1** and **Man 1** and **2** huddled together as if in an elevator. **Woman 2** steps among the three and turns as if getting into an elevator.)*

Woman 2: Good morning.
Man 1: Good morning.
Woman 2: Nice weather we're having. *(looks beside her at **Woman 1**, who is clutching her purse in obvious terror)* You seem to be a bit frightened.
Woman 1: *(afraid and suspicious)* What makes you say that?
Woman 2: Well, you're clutching that purse as if it were your salvation.
Man 2: She's right, you know. I noticed that when you got in.
Woman 1: Really? *(all nod)* Well, I guess I am a little afraid. I'm just not used to elevators.
Woman 2: You needn't worry. I ride on them all the time, and nothing has ever happened to me.
Woman 1: But what if it gets stuck?
Man 2: Yeah. You know, I heard of a bunch of people being stuck in an elevator like this one for hours before anyone even knew they were there.

Woman 1: *(gasping and clutching her purse more tightly)* Really?
Man 1: Yeah, it's true. I read about it in the Daily Post. It sounded awful.
Man 2: Just terrible. I once saw this movie where the cable broke, and the elevator dropped all the way to the bottom of the building.
Woman 1: Really? *(growing more nervous with every anecdote, beginning to look around as if for a way to escape)*
Woman 2: Oh, that's just in the movies.
Man 1: But it could really happen.
Woman 2: Maybe. But it doesn't worry me.
Woman 1: It doesn't?
Woman 2: Of course not. I've got the peace that passes understanding.
Man 2: What?
Woman 2: Jesus lives in me. He gives me strength and assures me that he'll care for me and that I'll always be in his sight.
Woman 1: Sounds wonderful.
Woman 2: It is wonderful. He takes all my anxiety away. I'm never afraid, never worry about anything.
Woman 1: That sounds so good, I'm going to try it. What do I have to do?
Woman 2: Just close your eyes and ask God to comfort you. Then believe in your heart that he controls your world and trust him to take care of you. He'll never fail you or let you down.
Woman 1: That's it?
Woman 2: Just believe. Faith is the key.
Woman 1: Well, if you say so.
Woman 2: Trust me—or rather, trust God. That's what I do. *(Everyone is jostled a bit as if the elevator has just stopped. **Woman 2** clutches at the arm of **Woman 1**)* What happened?
Woman 1: *(calmly, now)* I don't know, but it sure feels good to just trust.
Man 1: That's nice.
Man 2: Yeah, that's nice—because I think we're stuck.
Woman 2: *(frantically)* Stuck?
Man 2: Stuck.
Woman 2: *(hysterically)* We're stuck! Oh, God, we're all going to die! Get me out of here! I think I'm going to be sick...HELP! *(lights down)*

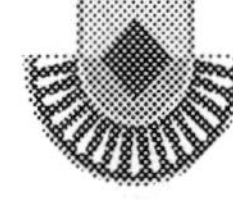

Faces R Us

This crazy skit can be used to introduce a lesson on appearances, attitudes, or related topics.

In a table top or sheet of plywood, cut four holes, each big enough for someone's head to fit through. Set up the table and cover its front and sides with a sheet of butcher paper. Place a cardboard box big enough to cover someone's head over each hole.

Decorate the table like a department-store display of faces for sale. Perhaps label the boxes according to the types of faces "inside," and place price tags on each box. With some kind of sign identify the name of the store—Faces R Us.

Prepare several kids to act out the types of faces you choose to describe. They will be hidden under the table and stick their heads up through the holes in the table top. (It's even more hilarious for **one** person to act out **all** the faces by moving from one hole to the next as the boxes are lifted and lowered by the salesperson.)

The action begins as a salesperson dusts off the boxes on the table as a customer comes in. The skit can run something like this:

"I'm interested in buying a new face. The one I have now is really worn out, and...well, people have been making fun of me lately."

"You've come to the right place—we've got several great faces for you to choose from."

The salesperson describes each face one at a time, lifting a box to reveal the actor underneath. To keep it simple, the actors may attempt to hold a "freeze frame" expression that looks like the face that the salesman is describing. For a more elaborate skit, actors can wear makeup, wigs, glasses, or other props that enhance their characters.

The salesperson can start his description of the different faces with lines like these:

- "Here's our **Intimidator** model, which as you can see, is the face of someone you wouldn't want to mess with..."
- "This is our **Professorial** model...extremely intelligent-looking. Everyone will think you graduated summa cum laude or are a Mensa member. They'll flock to you for advice..."
- "Here we have our **Playboy** model, which

girls find irresistible. Notice the enticing eyes...You can see why this is a most popular face..."

- "This face just might get you on the cover of *Rolling Stone.* It's our **Heavymetal** model, complete with makeup, hair dye, nose ring, and tatoos..."
- "I'm sure you recognize the **Bornagain** model. Notice that the smile is permanent, regardless of how you feel on the inside...the perfect expression to fool people into thinking you have no problems..."

Depending on the direction you want to take, the final face may be that of a street person, a Third World refugee, Christ himself—in short, an undesirable face by popular standards. The salesman can conclude along these lines:

"Well, that's all the popular models...what? None of these are exactly what you're looking for? That's funny...they fit everybody else. Well, there *is* a discounted face here somewhere...let me see if I can find it...ah, yes, here it is. We don't sell many of these, for, uh, obvious reasons. It's the cheapest face we carry...though the few who've bought these have told me later that it was the most expensive purchase they ever made. Can't figure it out..."

(Contributed by Danny Greer, Nashville, Tenn.)

Fishers of Men

Kids can learn that sharing their faith needs to be as specialized as the fishing styles and equipment of avid anglers.

Find some professional or sports fishermen in your congregation or among your young people's families. Ask to borrow some of the specialized gear they use to go after different fish—different kinds of tied flies, wading boots, a deep-sea fishing pole, a more common rod and reel, a simple cane and can of worms, a casting net—even a piece of the rope used in nets of professional deep-sea fishermen. If some of the owners of the equipment are willing, invite them to come to the meeting to model their own gear and explain why fishermen need such equipment in order to catch the particular kind of fish they want to hook (or net). If you haven't got any takers, dress up several of the kids in either borrowed or makeshift

gear.

Introduce each fisherman or each style of fishing, describe the equipment on display, and explain (or ask the fisherman to explain) the method used to catch the desired kind of fish. Ask the fishermen to demonstrate their techniques.

Then explain that, in their attempt to catch fish, fishermen change their approaches according to the kind of fish they want. The goal of Christians is to be fishers of men. Our choice of equipment and methods must reflect the needs and background of the individuals we approach. Sometimes a simple, straight-forward approach will do the job—like the cane and the can of worms. Some fish respond only to refined bait that flicks their attention your way long enough to give the message. Sometimes you must wear thigh-high boots to wade in to meet people where they are. Those under the influence of deeply addicting sins require heavy-duty equipment to counter their intense resistance to the gospel—but they, too, need to know and experience the love of Jesus. (Contributed by Russ Porter, Rosenberg, Tex.)

Fold-a-Lesson Bible Studies

To make the most of kids' fascination with the unpredictable and unconventional, prepare this lesson aid. On a large sheet of newsprint, list the concepts from your lesson in the order you'll present them.

Take the Beatitudes, for instance (Matt. 5:3-12). Each verse has two parts—"blessed" and "for theirs is"—for a total of nine of each. Using two sheets of newsprint, create five long rectangles by folding the paper from the bottom to the top in segments of about two inches. Unfold the sheet, then in the top rectangle write the lesson's title ("The Beatitudes"). In the next four rectangles on the sheet, write each verses' "blessed" on the left half and their corresponding results next to them in the right half. On the second sheet, follow this pattern for the last five verses. Then refold the sheets and secure each one with a paper clip to keep it from unfolding.

When you're ready to teach, tape the folded and paper-clipped sheet to the wall. As you teach the lesson, simply remove the paper clip and unfold each section as you're ready to expound on it. Some kids may wish to follow along in their Bibles, but the fold-a-lesson helps the resistant see and hear the Word. Tip: Use lots of colors in writing up verses in the sections. (Contributed by Mark Simone, Ravenna, Ohio)

Giftedness

Need to illustrate the value of the spiritual gifts God has given each of us? Choose eight volunteers; of them form two teams of four. Tell both teams that they have 10 minutes to build a house out of two sheets of paper. Give the first team their paper and send them to a separate room to work, emphasizing that they can only use the paper they were given—nothing else.

After team one leaves, give the second team two sheets of paper—and also scissors, crayons, and tape. Now send that team to a separate room to work on their house.

When you call time, the two groups return to show off their houses. The team that received "gifts" will have produced a more interesting and intricate house than the team that received no gifts. Explain to the kids that in the same way God has gifted each one of us with spiritual gifts to build up our youth groups and churches to be the best they can be. (Kurt Staeuble, Canyon Lake, Calif.)

Global Proverbs

Does your teaching calendar call for a discussion on world missions? Or on wisdom? Or do you need a lively introduction to a study of the book of Proverbs? Give your students a copy of the "Global Proverbs" on page 83.

Answers:

Habits are first cobwebs, **then cables**.

God save you from a bad neighbor and from **a beginner on the fiddle**.

A trout in the pot is better than **a salmon in the sea**.

Before you marry, keep your two eyes open: **after you marry, shut one**.

Even a small star shines **in the darkness**.

Beauty in a woman without good judgment is like **a gold ring in a pig's snout**.

He who cannot dance puts the blame **on the floor**.

That which is brief, if it be good, is **good twice over**.

You always find something **the last place you look**.

If you want your dreams to come true, **don't sleep**.

Faults are thick where **love is thin**.

With time and patience the mulberry leaf

becomes a silk gown.
Too many captains may steer a boat **up a mountainside**.
Treat your guest as a guest for two days; **on the third day, give him a hoe**.
(Contributed by Keith Curran, Titusville, Fla.)

Guilty!

Need a skit that illustrates that Christ paid the penalty for our sins? Here it is! (Contributed by Rob Peterson, El Cajon, Calif.)

GUILTY!

Cast: Bailiff (dressed in uniform if possible)
Defendant One—Noriega Castro Sleaze
Defendant Two—Cindy Almost Pure
Judge (in robe, holding gavel)

Scene: Courtroom of Heaven

Bailiff: All rise! The court of heaven is now in session. The honorable Creator of all that is, was, and shall be, presiding.

Judge: Please be seated. Defendant One, please state your name.

Def. One: My name is Noriega Castro Sleaze, your honor. I'm guilty—I know that now. But I don't know why I'm here. I asked for your mercy and forgiveness. What gives?

Judge: Mr. Sleaze, everyone that's ever been born must appear before me. Bailiff, what is the sin of Mr. Sleaze?

Bailiff: Your honor, rape, murder, drug trafficking, and jaywalking—to name only a few of his many, many sins against humanity.

Judge: You have been found guilty of sin, Mr. Sleaze. The penalty is death. Defendant Two, please state your name.

Def. Two: My name is Cindy Almost Pure, your most wonderful honor, your holiness, sir. And I just want you to know that I'm guilty, too—I know that, and I'm sorry for what I've done. But I'm not nearly as bad as Sleaze, here. My sin is nothing compared to what he has done. Besides, I go to church every Sunday, say my prayers every day, and I obey the Ten Commandments—well, most of them.

Judge: Bailiff, what is the sin of Miss Almost Pure?

Bailiff: She is guilty of envy, your honor. She wanted the Mercedes 300 SL that belonged to her neighbor.

Judge: You have been found guilty of sin, Miss Almost Pure, and the penalty is death.

Bailiff: **(licking his chops)** They deserve it! Now they're gonna fry!

Judge: Bailiff, set them free.

Bailiff: What do you mean? I thought you said they were guilty and the sentence was death!

Judge: They are guilty, and the penalty is death. But the sentence has already been served. **(Holds up both hands, which are marked with red nail prints)**

Offstage voice: For God so loved the world that he gave his one and only Son, that whoever believes in him will not die but have eternal life.

Global Proverbs

Directions: The following columns list in two parts proverbs from several countries. Choose from the right the correct ending for each proverb, then write that ending on the line.

(Spanish)	Habits are first cobwebs, ______	in the darkness.
(Italian)	God save you from a bad neighbor and from ______	becomes a silk gown.
(Irish)	A trout in the pot is better than ______	love is thin.
(Jamaican)	Before you marry, keep your two eyes open: ______	on the floor.
(Finnish)	Even a small star shines ______	up a mountainside.
(Bible)	Beauty in a woman without good judgment is like ______	don't sleep.
(Hindi)	He who cannot dance puts the blame ______	on the third day, give him a hoe.
(Spanish)	That which is brief, if it be good, is ______	a gold ring in a pig's snout.
(American)	You always find something ______	after you marry, shut one.
(Yiddish)	If you want your dreams to come true, ______	then cables.
(British)	Faults are thick where ______	a beginner on the fiddle.
(Chinese)	With time and patience the mulberry leaf ______	the last place you look.
(Korean)	Too many captains may steer a boat ______	good twice over.
(Swahili)	Treat your guest as a guest for two days; ______	a salmon in the sea.

Guts and Glory

You need the guts to do the right thing if you want to receive God's glory. Let the kids experience this truth by taking their turn at the balloon pit.

Create the pit in a corner of the room (see diagram). Lay several sleeping bags or some other kind of cushioning on the floor of the pit. Inflate 50 nine-inch balloons and place them in the pit. Set a chair up at the end of the pit.

The **object** is for a person to stand on the chair, back to the pit, and fall backwards into the pit. The **object lesson** is that few are willing to be the first to do something difficult or scary. After the first one goes, others will see that no harm is done and they will eagerly follow. Talk with the kids about how they encouraged or discouraged the first person who wanted to attempt the feat. Notice that some never take a turn.

It's a wild sensation. The first layer of balloons shoots up into the air while the bottom layer breaks the fall. Balloons do break, so have plenty of extras to add to the pit. And be sure it's safe—don't use tables with sharp edges, don't permit unsupervised pit-jumping, etc. (Doug Partin, Lubbock, Tex.)

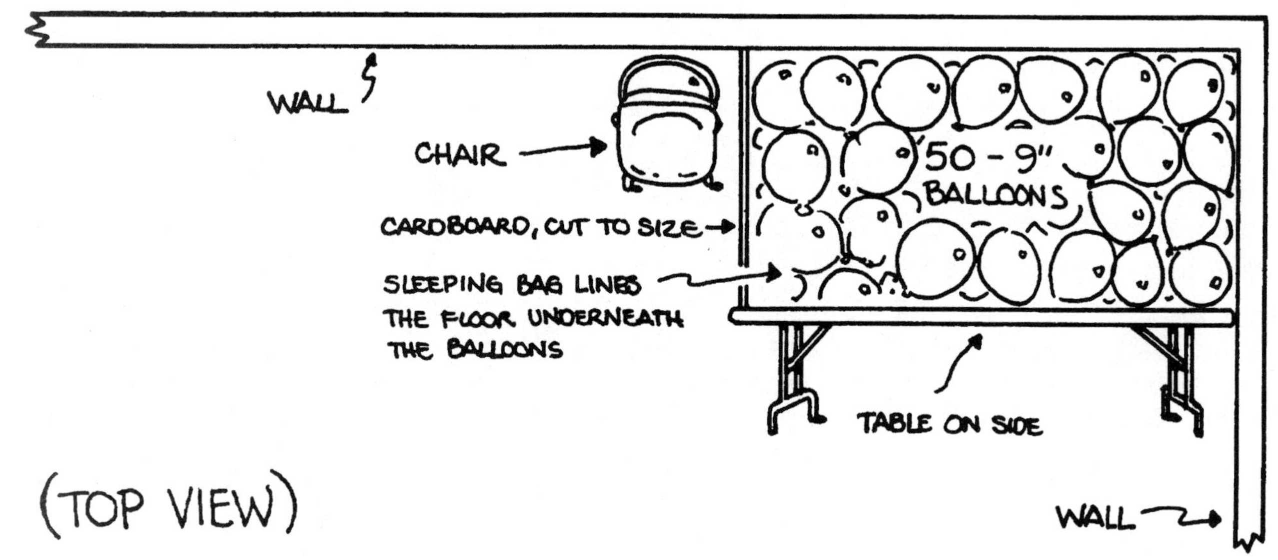

How Do You Feel?

To help kids express their feelings to each other in creative ways, form small groups in which students express how they are feeling in terms of, say, automobiles: "I feel like a red Porsche" or "I'm just about out of gas right now."

Here are more subjects and images to choose from:

Car
Flower
Song
Number
Toy
Color
Year
Day
Month
Season
Stone
Fruit
Vegetable
Flavor
Holiday
Sandwich
Candy
Road sign

Recipes
Sewing
Book
Clothes
Shoes
Time
Money
Jewelry
Furniture
Animal
Building
Sport
Movie
Cookie
Cake
Beverage
Fabric
Cereal
Ice cream
Feeling word
Temperature
Weather

(Contributed by Sherry Wingert, Oakland, Neb.)

Individual Tax Return for God's Gifts

This fake Form 1040 on pages 86, 87, and 88 is a discussion starter about using time and talents for the kingdom of God. Two warnings: It takes a while to fill out, and it works better with older teens than it does with junior highers. Since the one "filing the form" has to carry information to various other places on the form, different people can have different results. (Contributed by David R. Holmes, Lexington, Tenn.)

Kids on Campus

Here's a good way to identify different kinds of problems kids deal with. Bring in an assortment of common items to use as object lessons to generate discussion about the characters you describe.

• **Mr. Clean** represents church kids—those who think they have it all together. Though they look good on the outside, there can be a lot of struggles on the inside. How do we relate to kids like that?

• **Cover Girl make-up** represents kids who are preoccupied with their appearance. They want to look good, no matter what it costs. Why do you think some people are obsessed with their looks? What should our attitude be?

• **Beer cans** symbolize the party guys at school. Their idea of fun is getting wasted, getting in trouble, and acting like jerks. Is it possible that their behavior is a smoke screen for a lot of pain on the inside? How can we reach out to guys like this?

• **Chunky candy bar** illustrates overweight kids left out of certain circles or kids who may be loners for other reasons. Their isolation may be obvious, or they may hide it by laughing at themselves, pretending to be jolly and content. Any ideas about sharing Christ with kids like these?

• **Aspirin** portrays Johnny Advil—the kid who gives you a headache. He's obnoxious and seems to go out of his way to irritate you. You wish he'd leave you alone. But what do you think Johnny's *real* problem is?

• **National Enquirer** represents the person who spreads rumors about everyone. He or she has a tongue of fire and loves to cut people down. How do you feel when people spread rumors about you? What can be done about it?

These are only ideas—add others as you wish; the possibilities are endless. (Contributed by Tim Freet, Santa Barbara, Calif.)

1040G Individual Tax Return for God's Gifts 19____

LABEL

Your first name and initial ____ Last name ____

Home address ____

City, State, and Zip ____

FILING STATUS

1. ☐ Christian
2. ☐ Nominal Christian
3. ☐ Non-Christian
4. ☐ Nominal Christian filing as Christian, hoping no one knows
5. ☐ List name of person you think you are fooling ____

EXEMPTIONS

If your time value in this section is less than once per week, please use an appropriate fraction to represent the value of time for one week.

List use of your talents for God.

Event	Total the number of times the talent is used per week.
Example: Use of vocal talent by singing in choir.	2
6. ____	____
7. ____	____
8. ____	____
9. ____	____
10. Total........... Enter here and on line 30.	☐

If a line is blank, please enter zero (-0-) on the appropriate line.

List use of your time for God.

Event	Total time per week.
Example: Reading Bible daily for 30 min. each day.	3.5 hrs.
11. ____	____
12. ____	____
13. ____	____
14. ____	____
15. Total........... Enter here and on line 35.	☐

List use of your money for God. (Do not include the tithe.)

Event	Total amount per year.
Example: Money given to Christmas Missions Offering.	$50
16. ____	____
17. ____	____
18. ____	____
19. ____	____
20. Total........... Enter here and on line 44.	☐

INCOME

For talents include all possibilities: musical ability, helpfulness to a friend, ability to visit the sick, to visit shut-ins, to witness, etc.

21. Enter total number of talents you possess. .... ________

x7

____

x52

22. .... [ ]

23. Enter total number of hours God gives you per week. (If this is something other than 168, attach an explanation.) .... ________

x52

24. .... [ ]

25. Enter total monies available to you from all sources. ________
26. Multiply line 25 by 10% ________
27. Subtract line 26 from line 25. .... [ ]

TAX COMPUTATION

28. Enter amount from line 22 .... ________

x10%

29. This is the number of talents God expects you to use.. ________
30. Enter amount from line 10 .... ________

x52

31. This is the number of talents used for God ..... ________
32. Subtract line 31 from 29. This is the number of talents owed God .... [ ]

33. Enter amount from line 24 .... ________

x10%

34. This is the amount of time God expect.......... ________
35. Enter the amount from line 15 .... ________

x52

36. This is the amount of time given to God .... ________
37. Subtract line 36 from line 34. This is the amount of time owed God .... [ ]

38. Enter the amount from line 26 .... ________
39. Enter the amount you have given toward your tithe. ________
40. Subtract line 39 from line 38. This is the amount owed for tithe .... [ ]

41. Enter the amount from line 27 .... ________
42. Enter the percentage of your money you feel God wants you to give as an offering to him ... ________%
43. Multiply line 41 by the percentage on line 42 ... ________
44. Enter the amount from line 20 .... ________
45. Subtract line 44 from line 43. This is amount due God in offering...................................... [ ]

OTHER TAXES AND PENALTIES

46. If you have ever sinned, please check this box. (See instructions in Romans 3:23.) ☐

47. If you checked the box on line 46, then your penalty is hell for eternity. (See instructions in Romans 10:9, 10.) List your penalty here...... ________

CREDITS

a. If you checked box 1, then your penalty has already been paid by Jesus Christ. You qualify for a reward in heaven. Write "heaven" on line 48.

b. If you checked box 3, then you must eventually pay the amount on line 47. You may change your status to box 1 if you work out details with Jesus Christ. If you do not work out such details, then enter on line 48 the information from line 47.

c. If you checked box 2, then your penalty has already been paid by Jesus Christ—though you may not understand or appreciate the fact. (See the New Testament for details.)

d. If you checked box 4, Jesus Christ will audit your return. He knows the truth anyway—and he can set you free (see b. above).

48.. ☐

TOTALS AND PAYMENT

Enter the amount from line 32.........	☐	Due in Talent
Enter the amount from line 37.........	☐	Due in Time
Enter the amount from line 40.........	☐	Due for Tithe
Enter the amount from line 45.........	☐	Due for Offering

PLEASE MAKE ARRANGEMENTS TO FULFILL THESE REQUIREMENTS IN THE NEAR FUTURE. FAILURE TO DO SO WILL RESULT IN THE LOSS OF VALUABLE BLESSINGS THAT ARE ALREADY AVAILABLE FOR YOU. ADVANCE AND EXCESS PAYMENTS WILL BRING YOU THE BENEFIT OF ADDITIONAL BLESSINGS.

Enter the information from line 48 ____________________

IF THIS IS ANYTHING OTHER THAN "HEAVEN," THEN THE INFORMATION ON BLESSINGS AVAILABLE DOES NOT APPLY TO YOU. WE ENCOURAGE YOU TO CONSIDER FILING STATUS NUMBER ONE. IT DOES REQUIRE SACRIFICE ON YOUR PART, BUT IT ALSO COMES WITH A FULLY FUNDED RETIREMENT PLAN THAT IS TRULY OUT OF THIS WORLD.

For more information please see Romans 3:23; 6:23; 10:9,10,13.

Signed: ______________________________

The Kingdom Cross

When kids gain an insight or make a decision, creating an item for display—a modern memorial of sorts—can be a powerful reminder of the event.

Before the session build a wooden form for a modest-sized cross (see diagram). Just prior to the meeting, pour cement into the form. (A small amount of calcium chloride will make it harden quickly.) The cross should be somewhat mobile, so don't make it too large. Also have on hand two baskets of small stones—one basket containing common rocks, the second containing polished stones (you can pick them up inexpensively at rock and gem shops).

At the session discuss with your students how we experience the reign of God now in the ordinary joys and struggles of life, yet we look forward to the unveiling of the full glory of the kingdom. Then pass around the two baskets of rocks, allowing the teens to select one stone from each basket.

Ask them to reflect on how the two stones represent their own experience of the **now** and the **not yet**. Prompt them to focus on one or two specific examples of the struggle and joy they're experiencing right now, represented by the common stone. Then give them time to handle the polished stone as they consider their hopes for the kingdom to come.

After a few minutes of reflection, roll the cement cross up to the front as you explain how believers experience the kingdom of God through the cross. As music plays (perhaps Amy Grant's "The Now and the Now Yet" from **Straight Ahead**), invite the teens to come and set their stones in the wet cement in such a way that they are visible. You may want to read 2 Peter 2:4ff about being living stones in the temple of God. Once the cross hardens, it can be used as a centerpiece for future worship times. (Contributed by Bill Swedberg, Renton, Wash.)

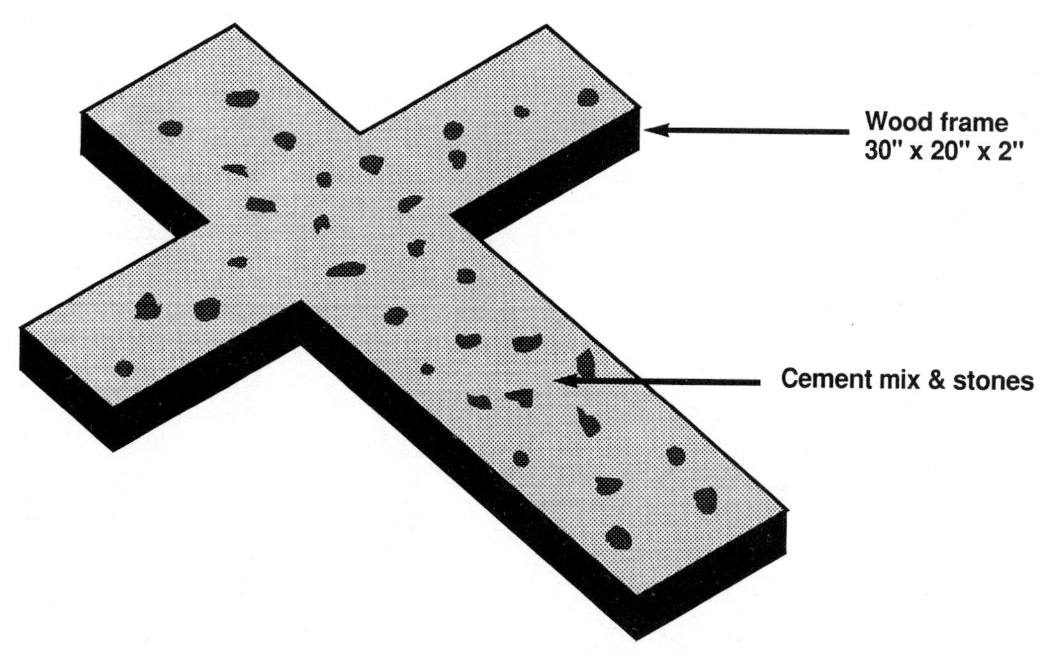

Lifesaver Night

In advance arrange at least four people to be special guests at your Lifesaver Night. Be sure they represent different age groups—college, young married, the 30-to-50 age group, and 50 or older. (Include a married couple to share together as one of the four.) Ask these people to talk from their hearts about a time in their lives when a Christian made their lives sweeter in some way—led them to Christ, helped them in a time of critical need, or modeled for them a quality of Christ that they in turn adopted into their lives. If you have a time limit or want to conclude with questions from the kids, let your guests know ahead of time.

On Lifesaver Night explain the format of the evening and introduce the speakers as they take their turns before the kids. Then close the meeting by bringing out a pack of Lifesavers. Explain that the package unit is made up of many different flavors and colors of Lifesavers, but they are all part of the same roll. Christians also come in many different flavors and colors, but we are part of the same body—Christ's body—and we all have the same purpose—to grow up to be like Christ. When we tell others about Jesus or others see Jesus in us, our particular flavor makes their lives sweeter.

Then pass around six-inch pieces of string (one per student) and packs of Lifesavers. The student can choose three to five of their favorite flavors and place the Lifesavers on the string. Challenge the youths to go out and be lifesavers. Each time they tell someone about Jesus or reach out to help someone in Jesus' name, they can bite a Lifesaver off the string and eat it. Tell them you trust them not to eat any of the Lifesavers unless they have met the requirements. Follow up by asking at the next meeting how long it took them to eat their whole string of Lifesavers. (Contributed by Danny Balint, Mobile, Ala.)

Lost and Found

This event will help your group discover what it means to find the lost even as they struggle themselves to walk by faith. It's a fitting activity to precede or follow a study of the three lost-and-found stories in Luke 15.

The objective is for each team to make it as far along a course as they can in five minutes—blindfolded—while in the process finding as many items as they can.

❖ Preparation ❖

What you'll need: large room with lots of tables and chairs, fishing line, ten items from your office (pencil, cassette, key, aluminum can, dart, coffee cup, coat hanger, book, etc.), Bible, masking tape, blindfolds (two to four), watch, prizes (optional).

Set up as follows:

1. Trash the room. Turn all the tables and chairs on the their sides. It should be hard to walk through.
2. The path through this chaos will be a fishing line. Tie one end of the fishing line to a chair leg just inside the door. Then run the line all over the room, wrapping it around numerous tables and chairs to keep the line taut. The line should not cross over itself.
3. Mark 10 locations along the path (though not on the fishing line itself)

with pieces of the masking tape. At these sites you'll put the "lost" items for each group to find; then you'll replace them after each group goes through the course.

4. Put your 10 items on the tape-marked sites.
5. Blindfold the teams before they travel the course.

❖ Introducing the Lesson ❖

If you haven't already studied Luke 15, tell the kids that Christians walk by faith. Though we do not always know where the Lord is leading us, yet if we study the Bible and stay tuned into the Spirit, we will be led to where God wants us.

One thing is certain—we will encounter the lost. Then share with your students the highlights of your study of the three lost-and-found stories in Luke 15.

❖ Playing the Game ❖

To start the game, divide your group into teams of two, three, or four. Tell them that in a nearby room you have lost 10 items; list them for the teams. Each team has five minutes during which to find as many of the 10 items as they can. When one team member finds an item, the whole team is to whoop it up (Luke 15:6-7,9,23-24,32). The catch is that the teammates wear blindfolds and the lights are out. On the other hand, there is a fishing line strung throughout the room that, if they can locate it by feel, will lead them to at least the vicinity of all 10 "lost" objects. Furthermore, they'll encounter obstacles along the way—they may have to step over chairs, tables, and the fishing line itself.

Blindfold the first group, release them into the darkened room, and let them have a go at their task. After five minutes, turn on the lights and allow the team to remove their blindfolds. Count the number of items they found, and how many (if any) finished the course. If the fishing line needs to be drawn taut again, have that team help you. Then allow this team to watch the next team go through.

After all the teams have finished, award a prize to the team that found the most items.

❖ Post-game Ponderings ❖

Assume that following the line represented walking by faith, and that the objects the kids found in the dark room were lost people we encounter. Your observations may resemble the following:

- "Brad made it almost all the way through, but he never found a single lost item. Walking by faith is a struggle in itself, and sometimes you struggle so hard that you go right past the lost."
- "When Lisa and Tanya lost the line, John helped them find it again. Sometimes we stray from our walk with God, and then we become ones who need to be found."
- "When Michelle started humming the theme song to 'The Twilight Zone,' it distracted Clay enough that he stopped following the line. It reminded me how the world diverts us from our walk with God."

Then turn it over to your group to share their own observations. You may want to close by reading the Great Commission.

(Contributed by Doug Partin, Lubbock, Tex.)

Maturity Hunt

At a camp, retreat, or lock-in where students can observe each other and their leaders over a period of time, do a lesson on Christian maturity. Following the study, give students a copy of the chart on page 92, listing several descriptions of maturity. Their assignment: to be on the lookout for examples of each description in the behavior of other people. After a designated time for observation, discuss the results. (Contributed by Ed Laremore, Medford, N.J.)

MATURITY SCAVENGER HUNT

What does spiritual maturity look like?

The following statements exemplify several aspects of maturity. During our time together, notice people around you whose behavior illustrates these different aspects of spiritual maturity. When you observe someone living out one of the following marks of maturity, summarize the incident (in the box next to the description), and then ask who you observed to initial the appropriate box. You may also list incidents that violate the different aspects. Record those incidents in the appropriate boxes as well. *No initials are needed in these cases!*

What maturity is	Circumstances surrounding the the mature behavior I observed	Initials
1. Maturity is the ability to control anger and settle differences without violence or destruction.		
2. Maturity is patience—the willingness to pass up immediate pleasure in favor of long-term gain.		
3. Maturity is perseverance—the ability to sweat out a project or a situation in spite of opposition and discouraging setbacks.		
4. Maturity is unselfishness—responding to the needs of others, often at the expense of one's own desires or wishes.		
5. Maturity is the capacity to face unpleasantness and frustration, discomfort and defeat, without complaint or collapse.		
6. Maturity is humility. It is being big enough to say, "I was wrong." And when right the mature person need not say, "I told you so."		
7. Maturity is the ability to make a decision and stand by it. The immature spend their lives exploring endless possibilities and achieving nothing.		
8. Maturity means dependability, keeping one's word, coming through in the crisis. The immature—confused and disorganized—are masters of the alibi. Their lives are a maze of broken promises, former friends, unfinished business, and good intentions that never materialize.		
9. Maturity is the art of living in peace with that which we cannot change.		
10. Maturity is knowing how to give and receive love.		
11. Maturity is the ability to learn from experience.		

Mission Possible

Introduce a Bible study on Christian fellowship and outreach by challenging your group to rediscover and recommit itself to a biblical purpose for its existence. Create and act out a scenario (see sample below) in which small groups of students must defend the youth group's existence before the governing body of the church. Emphasize that students must use Scripture to make their points. (Contributed by Jim Bell, Hamilton, Ohio)

MISSION POSSIBLE

At last week's church board meeting, several members raised some serious questions about First Church's youth ministry:

- Isn't this youth group costing us more than it's really worth?
- Aren't today's kids already so busy with school that they don't need activities piled on at church?
- What is this group accomplishing, anyway?
- Why should there even be a youth group—shouldn't the teenagers be involved in the regular church programs?

No one representing the youth ministry was there to answer these questions, and after 45 minutes of discussion, the board voted that unless someone could present at next month's board meeting a good case for continuing the youth group, the youth ministry will be ended.

The church board is willing to hear from someone who thinks the church's youth ministry is important and worthwhile. Your mission is to prepare a statement to present to the church board, answering their questions and telling why you believe First Church should continue its youth ministry.

A Modern Parable

The pressure of meeting goals is the subject of this discussion starter. Read "Bill the Boll Weevil" on page 94 (or assign a student to practice then deliver it) imaginatively. Here are suggestions for pursuing a discussion with your group.

Suggestions for discussion

- Who do you know who lives like Bill? Do *you?*
- Because of what people you respect tell you, your lives may be filled with demanding goals that you feel are important. For example, you've all heard these famous last words:

"You have to spend time studying to make good grades."

"You have to make good grades if you plan to go to college."

"You have to go to college if you want a good job."

"You have to get a good job if you want to live the good life (afford a spouse,

house, kids, cars, vacations, etc.)."
"You have to be a good steward if you want to retire comfortably."

• Imposed goals can make a life heavy, burdened, unenjoyable. They can even destroy a life by instilling the lie that no matter what you achieve, it is not enough. So you exhaust yourself trying to achieve goals someone else instilled in you—until you collapse under the pressure. It's not that the goals are evil—only that there's more to life than the goals may allow.

• True or false? Explain your answers.

1. One's goals inevitably affect one's attitudes.
2. Materialistic preoccupation is a necessary evil today.
3. The expectation of others often spurs us on to a better quality of life.
4. Peer pressure usually pulls you down.
5. The cost of success—that is, of reaching goals—is usually worth it.

• Let's read Matthew 6:25-34. *(Ask some students to paraphrase it.)* Consider these questions:

1. What should be your primary goal (or goals) in life?
2. Who imposes this goal?
3. What kind of life can you expect if you strive for this goal?
4. Why pray about reaching goals—whether about grades, jobs, etc.—when you could worry about them instead?
5. How much time do you spend *worrying* about reaching a goal? How much time do you spend *praying* about reaching a goal?
6. What should God's care for his creation teach you?
7. Will God take care of your physical needs if you don't work?
8. Will God take care of your physical needs if you work on seeking his kingdom and his righteousness? How do you expect this to be done?
9. If you took this Scripture seriously, how would it affect your life today?

(Contributed by Doug Partin, Lubbock, Tex.)

Bill the Boll Weevil

Way back when, there was a Bolivian boll weevil named Bill. Like other beetles, Bill was badgered by his parents about becoming better. So instead of being content living life one boll at a time, Bill set a goal of becoming the most famous boll weevil in all of Bolivia.

When Bill told his friends, they scoffed at his goal and told him to quit being such a Bolshevik. Well, Bill bolstered his belittled ambitions and decided to take a bold step. He determined to become the strongest boll weevil in all of Bolivia. Sure, he thought, that would make him the most famous boll weevil of all.

So while his bourgeois friends bloated themselves and basked under blistering beams and balmy Bolivian breezes, Bill was burning calories and building brawn. At first he could barely bench a discarded boll, and he had to learn how to breathe from his belly. As time passed, however, he became buff enough to heft basketballs and eventually bowling balls.

When Bill began bragging about his strength, his friends laughed at "Barrel Chested" Bill's bunch of balderdash. So Bill bet a bunch of bolls that he could bench the ball, and before a bewildered bunch of beetles, he performed the feat. As he bulked up, his fame broadened throughout all Bolivia. Beetles from around-about came to see Bill the boll weevil bench balls, bassoons, even boulders.

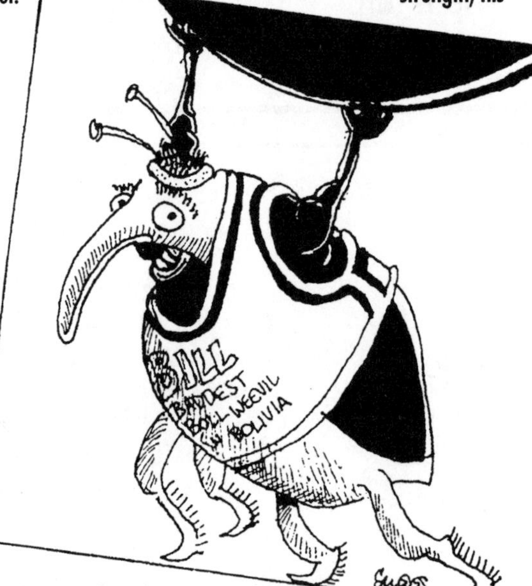

One day the bigwig of Bolivia, taking advantage of Bill's popularity, invited Bill to a command performance. Billboards announced the event, and ESPN was on hand to cover the sensation. Proud boll weevils wore B-shirts that billed Bill as the best boll weevil in all of Bolivia.

Excitement was in the air. The bigwig had given Bill his fill of barbecued bolls. Bill donned a bright bolero with matching bolo and bolted over to the Baldwin baby grand. Amid the oohs, aahs, and ballyhoos, Bill hefted the Baldwin up and balanced it on one finger. The crowd went wild. Bill was just beginning to bow when he let loose a gut-bursting belch. He bobbled the Baldwin, and it came down with a bang, leaving bashed Bill with broken bones and a badly bruised ego.

Name That Sin!

This game-show activity also makes an easy and entertaining opener for a weekly meeting—especially if your lesson is about one of the sins mentioned in this game.

The emcee (you or a sponsor) runs into the room and in typical Guy Smiley fashion shouts, "It's time to plaaaay…Name That Sin, the game where knowing your sins wins you big prizes!" The emcee then divides the group into two teams, or—if the group is large (50 or more)—selects a five-student panel from each team, and the rest of the students cheers for their representatives.

The game itself is simple: the emcee reads the question (see a sample list below; answers follow in parentheses), and the first player to raise a hand has a chance to answer. Remind players that they should respond with the **predominant** sin, not the related, subtle ones underlying the problem. If the answer is wrong, the other team gets a chance to answer the question—and so on, until there are three wrong answers, and then the question is thrown out. Award a point per correct answer—or three points if the answer is given on the first attempt, two points on the second attempt, and one point on the third attempt.

The emcee can toss a Tootsie Roll (or similar small treat) to players who give correct answers. All members of the winning team get a prize at the end of a round.

Or vary the game's title and questions to match your teaching series—Name That Old Testament Prophet, Name That Spiritual Gift, Name That Prophecy, Name That Parable, etc. (Contributed by Lynne Marian, San Dimas, Calif.)

1. Your best friend gets a new car and you wish she'd die of a disease and leave the car to you. Name that sin! **(covetousness or envy)**
2. Your girlfriend smiles at another guy, and you want to kill him. Name that sin! **(jealousy)**
3. Your parents forbid you to see a movie, but your friends talk you into it and you go. Name that sin! **(disobedience)**
4. During the prayer-and-share time in Sunday school, you mention your grandparents' $1000 gift and explain how you plan to spend it. Name that sin! **(boasting)**
5. You replay the bedroom scene three times in the video Top Gun. Name that sin! **(lust)**
6. When your friend tells you in confidence that she might be pregnant, you tell a couple of your friends at church—just so they can pray about it. Name that sin! **(gossip)**
7. You've just turned 21, you're out to dinner with some younger Christian friends, and to celebrate you order a beer with your meal. They wish they could have one. Name that sin! **(causing a weaker brother to stumble)**
8. Your curfew is midnight. You get home at 12:20 a.m. In the morning your parents ask what time you got in, and you answer, "Around twelve." Name that sin! **(lying)**
9. You reject Jesus as Savior and Lord. Name that sin! **(unbelief)**
10. Your sister borrows your best sweater without asking you and accidentally ruins it. She's miserable about it, apologizes to you, and even offers to replace the

sweater. You don't speak to her. Name that sin! **(unforgiveness)**

11. When you get a new car, you spend most nights and weekends either working on it or working at a job for cash to spend on the car. Name that sin! **(idol worship)**
12. You figure that as long as you and your girlfriend don't go all the way, it doesn't really matter what else you do. Name that sin! **(sexual immorality)**
13. You "accidentally" let a newspaper clipping about your recent football accomplishments fall out of your Bible during Sunday school in front of the girls so they will comment on your achievements. Name that sin! **(pride)**
14. You tell your little sister never to touch your things—but when you're out of hair spray, you use hers without asking. Name that sin! **(hypocrisy)**
15. You're mad at your little brother, so you purposely leave his hamster cage open so it can escape. Name that sin! **(malice)**

Opened Eyes

Complete with activity and discussion starters, this meeting begins when the kids make a pair of glasses out of exotic colored pipe cleaners. All students receive four pipe cleaners each, and they must wear the resulting pair of eyeglasses for the rest of the meeting.

Start a discussion this way: suggest that all imagine what they might see if the glasses they are wearing enabled them to clearly observe the **spiritual** realm. What might they see when somebody dies? When conception happens? At a heavy metal concert? What would heaven look like? Or the Devil? Or angels?

Follow up the discussion by studying spiritual warfare, emphasizing that God has given us authority over all the works of the enemy. Examine the Christian's armor in Ephesians 6:10-18, and tell the story of Elisha and his servant seeing the army of God surrounding them (2 Kings 6:15-17). Conclude the meeting by listening to part of the audio version of Frank Peretti's **This Present Darkness**. (Contributed by Gene Stabe, Canyon Country, Calif.)

The Parenting Game

Give your youths an idea of what it's like to be a parent. Form families of three—one person plays the role of the father, one the mother, and one the child. The object is for each pair of parents to lead their blindfolded child "home" (a designated spot), directing the child by verbal guidance only.

But you tell the **"children"** and the **"parents"** two different things. Take the "children" to a separate room to blindfold them. Before they return to play the game, tell them that they must attempt to get home and that their "parents" will attempt to mislead them—even lie to them—about the directions to home.

Tell the "parents," however, that this game is a race and that the first child to reach home wins for the team.

Now bring the two groups together to the starting place. After disorienting the blindfolded children by spinning them, say "Go!" Parents may then shout directions to their child. What happens next allows your group to experience some of the frustrations parents often feel.

What you'll see:

• Parents screaming for their child to listen to them.
• Children frustrated by their parents' pushiness to go fast and win.
• Some parents may simply stop giving guidance altogether.
• Perhaps one half of a parental pair may get sufficiently frustrated with yelling directions that he or she gives up—leaving the other partner as a "single parent."

Follow the game with a forum on parent-teenager relationships. (Contributed by Mike Couvion, Venice, Fla.)

The Perils of the Prodigal

Here's a humorous version of the parable of the Prodigal Son, a melodramatic rendition intended to be an improvisational skit. One student or leader reads the narration on page 98 while several students act out what is being read as they hear it. The narrator should pause for the characters to repeat the dialogue attributed to them. The more exaggerated the acting, the more effective the skit. (Contributed by Mark Frost, Trenton, Mich.)

Pick a Compliment

When teaching on encouragement, get the ball rolling with Pick a Compliment. Photocopy the compliments on page 99, cut them out, and then do one of these activities:

1. Pass around a hat containing the compliments. Each person pulls out a compliment and lays it on the person on his or her right. Encourage players to ham it up.
2. Print each compliment on a full sheet of paper and pass out one sheet to each person. Announce a timed contest to see who can compliment the most people in the allotted time using the written compliment. After complimenting another player, the student offering the compliment gives his or her paper to the newly complimented person to sign.

(Contributed by Jack Hawkins, Sierra Madre, Calif.)

Postcard Home

After a retreat or a lesson that causes your kids to commit to something or change in some way, hand out to each student a prestamped post card (or a 4 X 6 index card—the post office won't take 3 X 5 cards). Ask your students to write to themselves what they feel God leading them to do or change—you won't need to tell them what to write. Then ask them to write their address on the other side. The next day you drop the cards in the mail. A perfect auto-reminder! (Contributed by Gerard Labrecque, Staunton, Va.)

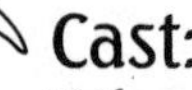

The Perils of the Prodigal

(A Melodrama)

Cast:

Wise and loving father
Faithful son Larry
Flaky son Daryl
Daryl's fair-weather friends:
Lisa Luscious
Amy Airhead
Heather Hot
Henry Hunk
Pigs (at least two)
Employees (played by the friends and pigs)

Once upon a time there was a wise and loving father who had two sons, Larry and Daryl. (He used to have another son George, but that's another story.) This wise and loving father was quite rich, owing to the fact that he was the founder of Jeans R Us at the nearby mall. (He used to own The Gap, too, but that's another store.)

The older son of this wise and loving father was a hard worker. Larry went to his father's store each day to put out new merchandise, operate the cash register, and answer the phone. The younger son of the wise and loving father, on the other hand, was spoiled. Daryl went to the store each day, too—but only to flirt with the female employees, tease his brother Larry, and "borrow" from the cash register to buy donuts at break time. But when their father came to look in on the store, Daryl started to work like crazy. Then Dad would pat both his sons on the back and exclaim, "What fine sons I have!"

One day Daryl went up to his father's office on the second floor of the mall. (His father's office used to be on the third floor, but that's another storey.) Daryl got down on his knees, clutched his father's hand, and pleaded, "Father, dearest—when you die, who will get your money?"

"I'll split it between you and Larry," replied the father.

Daryl, looking earnestly into his father's eyes, said, "Can I have my half now? I want to start my own business."

The father looked like he was almost ready to cry. "I'm not sure, son," he said.

But Daryl was persistent. He wrapped himself around his father's knees and pleaded pitifully over and over again, "Please, Daddy." Finally the father agreed. He took his money and gave half to Daryl. The other half he gave to Larry.

Daryl decided to open his own Jeans R Us franchise in L.A. So he caught the next plane (narrator throws paper airplane for him to catch) to the coast. When he got there, he scratched his head and thought aloud: "There's time for work later. First I'll check out the beach." So he headed for the ocean, stopping first to pick up a new sports car (narrator rolls him a toy car for him to pick up).

When he got to the beach, a beautiful girl came up to him. "Hi," she said, tossing her hair over her shoulder. "My name is Lisa Luscious."

Lisa took his hand, placed it around her waist, and led Daryl off to meet her friends Amy Airhead, Henry Hunk, and Heather Hot. Looking at Daryl, they all said in unison, "Hey, dude, let's party."

They all piled into Daryl's car and went cruisin'. Every day the four of them partied late into the night. Daryl bought them clothes, booze, drugs, Guns 'n' Roses. They were so happy that they picked Daryl up and carried him on their shoulders as they sang, to the tune of "For He's a Jolly Good Fellow," "Daryl likes to party—all the time."

One day as they were carrying Daryl around on their shoulders, he said laughingly, "Guess what guys? I'm out of money."

They dropped him like a bad habit.

Now Daryl was all alone, far from home, and broke. He lay face down on the ground and pounded it with his fists as he cried aloud, "What shall I do? What shall I do?"

Soon he found himself feeding pigs for a local farmer. The pigs were messy, and they made disgusting pig noises. Daryl paced back and forth among the swine, wondering aloud, "How could I ever have been so stupid?"

Then one day an idea hit him. He slapped his forehead so hard it knocked him backwards onto one of the pigs, who made angry pig sounds at him. But that didn't bother Daryl. He picked himself up, gazed intently into the distance, and said, "I'll go back to my father. Even the stock boys in Dad's store have it better than this!" Daryl began to dance around the pig pen while the pigs squealed with delight.

The next morning Daryl got out of bed and started for home. He couldn't afford to take the plane, so he borrowed a friend's bike and pedalled feverishly. When the bike broke down, he hitchhiked. When his ride dropped him off, he bought a used skateboard and rode it. When the bearings fell out, he began to run. Exhausted, he slowed to a walk. When the mall finally came into view, it was all he could do to crawl the last few yards to get to his father's store.

Meanwhile, his father was looking way down the length of the mall, hoping to somehow recognize his son among all the shoppers. So when he saw Daryl, he leapt for joy, let out a whoop like a banshee, and danced around in circles, jumping and clicking his heels together. Then he ran to meet his son.

Daryl wrapped himself around his father's ankles, sobbing violently while his father patted him on the head. "Father," he finally blurted out. "I am not worthy to be called your son. Make me a stock boy!"

The father took Daryl's face tenderly in his hands and lifted him to his feet. "My son is home!" he exclaimed. They embraced.

Daryl's dad took him in the store and gave him a brand new pair of Guess jeans, a pair of Air Jordans, and Oakley sunglasses. Then he invited all the employees in the store to join him and Daryl at Baskin-Robbins for ice cream. They all formed a circle around Daryl, joined hands, and danced around him singing, "For He's a Jolly Good Fellow."

But the father left the party because someone was missing—Larry. He found Larry sulking outside Baskin-Robbins, feeling sorry for himself, and sucking his thumb. As his dad approached, Larry yelled, "You don't love me! You never loved me! You always liked Daryl best! You never bought ice cream for me and my friends!" Then he put his thumbs in his ears, stuck his tongue out at his dad, and made the ugliest face you ever saw. He was so angry he fell to the floor kicking and screaming.

The father reached down and lifted Larry to his feet. "Larry," he said "everything of mine has always been yours. But we have to be happy. My son was lost and now is found!"

Then the father and his two sons spent the next six hundred years building an ark—no, wait, that's another story.♦

PICK A COMPLIMENT

You have the greatest teeth.

Your liver holds a lot of bile.

You have really cool ears.

I like the scent of your deodorant.

You have the nicest nostrils I've ever seen.

You have the most hairs on your head per square inch that I've ever seen.

You have the prettiest pinky I've ever seen.

Your clothes have really cool pockets.

You have a great sense of smell.

You have hardly any dirt between your toes.

I really like your shoe laces.

You have great eyebrows.

You have the prettiest middle name I've ever heard

Your fingerprint is a piece of art.

Your ears hardly build any ear wax.

You have the cleanest neck I've ever seen.

Your tongue has more taste buds than anyone else's.

You have a great intestinal tract.

I wish my stomach digested food as quickly as your does.

When you belch it smells like a bouquet of flowers.

Puzzling a Youth Group

Here's a group-building exercise. Purchase at an art store a large piece of bristle board that is mounted on ¼-inch-thick Styrofoam. Before the session cut the Styrofoam with a sharp blade into enough puzzle pieces for the number of kids expected to attend. Make it as difficult as you wish.

When the kids arrive, ask them to each decorate with marking pens one piece of the puzzle. (Use fruit-scented markers for more sensory appeal!) Decorations should include the artist's name, age, grade, school, and a drawing of a favorite activity (or any other aspect of identity you may choose).

When all have completed their pieces, put the puzzle together. Add in any blank pieces to represent the potential for new members. Take a picture of the finished puzzle with the contributors lying around it. (Contributed by Susan and David Johnson, Kitchener, Ontario, Canada.)

A Puzzling Church

If you liked "Jigsaw Puzzle" (**Ideas 9-12**), you'll love this elaboration of the idea.

Set up tables around the room. Divide your group into teams of three to six people, and provide each team with a 250-300 piece jigsaw puzzle. All of the puzzles should have the same number of pieces but should be of different scenes. Announce that the first team to complete their puzzle will win a prize.

After 10 minutes or so, announce a team shift (actually, the first of three—but don't let on that there will be any more). Gauge the timing of the subsequent shifts on the speed at which the puzzles are being completed.

- **Shift 1**—Each team moves to another puzzle, but everyone must work without talking among themselves.
- **Shift 2**—The teams move to yet a different puzzle—but just before they rotate, you remove the puzzle box with the picture on it. They may resume talking to one another, however.
- **Shift 3**—This time everyone scrambles themselves into new teams as they each move to a puzzle they haven't worked on yet. Return the puzzle boxes to each table as they're settling in.

As soon as the first puzzle is completed, stop the activity and award the prize. Conclude by discussing any of the following: Reaping what you have not sown...the importance of the Bible and the life of Jesus as a model for Christian living...division of duties in the body of Christ...unfinished business at the second coming of Christ...commitment to ministry and the church in a transient culture...competition/cooperation...leadership in the body of Christ...unity and diversity...the task of the church...denominations. (Contributed by David Shaw, Laurel, Md.)

Quick-Draw Bible Basics

If you teach junior high Sunday school, you know you can no longer count on your students knowing basic Bible stories. To quickly ground the novice in who's who in the Bible while keeping more knowledgeable students motivated, try this quick-draw game.

Assign one or two chapters for the kids to read as homework (creation story, early life of Samuel, excerpts from the life of Christ, and so on). The next Sunday play a modified version of Pictionary, using the words from the assigned reading as the source of the drawing clues.

With the story of Joseph, for example: assign Genesis 37 and 39 to read. Write out the following clues for the artists: "He made a richly ornamental robe for him" (37:3); "...binding sheaves of grain in the field" (37:7); "Throw him in the cistern here in the desert" (37:22).

Tell the kids before they start how long they have to draw and how accurate the guess has to be. If the group is willing to slow the pace of the game, ask those drawing to explain the situation around what they drew. (Contributed by Joyce Vermeer, Coaldale, Alta., Canada)

Race of Life

This game doubles as a parable. It speaks to the common response of teens to the demands of discipleship: "If all I need to gain eternal life is to claim Jesus as my Savior before I die, then why shouldn't I just have the best time I can and save religion for the deathbed?"

Explain to the group that they're going to race to a determined finish line. They all must start when the whistle blows, must walk (not run), and must freeze when the whistle blows a second time.

Make it equally clear, too, that they **may** cheat.

➡First Round

1. Blow the whistle to start the race.
2. When a few reach the finish line, blow the whistle a second time.
3. Now announce that those who cheated (either by running or by not freezing in time) are hunchbacked. For the remaining rounds they must walk with their hands on their knees.
4. Announce to the kids who made it to the finish line fairly that, because they seem to have a natural advantage, they must be handicapped—so they also will have to walk hunchbacked for the remaining rounds.

➡Second Round

Repeat the race and follow the same procedure. Only this time, however, the cheaters and the winners become crippled—that is, they have to hold onto one foot and hop on the other for the remaining rounds. Those who are already hunchbacked must keep one hand on a knee as well as hold one foot with the other hand.

➡Third Round

Repeat the race. This time the cheaters and winners become blind and have to close their eyes for the fourth and final round.

➡Fourth Round

After this round ask everyone who is not hunchbacked, crippled, or blind to come forward. **These** are the actual winners. Explain that the objective was never to be first to the finish line; **the objective was to finish the race as a whole person.**

Explain to the kids the "save it for the deathbed" approach to Christianity. Read them the quote from the first paragraph of this idea, then ask them, "How does this game answer this question?" First of all, what may appear to be the obvious objective in life is not the real objective. The real objective in life is not to satisfy our appetites for sex, money, or power, but to be a whole person.

Second, sin cripples us. We suffer from the guilt, shame, and consequences of our sins in **this** life regardless of the life to come. Sin keeps us from reaching the real goal in life.

When the kids respond, "But you said we could cheat," explain that the game also illustrates free will—we are free to live in the manner we choose. Finally, you may want to add that sin inhibits us from reaching even the illusory goals—overindulging our appetites bring us to a point of diminishing returns. (Contributed by Andrew Parker, Abilene, Tex.)

Rap Sermon II

Here's another Old Testament story in rap (see **Ideas 48**). It's especially appropriate for children's sermons performed by you or your high schoolers to the accompaniment of a rap track or to a couple of people who can vocalize the rhythm-heavy, percussive rapping sound. (Contributed by Lyn Wargny, Palmyra, N.J.)

DAVID AND GOLIATH

Once upon a time, when the Hebrews were at war,
Their soldiers met a foe they had never met before.
He fought for the Philistines and his name was Goliath,
And they could not defeat him, no matter how they trieth.
Goliath was a giant. He was huge and he was scary.
His face was really mean and his arms were big and hairy.

King Saul promised a reward to anyone who'd beat him,
But all of the soldiers were too petrified to meet him.
They'd start out to fight, but then quickly run away
As soon as they heard what Goliath had to say.
He said, "I'll fight you, one to one, if anyone is willing,
And victory will be determined by who does the killing.
If I win—and I know I will—then you'll be slaves of ours.
If I should lose—preposterous!—then we'll be in your powers.
I'm ready to get going; come on, let the fight begin!
Or are you all too chicken?" said Goliath with a grin.

Now David had three brothers in the army of King Saul.
His father asked if he would go and check up on them all.
He heard Goliath's threats and he saw the Hebrews fleeing,
And he could not believe that these were soldiers he was seeing.
For David, though a shepherd boy, was full of faith and courage,
He was shocked and dismayed at the soldiers' show of worriage.
"This fellow has a lot of nerve—why, he insults our God!
And none of you will stop him? I find that very odd.
Heck, I'll go out and fight him. If you agree, then I'll
Go out and beat Goliath, for God is on our side."

D-A-VID, D-A-VID, D-A-VID, yay, David!

Saul was just delighted. "Good for you, son—I approve!"
And he loaded Dave with armor till the poor kid couldn't move.
David said, "Hey, I don't need this. I don't want anything.
I'll just take five little stones and my old shepherd's sling."

D-A-VID, D-A-VID, D-A-VID, yay, David!

(Referee:) Now in this corner, weighing in around 100 pounds,
David, the brave shepherd boy, going for tenrounds.
And in the other corner, very heavy, very tall,
The Philistine called Goliath. Which one of them will fall?

(Sadly) D-A-VID, D-A-VID, D-A-VID, good luck, David.

Goliath said, "You're just a kid! I hardly need my sword!"
And David said, "That might be true were it not for the Lord.
I'm doing this one for our God, his might and power to show.
Hope you have life insurance, for we will win, I know."

(Referee rings a bell)

So David threw a little stone, and hit him in the head.
And down fell Goliath, absolutely stone-cold dead!

D-A-VID, D-A-VID, D-A-VID, YAY DAVID!!!

(Referee counts 10 and holds up David's hand)
And that's how little David slew Goliath, saved the day,
And showed his people, "Trust in God, and you will be okay."
He did it for the Lord, and not to gain fame and glory.
And so we come at last to the moral of our story.
Although you may feel helpless, and although you may be small,
With God you can do anything—anything at all.

Well, now our story's over; that's all, my friend,
So you can go sit down again.

The Rich Fool

Here's another extemporaneous drama in which volunteers (or recruits!) play their assigned roles by acting out what the narrator reads. Use this on-the-spot, no-rehearsal sketch on page 104 (based on Christ's parable) as a discussion starter about possessions or materialism. Here are some questions you might want to use after your group enjoys the drama.

Discussion Questions

- Describe how important it is to you and your school friends to have the "right" things or possessions.
- Why do you think our society is so stuck on **things**?
- What priority have you lately given to seeking first God's kingdom?
- Describe some of the difficulties you face in storing up treasure in heaven versus storing up treasure on earth.
- Brainstorm realistic ideas that could help you to become rich toward God. List these ideas.
- Choose one idea from the list that you will try this week in order to escape the trap of materialism.

(Contributed by Jim Liebelt, Hingham, Mass.)

Saying Good-bye

The worksheet on page 105 will help your kids discover the good in good-bye. (Contributed by John Morgan, Caldwell, N.J.)

Spiritual Vision Test

Use the test on pages 106 and 107 to move your group to evaluate their spiritual condition. After they've taken the test, read aloud the diagnoses and discuss the Scriptures that apply based on their test results. (Contributed by Larry Stoess, Crestwood, Ky.)

Stump the Speaker

Here's a youth group version of Stump the Band, a game that's been featured on "The Tonight Show" for many years.

Ask kids to find objects in their pockets, purses, or around the room. Call on students one at a time to give you their objects. You then have 15 seconds to think up a thirty-second object lesson, using that item to teach a spiritual truth. If you can't do it, but the student can, the student wins a prize.

This game will get your creative juices flowing—plus, it's a great way to pass the time if you finish your Sunday school lesson early and are waiting for dismissal. Variation: Select kids to be the "speaker." (Contributed by Michael Frisbee, Hobbs, N. Mex.)

The Rich Fool

Luke 12:16–21

Cast:

Rich man (one person)
New wood for the barn (two more people)
Easy chair (one person)
God (one person)
Barn (two people)
Crop (two people)
Workers (two big, strong guys)
Narrator

Jesus told them this parable (well, his parable was *sort of* like this):

Once there was a rich man who went out into his field one day to look at this crop. He was very fond of his crop. You could tell he was fond of his crop because he would look over his crop lovingly. He would touch his crop. He would smell his crop—even though he was allergic to his crop. So whenever he smelled his crop, he sneezed on it. This made the crop sway back and forth. As he looked over his swaying crop, he would sneeze and say, "What a great crop!"

Then he said, "But what shall I do? My barn is too small for my crop!" Disappointed, he walked over and kicked the barn—which only injured his foot. He hopped around in pain, his face contorted by the anguish. Then he said, "I know...I'll hire workers to tear down this old barn and build me a bigger barn."

So that's what he did. The workers came out and tried tearing down the old barn. But the barn was strong and resisted. No matter how hard the workers tried to demolish the barn, it just kept on standing there. Yet the workers finally prevailed, the barn reluctantly yielded to the efforts of the workers. The old building crumbled—right on top of the workers. After a long struggle, however, the workers were able to squeeze out from underneath the ruins of the old barn.

Next, the workers carried in new wood to make a bigger barn. But they ran out of new wood—so they used the wood of the old barn to finish the new, bigger barn. The only problem was that the wood from the old barn was *very* heavy and was difficult to put into place.

Once the new barn was in place, the rich man said to his workers, "Hey, guys—nice barn." Then he said, "Why don't you come out and help me bring in my crop?"

"We'll do it!" said the workers.

"Great!" said the rich man. "This way, guys." The rich man turned and hopped off toward the field. The workers followed the rich man, also hopping as they went. When they were in the field, the rich man showed them his beautiful crop. He told them to touch the crop. He told them to smell the crop. The workers, also allergic to the crop, also sneezed on it. The crop swayed in the wind.

"Well, boys," said the rich man. "Take my crop into the barn." So the workers picked up the crop and carried it into the barn, sneezing all the way along and causing the crop to sway back and forth—which made it difficult to carry.

Once the crop was safely in the barn and the workers had gone home for the night (sneezing all the way home), the rich man said to himself, "Now I have plenty of good things. This stuff will last me for many years. I can take life easy. I'll eat, drink, and be merry."

With that, he reclined in his easy chair. But for some reason the easy chair was wobbly. The rich man tried to get comfortable, but he couldn't. Suddenly the chair collapsed under the weight of the rich man. He hit his head on the floor and passed out.

In a dream he saw God stand above him and say, "Yo, rich dude. You be a fool. This night you gonna die. Then who's gonna own all that stash of yours?"

The next morning the workers sneezed their way to work—and found the dead man. They gasped. They sneezed. They carried him to the barn and threw him in among the swaying crop.

The moral of the story? It's in Luke 12:21: "This is how it will be with anyone who stores up things for himself but is not rich toward God."

SAYING GOOD-BYE

1. THINK: Is there anything good about good-bye?
   WRITE: Describe the last time you had to say good-bye.

   ____

2. THINK: Think of a friend who has moved away with whom you still have a good relationship.
   WRITE: What was hard about that good-bye? Why is your relationship still strong?

   ____

3. THINK: Think of someone to whom you said good-bye and with whom you no longer have a relationship.
   WRITE: How did you say good-bye? What led to the loss of that relationship?

   ____

4. THINK: Read John 13:33 through 14:4 and John 14:15-31.
   WRITE: How does Jesus say good-bye? What does Jesus tell the disciples about how they should feel about his leaving?

   ____

5. Discuss with the group what people can do to make good-byes better.

SAYING GOOD-BYE

1. THINK: Is there anything good about good-bye?
   WRITE: Describe the last time you had to say good-bye.

   ____

2. THINK: Think of a friend who has moved away with whom you still have a good relationship.
   WRITE: What was hard about that good-bye? Why is your relationship still strong?

   ____

3. THINK: Think of someone to whom you said good-bye and with whom you no longer have a relationship.
   WRITE: How did you say good-bye? What led to the loss of that relationship?

   ____

4. THINK: Read John 13:33 through 14:4 and John 14:15-31.
   WRITE: How does Jesus say good-bye? What does Jesus tell the disciples about how they should feel about his leaving?

   ____

5. Discuss with the group what people can do to make good-byes better.

SPIRITUAL VISION TEST

Measure your spiritual vision with this spiritual  test.

1. When you look in the mirror, what do you see? (Ps. 139:13-16)
   a. The handiwork of God
   b. Zits
2. When you are walking in the woods and come across a mulberry bush, what do you see? (Ex. 3:1-3)
   a. The burning bush of Mt. Horeb
   b. Mulberries
3. When you lay on your back in an open field and look into a cloud-filled sky, what do you see? (Ps. 19:1)
   a. The majesty of God
   b. A chance of rain
4. Which of these most resembles God to you?
   a. A rainbow
   b. A thundercloud
5. What do you see in this picture?
   a. A devil
   b. A kitten
6. In this picture the glass is—
   a. Half full
   b. Half empty
7. What do you see in this picture?
   a. Three crosses
   b. An algebra equation

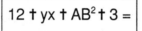

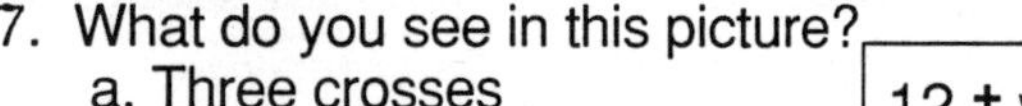

12 † yx † AB^2 † 3 =

8. What do you see in this picture?
   a. A cross on its side
   b. An asymetrical X

9. When you see a driver cut you off, then direct an obscene gesture at you, what's your reaction?
   a. A feeling of compassion for someone so driven by anger.
   b. To return an obscene gesture.
10. What do you see in the numerals below?
   a. The combination to a gym locker
   b. A girl's statistics

34 26 34

11. What is your reaction when you're in a group that's passing along bad but true gossip about someone you know?
   a. Suggest that there are two sides to every story, and that you're withholding judgment until you talk to the acquaintance personally.
   b. Just listen—and be thankful you're not the subject of this gossip.
12. What do you see in this picture?
   a. Money to help someone in need
   b. Money to spend on yourself

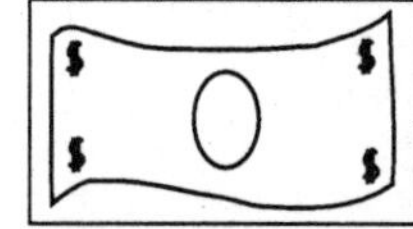

13. When you look at peoples' faults, what do you see first? (Matt. 7:1-5)
   a. The log in your eye
   b. The speck in their eye
14. What kind of movies do you like to see?
   a. Movies about adventure or relationships
   b. Movies characterized by sex or violence

15. Which would you rather watch?
    a. Sunsets
    b. TV
16. Which would you rather watch?
    a. PBS nature documentaries
    b. "Days of Our Lives"
17. Which would you rather watch?
    a. The six o'clock news
    b. A TV evangelist
18. Which would you rather read?
    a. The Bible
    b. A Stephen King novel
19. Which would you rather read?
    a. *Campus Life*
    b. *Seventeen*
20. Which would you rather read?
    a. A comic book
    b. A fund-raising letter from TV evangelists

Diagnosis

1. Total the number of a. answers you circled, multiply the sum by two, and write this number on the left side of the slash below.
2. Total the number of b. answers you circled, multiply the sum by two, and write this number on the right side of the slash below.

_________/_________

Refer to the chart to receive your diagnosis and treatment.

SCORE	DIAGNOSIS	TREATMENT
40/0 38/2 36/4 34/6	***Heavenly vision.*** Blessed are your eyes...For I tell you the truth, many prophets and righteous men longed to see what you see but did not see it. (Matt. 13:16-17)	To keep your spiritual vision clear, apply 2 Corinthians 4:16-18.
32/8 30/10 28/12 26/14	***Spiritual farsightedness.*** Your eyes are good; therefore you are full of light. Yet because you are farsighted, you overlook the kingdom of God when it is near (see Matt. 6:22).	To correct farsightedness, apply Mark 1:15.
24/16 22/18 20/20 18/22 16/24	***Laodicean vision.*** Your eyes are neither good nor bad, neither farsighted nor nearsighted. You therefore run the risk of losing your sight altogether (see Rev. 3:14-16).	Apply Revelation 3:17-18 immediately.
14/26 12/28 10/30 8/32	***Roamin' eyes.*** Your eyes have been darkened because they have roamed from the things of God to the passions of this world (see Rom. 11:8-10).	Apply 2 Peter 1:5-9 three times a day.
6/34 4/36 2/38 0/40	***Spiritual glaucoma.*** You're just plain blind—spiritually, that is. Your eyes are shot, and the darkness of this world is all around you (see 1 John 2:9-11 and Matt. 6:23).	Your only hope is Jesus' advice in Matthew 5:29.

Target Togetherness

To show that the church needs the talents of all of its members to succeed in completing God's mission for it, let the kids experience depending upon each other. They'll learn it's not always easy to work together, but when everyone persists in contributing to the effort, their goal can be achieved.

For each group you'll need three ping-pong balls, three wide rubber bands, and two blindfolds. You'll also need masking tape, Dixie cups, and one table for every three groups. Set up pyramids of stacked Dixie cups on tables as targets for the teams.

To start, divide the group into threesomes. Ask each trio to construct a slingshot by tying the rubber bands together and taping a "pocket" on the center rubber band. Assign body parts to the three teammates—one is the eyes, one is the right arm, and one is the left arm. Blindfold the "right arm" and "left arm," and give the "right arm" the slingshot.

Play begins with all the "right arms" sitting on the floor facing the table and holding the slingshot with both hands over their heads. All the "left arms" kneel behind the "right arms," loading the slingshots with ping-pong balls, and firing at the targets. All "eyes" stand behind the "left arms" and verbally direct them in aiming for the targets. The first group to hit a stack of cups wins that round.

After three shots, allow the group members to switch roles within their own group. Go several rounds and keep a running total of hits. (Contributed by Doug Partin, Lubbock, Tex.)

Ten Plague Relay

Whether you're studying the life of Moses or just playing for fun, your group will know the 10 Egyptian plagues when they finish this relay. Before playing, create a set of game sheets for as many teams as you expect will play. Each "set" consists of 10 sheets (index cards will do); on each sheet write one of the 10 plagues along with its corresponding

task.

The Plague of Blood—Drink a glass of red punch before returning to your team.

The Plague of Frogs—Hop like a frog all the way back to your team.

The Plague of Gnats—Return to your team waving your hands in front of your face as if swatting gnats.

The Plague of Flies—Make buzzing sounds, flap your arms like wings, and fly back to your team.

The Plague on Livestock—Get down on all fours, moo like a cow, and roll over dead before returning to your team.

The Plague of Boils—Place four Band-Aids on your body and then return to your team.

The Plague of Hail—Empty a cup of ice on your head before returning to your team.

The Plague of Locusts—Flap your arms like wings and fly in circles back to your team.

The Plague of Darkness—Keep your eyes closed as you return to your team.

The Plague on the Firstborn— Drop to the floor as though you are dead.

When you're ready to play, divide your group into teams of 10 or less. Place each team's set of game sheets on a chair 30 feet or so in front of each team. A few feet beyond the chairs, place on a single table one glass of red punch and one cup of ice per team, and four Band-Aids per team. Instruct players to line their teams up behind the starting point.

At a signal, the first member of each team runs to the stack of game sheets (stacked, by the way, in order of plague) on the chair in front of his or her team, grabs the top sheet and reads it, yells out the name of the plague, and then follows the instructions on that game sheet. When the first player tags the next person on the team, that person runs for the chair of game sheets and follows its instruction, and so on. (If there are less than 10 team members, let some run twice.)

The first team to have a team member drop to the floor as though dead is the winner. Capture this relay on video for a hilarious promotion of youth group activities. (Contributed by Tommy Baker and Jeff Baker, Florence, Ky.)

To Tell the (Holy Spirit) Truth

Divide the group into small teams. Choose two students to be readers; one reads the Holy Spirit statement in the left column; the other, the corresponding statement in the right column. After each pair of statements is read, the groups must decide among themselves which of the two statements is correct. Warn them to be cautious: **both** statements in some pairs may be correct.

The correct statements are those with Scripture references. (Contributed by Mark C. Christian, Long Beach, Calif.)

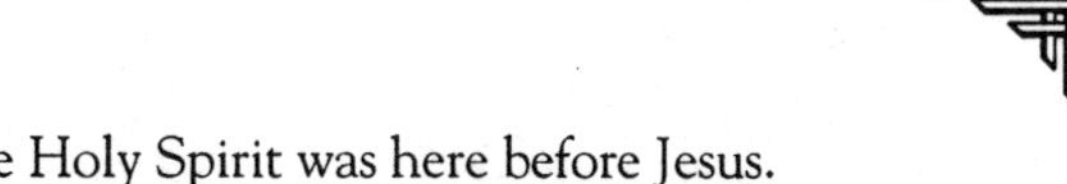

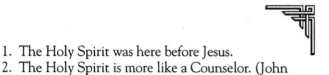

1.	The Holy Spirit came after Jesus. (John 16:7)	The Holy Spirit was here before Jesus.
2.	The Holy Spirit is like a gentle mother.	The Holy Spirit is more like a Counselor. (John 14:16)
3.	It's easy to see and know the Holy Spirit.	No way! You can't know him or see him. (John 14:16)
4.	The Holy Spirit came like wind. (Acts 2:2)	Better than that, he came like fire. (Acts 2:3)
5.	The Spirit helps to keep you from sinning. (Rom. 8:9)	No way! Nothing can keep you from sinning.
6.	The Holy Spirit prays to God for us. (Rom. 8:28)	No one prays to God for me but me alone!
7.	The Holy Spirit teaches us about God. (John 14:26)	Better than that, he guides us in life. (John 14:13)
8.	The Holy Spirit is an external force only.	The Holy Spirit lives inside every Christian. (1 Cor. 3:16)
9.	The Holy Spirit is called the Spirit of Knowledge.	Nope. The Holy Spirit is called the Spirit of Truth. (John 16:13)
10.	Okay, then how about the Spirit of Promise? (Eph. 1:13)	Nope again. He's the Spirit of Dreams.
11.	The Holy Spirit is the Spirit of God. (1 Cor. 3:16)	Dream on. He's the Spirit of Christ. (Rom. 8:9)
12.	The worse sin of all is murder.	Not so. The worst sin is swearing at the Holy Spirit. (Matt. 12:31)
13.	A Christian is one who is born in God's Spirit. (John 3:5)	A Christian is one who attends church and does good.
14.	The word *spirit* means *breath.* (this is correct)	With breath like yours, a better definition is *wind.* (this is also correct)
15.	One of the results of the Holy Spirit in my life is I'm full of joy. (Gal. 5:22)	The Holy Spirit makes me more competitive and determined.
16.	The fruits of the Spirit include love, peace, kindness, and faithfulness. (Gal. 5:22)	You forgot gentleness, self control, and kindness, didn't you? (Gal. 5:22)
17.	God's Spirit gives me power to be just a bit better than others.	God's Spirit gives me power to share my faith. (Acts 1:8)
18.	The Holy Spirit keeps bad things from happening to me.	The Holy Spirit shows me the things I am doing that are bad. (John 16:8-11)
19.	Sin will kill us. (Rom. 8:13)	The Holy Spirit helps destroy our sin and gives us life. (Rom. 8:13)

The Ultimate Ken and Barbie

Form small groups of three to six kids, and give each group the following supplies: old magazines (**Sports Illustrated**, **Glamour**, **Vogue**, **Seventeen**), glue, scissors, and newsprint. Assign each group the task of creating from magazine cutouts the perfect Ken and Barbie. From different models they should cut out the best pair of legs, the greatest biceps, the most beautiful hair, the most alluring eyes—in short, they should create the ultimate body (which will appear deformed and add to the fun).

After gluing these parts to the newsprint, create the ultimate setting of beautiful home furnishings, exotic cars, electronic toys, landscape artistry—everything society says we need in order to be happy. Once the small groups have hung their contributions on the wall, let the whole group vote on the best collage. Conclude by helping the "artists" look at our society with God's perspective: he looks at the heart (1 Sam. 16:7). Besides, after he had made us—and before Sony, Guess, and Toyota had cluttered our lives—he said his creation was good. (Contributed by Chuck Hawkins, Nashville, Tenn.)

Wannabe Bingo

As a crowd breaker or a discussion starter, this variation on bingo can be used as is or with your own fill-ins. Make copies of the bingo sheet on page 112 to hand out (one to each player), give players a pencil, and let everyone mingle.

The object: players find people who want to be like the person or trait written in one of the squares, and then ask that person to put his or her initials in the appropriate square. The winner must get initials in four squares in one horizontal or vertical row or in one diagonal row. Players can initial only one square on their own bingo sheet. The rest of the squares must be initialed by different players. (With a bigger group ask for two players to initial each square.)

Waterproof Devotional

After your next water event—pool party, beach trip, etc.—run off enough copies of the following "Waterproof Devotional" on pages 113 and 114 for each attender. Fold the devotional so that the title shows, and then stuff each one in a Ziploc sandwich bag. The note at the end of the devotional promises those who turn in the completed devotion by a certain date will receive a prize that will save their life (give 'em a pack of Lifesavers). (Contributed by Mark Adams, Derwood, Md.)

Wannabe Bingo

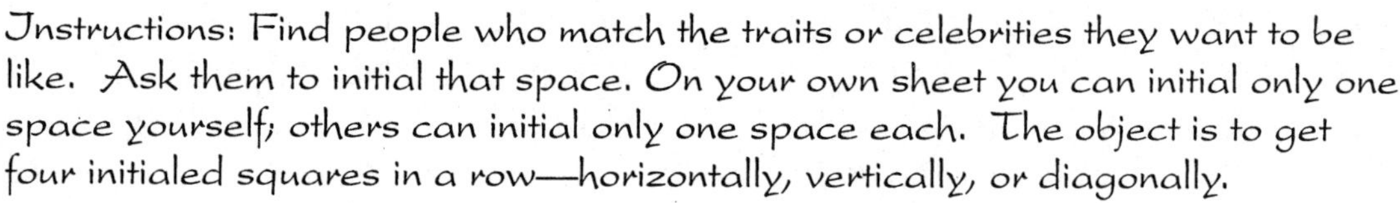

Instructions: Find people who match the traits or celebrities they want to be like. Ask them to initial that space. On your own sheet you can initial only one space yourself; others can initial only one space each. The object is to get four initialed squares in a row—horizontally, vertically, or diagonally.

Arnold Schwarzenegger	Teenage Mutant Ninja Turtles	Normal	Mr. Universe
Athletic	Paula Abdul	Blonde	Taller
Blue-eyed	Thinner	More motivated	Brown-eyed
Popular	Miss Universe	Prettier	Brunette

YOUTH AQUATIC DAY, TAKE-HOME, DO-IT-YOURSELF WATERPROOF DEVOTIONAL

By now, hopefully, all the water has drained out of your ears and you are contentedly relaxing, remembering the fun we had in the water. Yet before you hit the sack, take a few minutes to see what can be learned from this event that can help you be a better Christian.

"What can a day in the water teach me about Jesus?" you ask. You may be surprised—Jesus has a lot to do with water. In fact, the Gospels explain at least 10 significant liquid incidents in Jesus' life.

If you look closely at Jesus and H^2O , you just might wring out a spiritual truth or two. Here goes.

Now here's what you do:

- Get your Bible.
- Read *each* reference.
- In the space provided after each statement, write down what this example has to do with your life—what lesson can you learn that will make wakin' up tomorrow better?

Need a hint? The first example (Jesus was born of water) reminds us that, although Jesus was a hundred percent God, he was also a hundred percent human. That means he was born just like any human, lived life just like us—and so he knows what it is to suffer pain and bust a gut laughing. It also means that when you pray, you pray to someone who understands.

You do the other seven examples yourself. ***If you bring me your completed devotional this Sunday, I will give you a tasty prize that will save your life!***

Jesus...

1. Was born of water. (Luke 2:7)

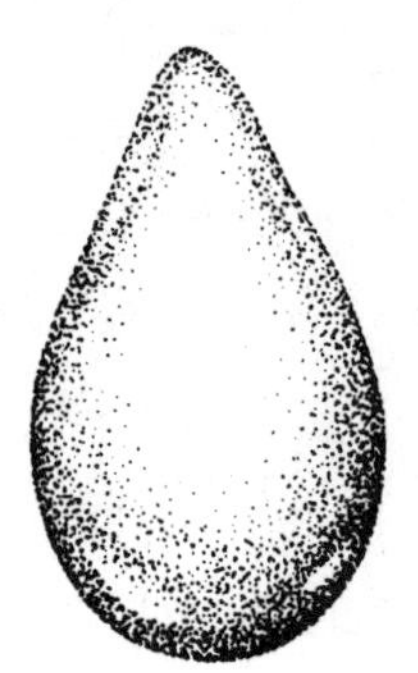

2. Turned water into wine. (John 2:9)

3. Was baptized in water. (John 3:21)

4. Drank water. (John 4:7)

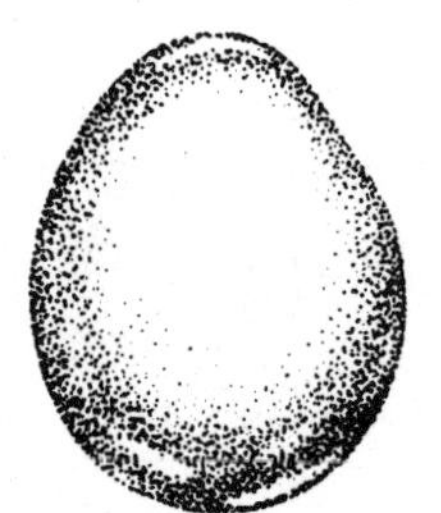

5. Calmed stormy water. (John 8:24)

6. Wept water. (John 11:35)

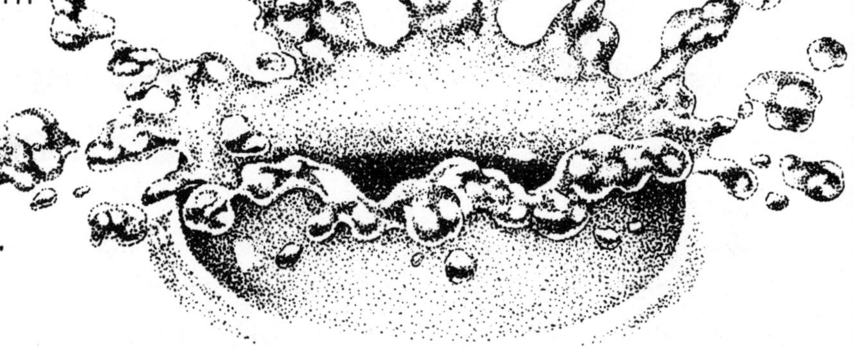

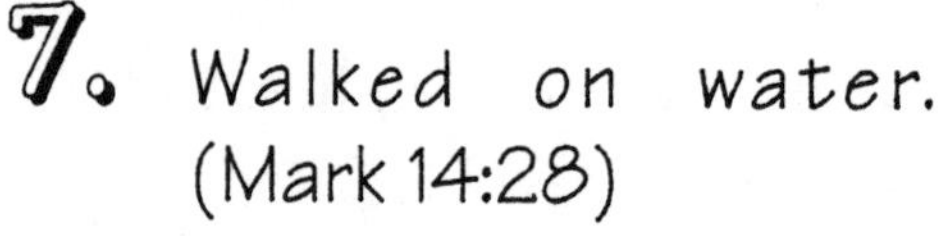

7. Walked on water. (Mark 14:28)

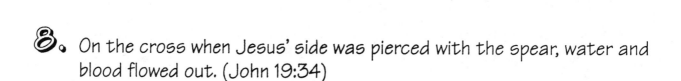

8. On the cross when Jesus' side was pierced with the spear, water and blood flowed out. (John 19:34)

Where Can I Put the Kingdom of God?

The directive of Jesus in Matthew 6:33—"seek ye first the kingdom of God"—is illustrated with this creative devotional.

Make a mental list of all the sports, jobs, hobbies, interests, etc., that kids in your group involve themselves in. Then collect lots of objects that symbolize or depict those interests—a basketball, football, Nintendo cartridges, videocassettes, time card, pizza box, CDs, comic books, textbooks, fashion catalogs, phone books.

Open the devotional by placing on the floor a Bible opened to Matthew 6:33. For starters, ask the group what sports they enjoy playing. When they answer, pull from a big box the corresponding object and toss it onto the Bible. Continue the interaction, asking what classes they like the best, how they prefer to spend their leisure, the extra-curricular activities they live for, etc. Each time, grab the appropriate object from the box and toss it onto the pile (which by now has probably covered the Bible completely).

A few minutes into this, ask your young people, "What happened to God?" The answer to this object lesson is obvious: God got buried under all the stuff. Once they acknowledge that, pull out the Bible from the stack of stuff and read Matthew 6:33. Ask them, "What would happen if you put the Bible—or God—on **top** of the pile?" Point out that if believers put God first, they still have all the other activities, but now they can see God, too. (Contributed by Chuck Hawkins, Macon, Ga.)

Willy the Prodigal

The actors in your group may either read or memorize the lines to this humorous retelling of the parable of the Prodigal Son. Even the audience gets involved when the narrator holds up various cue cards. (Contributed by Kyle Goodsey, Midwest City, Okla.)

Willy the Prodigal

Cast:

Narrator	**Willy**
Sissy	**Dad**

Cue-card indicators for audience participation:

✷ **"Beanhead!"**	✌ **"Wow, that's beautiful!"**
● **"Uh-oh"**	❀ **"Gosh, Beav—I think you really screwed up this time!"**
☆ **"Wow!"**	✠ **"Oooohhh, ick!"**

Narrator: For our Sunday school lesson today, we'd like you to meet a family: Dad and his two kids—Sissy and Willy.

Willy: I don't care what you say—life is out there for the taking, and I want to take it. Now. I don't want to waste my money and my time in college.

Sissy: But what about your future? ✷

Willy: There is no future. ☆ There's only today. I'm tired of wasting all my todays for a tomorrow I may never see. ✌

Sissy: If you don't slow down and look where you're going, you'll wind up lost. ✷

Willy: My money will be my guide. I'll go where it takes me. ✌

Dad: Hey, kids! What are you two arguing about?

Sissy: Oh, not much. Just life, liberty, and the pursuit of nothing. ✷

Dad: What do you mean?

Willy: What she means is I want my freedom, Dad. I want my half of the money you put in the bank for us.

Dad: But you haven't decided where you're going to college.

Willy: I don't want to go to college. I want to start enjoying life before I get old and gray like you. ●

Dad: Pardon me? ❁

Willy: I mean, uh, before I get too mature to remember what living is really like. I want to live while I still look good. I want to laugh. I want to boogie. I want to—

Dad: I get the point. All right, I'll give you a check for your half, but that's all you get. All the rest of the money belongs to your sister. ***(Pause)*** You know, son, you're really hurting me. I hate to see you do this to yourself. But, as you say, it is your life and you must live it. My only hope is that you live it wisely.

Willy: Thanks, Pop.

Narrator: Well, as you can probably predict, Willy went out and lived, but not wisely. He spent money right and left. First he bought a fancy sports car from a guy named Happy Sam. This tells you how wise he was being. Next he bought a new wardrobe. He didn't really look at the clothes much. He just made sure that they had a designer label and were expensive—because, he said, "to be good, you gotta look good." No swinging bachelor is complete without a swinging bachelor's pad. So Willy purchased a condominium from—guess who?—Happy Sam. Finally, Willy began "living." Caviar and lobster for breakfast, lunch, and dinner. $20 tips. ☆ He'd go to Baskin-Robbins and buy all 31 flavors for dessert. ☆

Happy Sam took Willy to all the night spots, where he spent his money gambling, drinking, and dancing until dawn. Willy was so busy spending his money on "living" that he didn't notice he was running out. He went to an ATM, punched in his 4-digit code—and got not cash but an "INSUFFICIENT FUNDS" notice. ●

The next day he opened an envelope from his bank to discover that his checks to Happy Sam had bounced. Life became even more difficult for Willy when he heard that Happy Sam had an unhappy friend named The Mongol. ❁

Willy stopped "living" and started surviving. Happy Sam repossessed the sports car and the condo. He pawned his wardrobe for food. Things got so bad, he placed his last 10 bucks on a 20 to 1 shot in a goldfish-swallowing contest. His man lost it—I mean, really lost it! ✠

Willy was plummeting, riding an express elevator straight to the bottom of his soul. ✌ Why, thank you! He realized he had to do something fast. All the good positions in the classifieds ended with the words, "College degree a must." Willy abandoned his search for the perfect job that provided instant wealth. He accepted the first offer he got.

Willy: SuuuuEEE! SuuuuEEE! C'mere, pig pig pig! Boy, I tell ya, those hogs are slobs—and they don't smell so sweet, either. This is horrible. I can't believe I'm working for a pig farmer, and for what he's paying me, too...those pigs eat better than I do. Of course, he did tell me I could have their leftovers. And I've been hungry enough to appreciate the offer. ✠ The only problem is that pigs don't leave leftovers. I am so depressed.

Narrator: Willy began crying as he walked toward the sty gate, not looking where he was going. He felt something cold and mushy on his ankles, on his knees, on his waist, his chest, his chin...he was sinking and sinking fast.

Willy: Great...just great. This is really the pits. Here I am up to my neck in muck, and no where to take a bath. I am so sick of living this way. Why didn't I listen to my dad? Why didn't my sister argue with me harder? Why didn't they just tie me up and force feed me and make me go to college? I know why: because they love me. ✌ I feel so foolish. I've wasted all the money my dad worked hard to earn. I want to go back home. I want to go back in the worst way and that's just the way I'm going.

Narrator: Willy pulled himself out of the mud and headed home. And I've got to tell you, folks, he looked and smelled disgusting. ✠ As he walked the long walk home, people stared, children pointed fingers, and a chihuahua bit him. He was miserable.

Willy: I sure hope Dad and Sissy take me back, or at least let me stay in the garage. Maybe Dad could hire me as a gardener or something. Maybe if I'm lucky, Sissy will give me a dollar or two to wash her car. I am so sorry I did this. If they only knew what I went through. ***(Singing mournfully)*** "Nobody knows the trouble I've seen..." All of this just goes to prove them right. I wish they would have just shown me pictures or a video or something that would have given me an idea of what to expect. Oh well, as my grandpappy used to tell me—"Wish in one hand, spit in the other, and see which one fills up first." ✌

Well, here I am, Dad...Dad? It's me, your dumbest child, remember? I'm not worthy to be your son. Dad, I'm sorry. I've been a real pain in the—I mean, I've been a real jerk, Dad.

Dad: Willy...Willy, is that you?

Willy: I'm afraid so.

Dad: Willy my son—whoa...pee-yew, you smell—and look—disgusting. ✠

Willy: I know, Dad. People stared at me, kids pointed at me, and a chihuahua bit me.

Dad: Well, I'm just glad you're home. Sissy, come here! Willy's home!

Sissy: Hi, Willy! Boy, you smell—and look—disgusting. ✠

Dad: He knows, dear. People stared at him, kids pointed at him, and a chihuahua bit him. But he's come home! Come on, Sissy, let's take Willy out and buy him some new clothes, a new car, some dinner. How about some lobster, son?

Willy: I think I've had enough lobster to last me a while. And if it's all right with you, no pork, either.

Narrator: So they took Willy out and bought him new clothes and a new car. By the way, they ate Italian that evening. Everyone was happy to see Willy back at home, but Sissy was a little upset.

Sissy: Dad, I'm really glad Willy's back and all, but I'm a little upset. ● He took all his money, ran off, had a good time, spent himself down to nothing, crawls back here—and look at the treatment he's getting! I've been here the whole time, I'm going to college—but you've never given me a party like this.

Dad: Look at it this way, honey. Willy didn't actually have that great of a time out there, and he's really sorry now. Besides, he's spent all his money and you've still got most of yours. You've got a lot more than him. What I'm trying to tell you is when someone is truly repentant and sorry for what he did, don't close the door on him. Rejoice!

Narrator: And that's the story of Willy the Prodigal.

Youth Group MVP

Hand out a slip of paper to each student and announce that they are going to vote for the Most Valuable Person in the youth group. Voters may list on their slips their first, second, and third choices. Each first-place vote is worth three points, a second-place vote is worth two points, and third-place votes receive one point each. (For example, Judy Smith received two first-place votes, seven second-place votes, and six third-place votes. Her total score is 26 points.)

Don't explain the balloting in any more detail. Let the students judge on the basis of their own standards.

Collect the ballots when they are completed and total the individual scores. Announce the top three finalists for MVP, and ask each of them to prepare a 15-to-30-second speech on "Why I Should Be Chosen Most Valuable Person to the Youth Group."

Following the speeches, read aloud Luke 9:18-36. Ask:

Who would you have voted for as MVP among the 12 disciples?

Discuss the reasoning behind their choices.

Read Luke 9:37-46. Ask:

Why do you think the disciples were arguing about who was the greatest?

(Hint: Think about Peter's confession, the "privileged" disciples taken by Jesus to witness the Transfiguration, and the testimony of the father of the child—"I begged your disciples to drive it out, but they could not.")

Conclude by reading Luke 9:47-48 and Matthew 20:26-28. Ask:

If we were to vote again for MVP in the youth group, would you vote differently this time? Why or why not?

Just before dismissal, either lead the group in a foot-washing service or distribute a small piece of towel to each student: ask them to carry it with them until the next meeting to remind them that the greatest is the one who serves. Close by praying for opportunities for the members to be MVPs in the coming week. (Contributed by James Wing, Niles, Mich.)

ABCs of Youth Ministry

Here's an alphabetical reminder to your staff workers and volunteers that you can post in your office, include in a mailer to them, etc. (Contributed by Bert L. Jones, Opp, Ala.)

ABCs of Youth Ministry

Attend to listening to your kids.

Be a model of one who serves others to teach kids service.

Coach—don't be a mere player. Leadership means getting kids involved.

Discipline when needed.

Encourage your young people.

Form fun activities to draw kids.

Grow in your own personal relationship with God.

Handle your ministry by the ninety-minute plan:

- One hour per week with one student.
- Fifteen minutes per week writing notes to three students.
- Fifteen minutes per week phoning three students.

Inform others of your plans (pastor, coworkers, parents, board, students).

Jeopardize no trust given to you.

Know your young people—by name, too.

Love Jesus and love kids.

Model for them the qualities you encourage them to exhibit.

Never lose sight of priorities—God, then family, then youth (others).

Open your home to your kids. Give away your telephone number and address.

Pray for your kids daily.

Quench overcommitment.

Reserve time in your schedule to build trusting relationships with kids. Share your faith with your group.

Team up with a support network. Don't go it alone.

Understand young people by reading books and magazines and by remembering what you were like when you were young.

Visit the places where kids are—malls, sporting events, school concerts.

Walk your talk.

E**X**perience regular time off.

Yield to being yourself.

Zero in on hurting, struggling, or lonely young people.

"And Tonight Our Speaker Is...You!"

To change the pace of your meeting, let your students teach the lesson. When the kids arrive, ask them to write down what they wish to discuss during youth group. List the suggestions on the chalkboard, and hand out ballots for the kids to privately vote for the topic they'd most like to discuss. Count the ballots and let them know which topic won. Then the fun starts.

Break the group into five smaller groups and give each group one of the following assignments:

- Come up with a crowd breaker that fits the topic.
- Create a role-play or skit that deals with the topic.
- Find several Scriptures that speak to the topic.
- Develop group questions concerning the topic.
- Illustrate the topic either from group members' actual experiences or from a story that gives insight into the topic.

Once the groups have completed their assignments, turn them loose—group by group—to provide their portion of the lesson.

Close the meeting by pairing students up to pray for each other regarding the topic. (Contributed by Michael Frisbie, Hobbs, N. Mex.)

"Come and See Me" Cards

Some of the best contact time with kids comes when you take time to attend your students' ball games, recitals, performances, contests, shows, and other events in which your kids shine. Tell kids you want to watch them (and get all the information you need to schedule yourself) by handing out "Come and See Me" cards. (They also serve as a record of your contacts.) Use the back of the card to jot down pertinent information that comes up in conversation or to record names of other related student contacts. (Contributed by Kevin Turner, Tacoma, Wash.)

COME & SEE ME!

Name ____________________ Phone ____________________

Date of Event ____________________ Time ____________________

Location ____________________ Name of Event ____________________

Compile Your Own Youth Ministry Book

Create your personalized resource of effective youth ministry ideas you've read about, handouts you've received, or notes you've jotted down during a seminar. Forget traditional stand-up files—instead, edit your own book. Get a three-ring notebook, and every time you read a good article, either photocopy it or cut it out and put it in your notebook. Your evolving handbook may not be on the best-seller list, but you'll have a personalized, practical youth ministry reference work that you can use for a long time. (Contributed by Bert L. Jones, Opp, Ala.)

Getting to Know You

Just arrived in your new youth-working position? Wondering how to get to know all those kids? Insert your name in the following offer, and include it in your next church newsletter or bulletin. You'll get lots of takers. (Contributed by Dan Lambert, Decatur, Ind.)

CHORES WITH DAN

I'd like to get to know all of you high schoolers here at Community Church better, so here's a plan to do just that (which I'll probably regret).

Remember that chore you simply hate or always wish you had help with? List below the date and time this month you have to do that chore—and I'll come help you. I figure that this way, I'll not only get to know you, but I'll better understand the things you do. (Not to mention the great stories you can tell about what you made me do.)

YES! I want Dan to help me, Todd Verro, on Sat. Sept. 19.

He needs to be at my house at 10 am. My address is 438 Grove Ave.

He should bring an extra set of clothes: ☐ yes ☒ no.

Special instructions: Can you bring your truck? We can use it to haul my grandmother's stuff to our house.

Have Phone Directory, Will Travel

Promote group organization and interaction with a "shrinked-wrapped" phone directory. Reduce your current youth group phone directory to a 2 1/2 x 4-inch rectangle. Print eight to a sheet on card stock and have the sheet laminated at a copy shop. You'll save money if you cut the sheet apart yourself after lamination.

The resulting cards fit into a wallet, pocket, purse, on a key chain, in an organizer—and they're waterproof. They'll survive a shove into the pool and even a spin cycle. (Contributed by Gene Stabe, Newhall, Calif.)

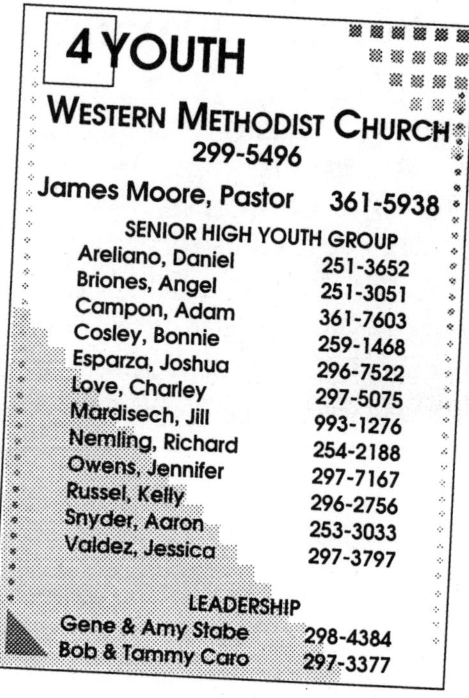

4 YOUTH

WESTERN METHODIST CHURCH
299-5496

James Moore, Pastor 361-5938

SENIOR HIGH YOUTH GROUP

Areliano, Daniel	251-3652
Briones, Angel	251-3051
Campon, Adam	361-7603
Cosley, Bonnie	259-1468
Esparza, Joshua	296-7522
Love, Charley	297-5075
Mardisech, Jill	993-1276
Nemling, Richard	254-2188
Owens, Jennifer	297-7167
Russel, Kelly	296-2756
Snyder, Aaron	253-3033
Valdez, Jessica	297-3797

LEADERSHIP

Gene & Amy Stabe	298-4384
Bob & Tammy Caro	297-3377

Yearbook

Here's a great way for your kids to get to know one another as well as the volunteers, sponsors, and other members of your congregation.

If you have access to a photocopier, your students can create a yearbook. It can be as sophisticated as high school annuals, or as simple as a collection of mug shots or write-up of who's who. First organize a student yearbook committee. Then assign some to take pictures of events, places, and people related to your church. Others write articles, design the book, lay it out, and paste it up.

It's even easier if your church or one of your students has a computer desktop publishing program. You can include photocopied newspaper articles featuring youth group members, collages of memorable events, "Most Likely To's," and personal trivia.

Sell advertisement space for a fundraiser, or sell each issue for a buck and cover some of the costs. To cut film cost, take pictures of two youths in one shot. (Contributed by Elliott Cooke, Nanuet, N.Y.)

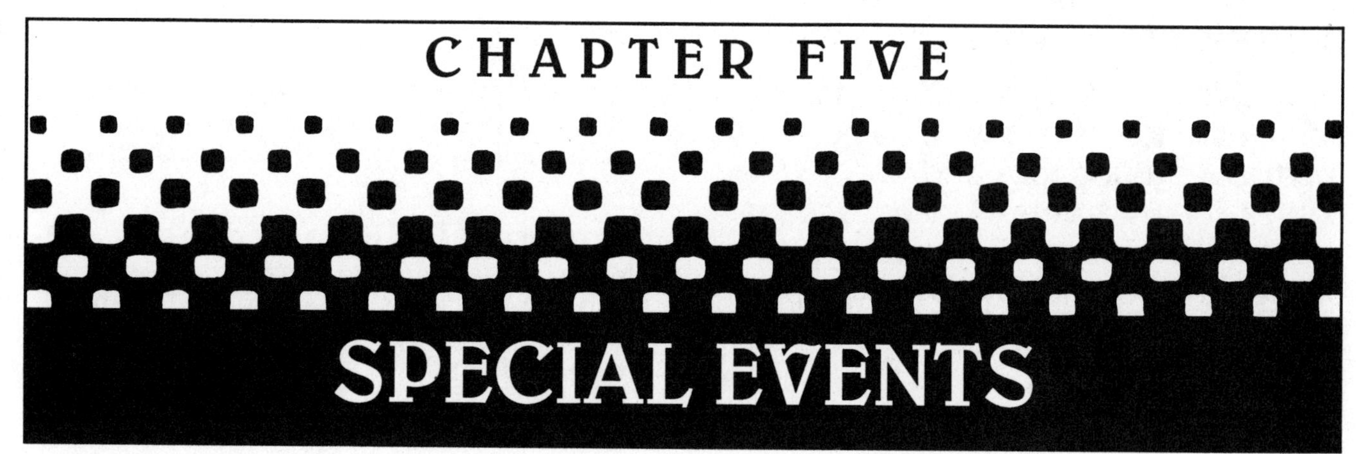

CHAPTER FIVE

SPECIAL EVENTS

Alphabet Fellowships

Plan a Sunday evening get together using a letter of the alphabet as your theme. Try one of the following ideas or make up your own. (Contributed by Greg Price, Maryville, Tenn.)

Food: Desserts
Activities: Decorating contest (teams decorate a cake or package or cookie)
Decathlon (10 quick events like dominoes, Delaware trivia quiz, dog-breed bingo, etc.)
Devotional: from Deuteronomy

Food: Tacos and trifle
Activities: Talent show and T-shirt auction
Devotional: Truth (John 8:32)

Food: Hoagies, Heath Bars, Hawaiian Sunrise punch
Activities: Homemade hats (prize for most original), humor (joke-telling contest)
Devotional: Hebrews heroes (or heavenly home, etc.)

C NIGHT

Food: Cookies, cakes, and candies
Activities: Card games, Christmas carol singing
Devotional: from Corinthians

Balloon Rodeo

Form two teams—guys versus girls—and let the teams choose a name for themselves (Buckaroos and Cow-patties, for instance). Allow each team to select contestants for the following events. Each event is worth 25 points to the winner and 20 points to the loser. (Contributed by Doug Partin, Lubbock, Tex.)

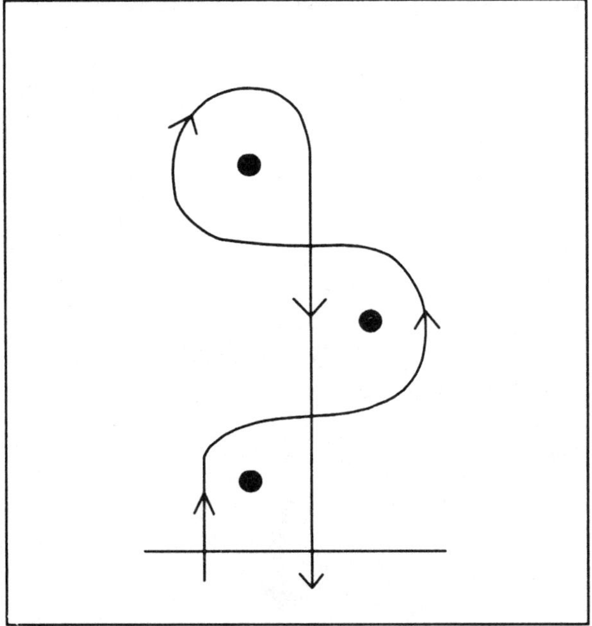

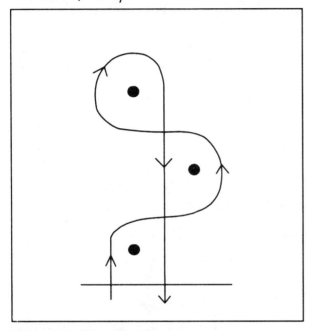

Barrel Racing

Place three barrels (or plastic cones or stacks of books) on the floor in a triangle shape (see diagram). Each team enters three racers. Blindfold both starting racers. At a signal, each one kicks an inflated balloon in a pattern around the barrels by following their team's shouted instructions. Each team adds up its three times; lowest total wins.

Bucking Balloon Riding

Mark off starting and finish lines about fifteen feet apart. Riders each place four balloons between their legs (you have to squeeze them down to hang on to all four). Then, with one hand in the air, the rider hops toward the finish line. Every rider who makes it all the way without losing a balloon gets credited with a full ride. Each team enters six riders. The team with the most full rides wins.

Balloon Lassoing

Tie a large washer on a long string, and wrap double-sided tape around both sides of the washer. This is the lasso; give it to the lassoer, who stands in the middle of the room. Place 35 or so balloons at one end of the room. The lassoer's opposing team attempts to herd the balloons to the other end of the room even as the lassoer tries to lasso as many balloons as possible. Each team enters two lassoers. The team with the most lassoed balloons wins.

Stompede

Now you don't want to pick up all those balloons on the floor yourself, do you? So send both teams to one side of the room, and gather the balloons on the other side. When you say go, both teams rush the balloons and begin stomping them and picking up the pieces. The team that collects the most balloon knots wins.

Barnyard Olympics II

Here are some more games to go with the Barnyard Olympics that appeared in **Ideas 21**.

Hay Toss

Open up a bale of hay and give a handful of hay to each player. The winner is the one who throws the hay the farthest. (There is a way to throw hay to make it travel father than you think. Experiment!)

Egg Scramble

Bring two dozen wooden eggs and a few raw eggs. Using barriers or tape, create a "chicken coup" with nooks and crannies for hiding eggs. It should be about 20 yards from one end to the other. Divide the group into two or more teams. One team at a time enters the coop; half the team searches for eggs at one end of the coup, and the other half searches on the opposite side. When players find an egg, they must throw it across the coop to their teammates who must catch it. If they don't catch the eggs, they have to do the toss over again until successful. The team who has all of their eggs found and tossed wins.

The catch, of course, is the few real eggs. Have paper towels on hand to clean up the inevitable mess.

Hen-Scratching Relay

Give each player a wooden building block. Arrange two teams in single file lines with the pile of blocks at the head of each team. On "Go!" the first players in line must pick up one block with their mouths, carry it across the "barnyard" to the "nest," and return to tag the next players in line. Play continues until the nest is full of eggs. The last player to deliver a block must sit on the nest and cackle, along with the rest of his or her teammates. The first team to cackle is the winning team.

Barnyard-Animal Relay

Divide the group into teams. Tape down a starting line and, across the room, a finish line. Have each member of each team perform the following actions in the sequence listed. Each player performs the actions when the teammate just ahead has completed the last action and crossed the line.

- **Dog** Roll over and bark
- **Rooster** Stand up, cock hands under arms, and crow
- **Pig** Lie on back, wiggle and oink
- **Cow** Get on all fours and moo loudly
- **Horse** Gallop to the finish line while neighing

Cow-Trough Relay

Best played outdoors, this game requires a large trough, several boxes of oatmeal, brown food coloring, large paper cups, lots of bananas, and a five-gallon bucket for each team.

In the trough mix the oatmeal with water, smashed bananas, and food coloring. Place the trough in the vicinity of the starting line, and the buckets about 100 yards away from the trough. Divide the group into teams, and give paper cups to all players. At "Go!" all the players run to the trough, fill up their cups, and then attempt to get to their team's bucket to dump the contents. The first team to fill their bucket wins. To guarantee a mess of fun, be sure to leave the oatmeal runny and make appropriate barnyard comments about the smell, color, texture, and so on.

(Contributed by Dale D. Hardy, Valparaiso, Ind.)

Blackbeard's Treasure Scavenger Hunt

Give your students the list on page 126 of piratical items. As in all scavenger hunts, define the boundaries and the deadline, then let them loose to "board and pillage" various homes for the donated items.

Your teenage cutthroats can use the occasion to leave fliers, brochures, or newsletters about upcoming events, regular meeting times, etc. For extra pizazz, design a flier especially for distribution during the scavenger hunt, and title it "Treasure Map"—which can be anything from directions to your church or youth group event to a gospel message.

When kids return with the booty, pour all the drinks they've collected into one punch bowl, and voila—Pirate Punch. With any luck, it will taste surprisingly good. (Contributed by Steve Smoker, Raleigh, N.C.)

BLACKBEARD'S TREASURE SCAVENGER HUNT

- ☐ Bread and water
- ☐ "Yo, ho, ho, and a bottle of—" four bottles of any soft drink
- ☐ Picture of a pirate
- ☐ Crow or parrot (real or pretend)
- ☐ Bandanna
- ☐ Polka-dotted head scarf
- ☐ Sea shell
- ☐ A message in a bottle
- ☐ Cannon ball (any ball will do)
- ☐ Container of beach sand
- ☐ Silver coin
- ☐ Treasure chest (any box will do)
- ☐ String of jewels or pearls (real or fake)
- ☐ Polly wants a **cracker**!
- ☐ Fish
- ☐ Large loop earring
- ☐ Walk the **plank**!
- ☐ Spade or shovel
- ☐ Button
- ☐ Orange or lime
- ☐ Eye patch (real or toy)
- ☐ Captain **Hook**
- ☐ Autograph of someone who wants to be a pirate
- ☐ Model of a boat
- ☐ Rope
- ☐ Flag
- ☐ Skull and crossbones
- ☐ Pistol (toy)
- ☐ Anything off a boat
- ☐ Chain
- ☐ Three strands of blonde hair from a fair maiden
- ☐ Ring
- ☐ Hurricane tracking chart
- ☐ Map
- ☐ Anything a pirate would use that is not on this list
- ☐ Prisoner

College Visitation

College. The mere mention of the word sets off stress for upper classmen who feel the weight of making a choice with life-long implications. But the church can do one better than the high school guidance office to defuse the threat. Provide college visitation weekends during which you not only visit former youth group members, but also expose juniors and seniors to various campuses within a day's drive of their hometown.

Plan trips to a variety of schools: public and private, large and small, Christian and secular, Bible and liberal arts. Contact the admissions office to arrange campus housing, tours, question-and-answer sessions, and written material. Most colleges are pleased to host potential students. If possible, line the kids up to attend several classes.

Before the trip contact any youth group graduates at the campus and arrange to visit them. Take advantage of their familiarity with the campus to break in the high schoolers to the college experience. This also assures the high schoolers that they won't be forgotten when they graduate, increasing the sense of community among both graduated and current members. Present the collegian with a care package put together by the youth group, and include their roommates in on fun activities. It may be their first experience with a Christian group of young people.

Groups such as Campus Crusade for Christ and InterVarsity Christian Fellowship generally have on-campus representatives as well as some sort of headquarters. Arranging for the kids to meet leaders of significant student ministries increases the likelihood of young people actually connecting with the group should they attend that college. Familiarize the students with recommended churches in the college community by driving by or by visiting a service.

Have fun on the trip—bring lots of tapes to listen to as you travel, watch for roadside attractions for fun stops and photos, attend a college sporting event together, eat at the local fast-food favorite. You could even arrange with several college students to "kidnap" the high schoolers for a late night donut party. Help the word **college** to inspire something other than fear. (Contributed by Kevin Turner, Tacoma, Wash.)

Hunt for Red October

Inspired by Tom Clancy's novel of the same name, this October scavenger hunt requires teams of five (plus one adult per team) to find as many of the following red items as they can in 60 minutes. To increase the competition, assign different point values to items based on the amount of ingenuity needed to obtain the items. (Contributed by Terry Martinson, Weymouth, Mass.)

red onion
red button
red lollipop
one red cent
piece of red construction paper
red balloon
boy wearing red lipstick
red toothpick
red shoelace
red paper plate or cup
red pencil
newspaper that has been read
lobster bib
girl in red pajamas
red apple
Red Sox baseball card
red stamp
red ticket or ticket stub
red Band-Aid
red pen

red kidney bean
red crayon
a copy of **The Scarlet Letter**
red soap
red game piece
fireman's autograph
red potato
picture of a submarine
valentine
candy wrapped in red foil
red M & M
Red Hot
red place mat or napkin
radish
test or assignment corrected in red
red marble
red cabbage
something typed with red ribbon
boy with red nail polish
red bandanna
red matchbook
red birthday party hat
6 inches of red ribbon
red birthday candle
picture of Santa Claus
red food coloring
red barrette
red comb or toothbrush
red licorice
red feather
6 ounces of tomato paste
paint chart with three shades of red
12 inches of red string
red plastic spoon

M.A.E. Day

It stands for **M**eet **A**nd **E**at. M.A.E. Day involves your kids in cooking, learning to cook, working together, eating, fellowshipping, and cleaning up a Sunday afternoon dinner in the church kitchen or at someone's home.

Once you choose the meal date, meet with the youths to plan the menu, organize the ingredients, and assign (or draw from a hat) the duties of cooking, washing dishes, drying dishes, sweeping floors, clearing tables, putting away dishes, and so on. Everyone should participate—even those who think they can't boil water or fear dishpan hands. Solicit food from parents, others in the church, or even local markets.

A good opportunity for discussion, ice breakers, or games is during the required cooking time for the main dish or dessert. The subjects brought up then often stir up meal conversation or provide interesting dialogue during cleanup. (Contributed by Greg Miller, Knoxville, Tenn.)

Make "It" a Date

Promote a fancy banquet to which everyone is required to bring a date—not the girl from third-period English, however, or the captain of the football team. Each date must be handmade—with broom sticks, paper bags, basketballs, and any other household items to construct a crazy, creative date. Award prizes for Best Male Date, Best Female Date, Most Outrageous Date, etc.

Have fun with the food you serve, too. Suck Jell-O through straws, spell words with alphabet soup, build crouton houses. You'll probably want to order pizza for later. (Contributed by John Fehlen, LaVerne, Calif.)

Out of Egypt Olympics

For this wacky theme event, first name each team after one of Israel's 12 tribes (though there are 13 names—remember?).

- **People Pyramids.** Build a pyramid using only people who fit certain criteria. For instance, call out, "Use seven people with white socks" or "...with birthdays in the summer" or "...with long hair."
- **Leap Frog.** Relay teams race leap-frog style in memory of the frog plague.
- **Mummy Making.** Each team selects a victim

to be wrapped in toilet paper until no part of the victim is showing.

• **Bug Bobbing.** Let a tray of red punch represent the Red Sea—then dump in a bag of Gummi Bugs. In this relay players must run up to the tray, bob for a bug, and return to their teams.

• **Horse Racing.** Riding piggyback on blindfolded Egyptian "horses," players coach their mounts through a sea of water balloons.

• **Speed-Eating Egyptian Treats.** The Israelites were always complaining about the food they left behind in Egypt. Let three volunteers from each team try to eat some of these delicacies at high speed—an onion, a clove of garlic, and a cucumber (all of them small).

• **Manna.** "What is it?!" will be the players' cry as they grab a foil-wrapped food item, unwrap it, and eat it as quickly as possible before running back to tag the next player on the team. Wrap carrots, crackers, Twinkies, marshmallows, and apples.

• **O, Ye of Little Faith.** Some people crossing the Red Sea didn't have much faith. Maybe they carried inner tubes—just in case. Make a relay out of cramming a tube over two people who must run to a point and back again before surrendering the tube to the next pair on their team.

• **Into the Promised Land.** The goal of this scavenger hunt is to bring back the biggest sample of everything on the list you compile. Give points to the teams with the longest piece of grass, the biggest pine cone, the largest leaf, and so on.

(Contributed by Lynne Hartke, Chandler, Ariz.)

Parent-Teen Banquet

Enhance parent-teen communication and create a family activity with an intimate, by-invitation-only evening for parents and their teens.

Invitations

First send out invitations to all mothers and their sons, to all fathers and their daughters, and to all single parents and their teens. Follow the invitation with a phone call a week before the dinner to find out who's coming for sure. Once you know which families will attend, hand write a personal thank-you note to parents: "Thanks so much for taking the time to share this evening with your teens…" Be sure to include a few lines about how their teens contribute positively to the group. Thank parents also for the privilege of serving their youths.

Dining

This is not an evening for parents to sit at a long banquet table and chat with other parents, or for the teens to socialize with their peers during dinner. So—set up the dining area so that each family sits at a separate card table, complete with table cloth, centerpiece, candle, and china. If your church doesn't have separate tables or attractive plates, borrow them and return them clean and undamaged. Do everything you can to make this evening unique and to make those who attend feel special and elegant.

Decorate the dinning area with streamers, and play contemporary Christian music in the background. Place on each plate a handwritten, personal note to the parent or student who will sit there, and next to the note place a chocolate kiss.

Ice Breaker and Dinner

Begin the evening in a room other than the dining area. When everyone has arrived, ask all the parents to link arms with their own teens and remain that way till the game is over. Give each parent-teen team a pencil and a sheet with the following list:

1. Find a family who uses Zest soap.
2. Find a family who has flown in an airplane together.
3. Find a family who had an argument today.
4. Find a family who moved here from out of state.
5. Find a family who eats frog legs.
6. Find a dad who uses Brute cologne.
7. Find a mom who buys any Avon cologne.
8. Find a teen who saw the same movie as the last one you saw.
9. Find a dad who has built something with wood in the past six months.
10. Find a mom who pumps her own gas.
11. Find a teen who wears her mom's or his dad's shoes.
12. Find a person who is hungry.

The teams mingle, find the family or person who fits the listed description, and request her or his signature following the item. The family who finishes first gets to lead all the others into the dining area (which no one has seen yet).

After a brief explanation of the purpose of the evening (to bring families closer together) and prayer, the youth staff serves the dinner.

Getting Together

Following dinner, escort the families into the youth room where kids award their parents with prizes that symbolize their parents' traits. Instruct the kids a week earlier to ponder what they most appreciate about their attending parent and have them bring, say, a peach for the peachiest mom, a light bulb for the brightest dad, an ear of corn for the best listener, a lollipop for the sweetest pop, corn flakes for the corniest dad, a rose for the mom with the rosiest personality, a heart for the dad with the warmest heart, grapes for the really "grape" mom, Pert shampoo for the pertiest mom, a box of Cheer for the most cheerful dad, etc.

Next play a parent-teen version of "The Newlywed Game." Ask the parents to answer five questions the way they think their teens will answer. Then ask the teens to answer five questions the way they think their parents will answer. The winning team is the pair whose answers show they know each other the best. Award them with a pear—"The Best Pair" award.

After the game prepare one of the youth staff to give the following vivid monologue about what it's like to live with a teenager. Before the evening begins, fill grocery bags with the items in capital letters in the monologue, and show them as you speak.

Living with teenagers can put a bit of a **STRAIN** [use a food strainer] on families. In fact, it could drive some people **BANANAS**. It takes very special persons to raise teenagers. People who are willing to **PLEDGE** their lives to God so he can make their hearts pure as **IVORY**. Our kids need to sense our faith just as they can smell the fragrant beauty of a **VELVETY ROSE**. Think of the **JOY** that we'd receive if we could look into the eyes of our teenagers and see the strong, firm faith in Christ that we've demonstrated to them **GLEEM** back at us. Oh, sure, we'll have our rough times when our kids will act like a **BULLY**, give us some **FIDDLE FADDLE**, and maybe even **SQUASH** our pride, but we'll get through it if we send a special **S.O.S.** to God, use a little common **CENTS** and a **BIG BATCH** of **LUV**. Don't think that God sent you a sour **LEMON** when things aren't going well. If you're very **WISE** and **QUICK** with understanding, you and your teen will begin to grow closer than you have ever imagined. Just hang in there, **EVER-READY** with a listening **EAR** [of corn] and give them lots of **HUGS** and even an occasional **KISS** would be nice. Be **BOLD** enough to help your teen make the right decisions. But at the same time do it with **CHEER** because teens love humor. Let your teens see your fun side. Act a little **CORNY** now and then, maybe even a little bit **NUTTY**. Teens are active, full of **ZEST** and **VIM**, so be sure to get your **TOTAL** daily supply of vitamins and iron. You might also want to encourage them to earn some of their own money because raising a teen does take a little more **BREAD**. Well, just hang in there and **ROLL** with the punches. These next few years will be a **CINCH** [sack garbage bags] if you follow this bit of advice.

I'm sure your kids will see you as real sweet **POPS** and absolutely **GRAPE** moms.

Lead the group to sing a few familiar songs and offer a talk on love and acceptance within a family, using 1 Corinthians 13 to explain what unconditional love between parents and kids is all about.

In conclusion, separate the parents and teens in two rooms, then present the following scenario to both groups: Imagine that the person in the other room (parent or teen) has just been told he's going to die—soon. What would you want to say to her? What would you want to thank him for? Distribute paper and pencils, and ask the participants to write a letter in which they express their thoughts to their partner for the evening. Tell them to write as if it will be the last words their partner will ever hear.

When the letter writing is complete, ask each parent-teen team to find a quiet spot within the church where they can be alone and read their letters to each other. The evening will end with many hugs and even tears as bonds are strengthened between parents and their teens.

(Contributed by Linda Dahr, Mechanicsburg, Penn.)

Personal Potato Awards

To honor teens at your next awards event, put together a personal potato trophy for each teen.

Working with staff or volunteers, gather a bag of potatoes and craft supplies: pipe cleaners, craft eyes, Styrofoam cups, tape from an old audio cassette (for hair), straight pins, markers, fabric, ribbon, yarn, Popsicle sticks, buttons. Create Mister and Miss Potato Heads complete with faces, hair, and even clothing and accessories. Present each teen with the trophy after the standard congratulatory remarks. (Contributed by Dave Mahoney, Indianapolis, Ind.)

Pizza Mystery Surprise

Spice up your next small-group pizza party with a little mystery. Buy personal-sized pizzas with strange combinations of toppings. The stranger the better—anchovy-pineapple, bacon-broccoli, onion-cauliflower. While the pizzas are still in their boxes, randomly place them in front of each youth.

Before opening the pizzas the kids may trade for a different pizza. When everyone's choice is final, let them open up their boxes.

All players/eaters must take at least one bite from the pizza before removing the toppings. (Contributed by Terry Fisher, El Cajon, Calif.)

Progressive Pool Dinner

In the heat of the summer, schedule several families to set up kiddie wading pools in their yards and to prepare one course of an evening meal for the youth group. Invite all the kids to come wearing their swimsuits and towels. At each house see how many kids can get into the wading pool, and then let everyone alternate between eating and cooling off in the pool. Plan so that the last house has a full-size pool, and after eating spend the evening swimming. (Contributed by Harl Pike, Sierra Vista, Ariz.)

Progressive Video Party

An intergenerational "get to know you" event, this activity can be played out among teams competing against a time limit or as a single group activity just for the fun of it.

Equip adult driver/chaperons with a camcorder and a collection of sealed envelopes, each containing a question like "What is your favorite Bible verse?" "When did you become a Christian?" "What is your most memorable church experience?" "In your opinion, what is the biggest problem facing teenagers today?" The group(s) visit as many homes of church members as possible within one hour. At each home the occupant chooses one envelope, opens it, and responds to the written question while being videotaped.

At the end of the hour, all meet at a home or the church and show all the taped interviews. The videotape serves as proof that the mission was accomplished—as well as offering all the groups the chance to get to know some adult church members better. (Contributed by Cheryl Ehlers, East Point, Ga.)

Sound Track

When you take your group to a fireworks display, prepare them ahead of time to provide a human sound track for the occasion.

There are usually three stages to each explosion of fireworks: the rocket shoots up, explodes, and then explodes again or dies. Tell everyone that when the rocket shoots up they are to say, "Ooooooooo." Upon the first explosion they sigh, "Ahhhhhhh." When it explodes a second time or dies they say, "Ohhhhhh." As the display continues, the overlapping explosions and just plain silliness makes things hilarious. (It's also a way to get more seating for the group—the noise drives the crowd to leave for another area.) (Contributed by Len Cuthbert, Hamilton, Ont., Canada)

Video Scavenger Hunt II

Borrow as many video cameras as you need for small groups of your teens to cruise the community and record on tape the funniest thing they can find. Place a 60-second time limit on tape footage. All the teams return at a predetermined time to view and judge which team's entry is funniest.

Round two is played in the same way, except that each team has 30 minutes to hunt, and they must find something funnier than the winning footage from round one. Play as many rounds as you want. (Contributed by Brad Strawn and Rick Bell, Ontario, Calif.)

Weenie Hunt and Roast

For this crazy version of hide and seek, recruit parents or adult volunteers to be the "weenies" who hide. Kids are the "hunters." Play where there are lots of places to hide, though within designated boundaries. If you play this at night, use flashlights.

Ask each of the weenies to choose a name for himself or herself. Use the names on the list below or let them make up their own. Weenies wear costumes that give subtle clues to their identity. Hunters divide into groups and choose team names. Give each team a score sheet (like the one on page 134).

Gather all players at a designated headquarters. At a signal the hunters close their eyes while the weenies hide. At a second signal the hunters begin searching for the weenies. Teams need not stay together to hunt. When hunters capture weenies by finding them, they bring them to headquarters and, judging from their captives' clothing, attempt to guess their names. Hunters who guess correctly win points for their team (see list below for suggested point values), and the identified weenie is out of the game. If players guess incorrectly, the weenies are allowed to hide again. Until they hide they are immune from capture. The team with the most points at the end of the time limit wins.

Then have a weenie roast—with hot dogs, that is. (Contributed by Mike Martinelli, Pillsburg, Pa.)

NAMES	POINTS	CAUGHT
Polka-Dotted Pottie Chaser	400	☐
Bearded Boom Fang	200	☐
Violent Violet Sissy Killer	700	☐
Purple Pitter Spitter	400	☐
Stripped Broom Stomper	300	☐
Blue Moon Growl	200	☐
Brown Ground Cobbler	500	☐
Black Jack Shalack	10000	☐
Lemon-Lime Lip Pucker	800	☐
Gold Mold Sucker	600	☐
Orange Ganu	400	☐
White No-Hair Sal	300	☐
Red Curly Pop	200	☐
Green Meenie	700	☐
Yellow Yippie	400	☐
Gray Granite Geek	500	☐
Slick Silver Quick	300	☐
Plain Padded Pansy	700	☐
Pink Puddle Plopper	400	☐
Terrible Tan Terror	900	☐

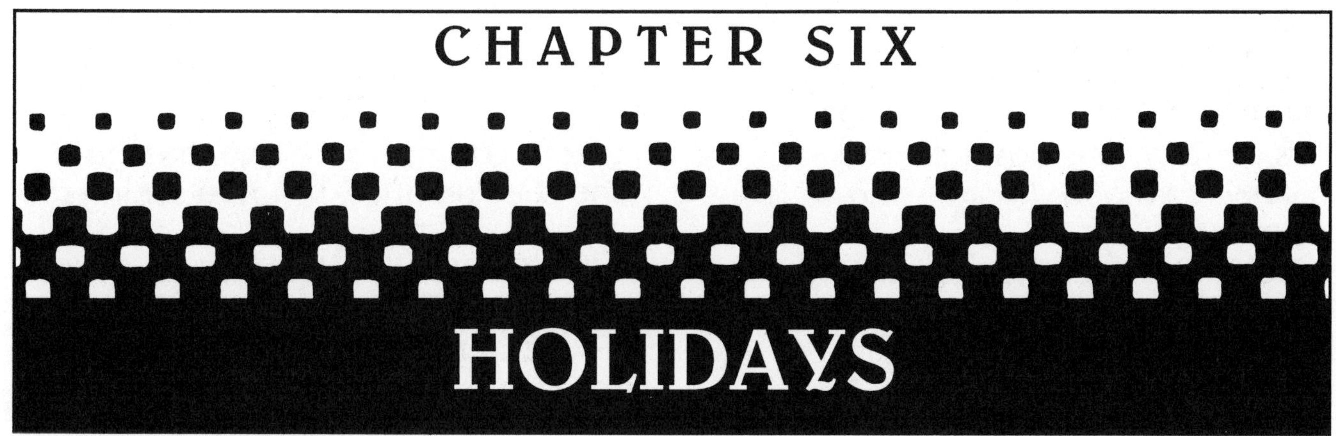

CHAPTER SIX
HOLIDAYS

HALLOWEEN

Dry Apple Bobbing

This variation of traditional apple bobbing is lots of fun and requires no water. Tie five blunt nails to strings of varying lengths and suspend them from a wooden frame, then pierce the apples with the nails. Ask participants to kneel beneath the apples and attempt to take a bite of the apples without using their hands. Add knee pads for comfort, or add blindfolds for a greater challenge. (And be careful of the embedded nails, even though they're blunt.)

If you use blindfolds, on the last round of five players allow one of the observers to randomly raise and lower the apples. Or replace an apple or two with a raw onion. Apples or onions, it's a nutritional game. (Contributed by Timothy Wilkey, Dayton, Tenn.)

Find the Pumpkin

All you need is a pumpkin for each team of three or four, a few flashlights, a dark and spooky place, and some advanced planning. Hide the pumpkins well (don't ask your teenagers to do this, because they probably can't keep a secret when it means winning or losing). Then backtrack to the starting point in as obscure a manner as possible, writing up riddling clues on 3 X 5 cards as you backtrack. Hide the clues. Repeat the process for each pumpkin and team.

Give the youths the first clue, and—using logic and navigation—they should be able to locate the second and following clues. The prep time required is significant (do you have adult sponsors who could do it?), but it's worth the unsurpassed fun of this nonsports-oriented challenge. (Contributed by Timothy Wilkey, Dayton, Tenn.)

Witch's Broom Relay

This game moves kids right into the Halloween mood quickly—and with a lot of laughs.

Provide each of two teams with a big witch's hat, a pair of ugly boots, a house broom, a long black skirt, a long black blouse, and a belt. The object is simple: each member of both relay teams must run the length of the course and back.

The twist is the get-up they must wear during their run. The first players to run must put on the entire witch's costume and "ride" the broom the relay distance. Upon returning to their teams, they must transfer the outfit to the next players in line, who mount their brooms and take off. The first team to finish successfully wins—the broom, that is. They can either mount it in the youth room as a trophy, or bequeath it to the losing team to use for the after-party cleanup. (Contributed by Timothy Wilkey, Dayton, Tenn.)

CHRISTMAS

Alternative Christmas Giving

Reinforce a noncommercial Christmas among your group! Design a Christmas card with the following message to give to members of your youth group. (Contributed by Randy Nichols, Inman, S.C.)

Dear Friend—

The annual rite of gift-giving is lots of fun for kids—but it can be just another stress for grown-ups.

So if you were gonna spend dough on me this year, instead remember me by just dropping me a note—you can even wait till after the holidays. And then spend the money that you were gonna lavish on a gift for *me* on something for the poor, the needy, or the lonely. (Matthew 25:35-40 makes this seem appropriate for Jesus' birthday.)

Who knows? Maybe we'll start a new stress-free tradition!

Pastor Randy

Away in a Modern Manger

Modernize the traditional Christmas story with this script. Fill in the blanks (see below) with the appropriate officials' names, youth group members' names, and towns and states near you. Let the kids videotape the action in different locations to produce a modern-day Christmas story. Show it at your Christmas party. Besides the good laughs, the experience can enhance the students' appreciation of the gospel message. (Contributed by Bert L. Jones, Lancaster, Ohio)

AWAY IN A MODERN MANGER

(based on Luke Chapter Two)

SCENE ONE

NARRATOR *speaks voice-over, or else on location in Mary's bedroom with a microphone, like a news reporter.*

NARRATOR: About this time __________, the president of the United States, decreed that a census should be taken throughout the nation. (This census was taken when ______________ was governor of __________.) All citizens were required by the U.S. Census Bureau to return to their permanent residences for the sake of this census. Joseph was working out of state on a long-term project (the Defense Department had subcontracted to him the construction of an office complex in ______________, ______________), so he had to return to his own town— ______________ in ______________. He took with him Mary, his fiancée, who was obviously pregnant.

JOSEPH: Everything packed? I'd like to leave before rush-hour traffic begins.

MARY: Yes, Joseph. You know, while we're in ________________, we need to go shopping for the baby. There is so much we still need to buy.

JOSEPH: All I have to do is check the oil and

tires, and we're ready to go. It'll take us ____ hours to get to ___________. The baby could come while we're home for the census, so make sure you have everything you need. *(Close-up of* **MARY** *closing suitcases. Pull back to follow* **MARY** *and* **JOSEPH** *walking out the door to their pickup, loading it, getting in, and driving away.)*

SCENE TWO

*(***MARY** *and* **JOSEPH** *have arrived in their own city. Film several landmarks of the city, then catch the car.* **MARY** *and* **JOSEPH** *ad lib small talk while film rolls: "They've put in a new Burger King there!", "So much has changed in a year," etc.)*

NARRATOR: And while they were driving around ___________, the time came for Mary's baby to be born.

MARY: *(Move shot to inside the car, where Mary's eyes go wide and she puts a hand quickly to her belly)* Ooohh!

JOSEPH: What's wrong?

MARY: It's time.

NARRATOR: And so Joseph floored it all the way to the hospital.

SCENE THREE

(Their pickup squeals up to a hospital's emergency room door. **JOSEPH** *leaps out, runs around to the passenger door, opens it, helps* **MARY** *out and into the hospital. A member of the youth group is at the admissions desk.)*

CLERK: May I help you?

JOSEPH: *(frantically)* My wife is going to have a baby any minute.

CLERK: We don't have obstetrics or maternity at this hospital. But the general hospital at the far end of town can—

JOSEPH: She'll never make it that far.

MARY: *(panting heavily)* Joseph...there's a...Motel 6 next door *(here and throughout script, use the name of a budget motel in your area)*...I saw it as we drove in...take me there...

JOSEPH: A Motel 6? Look, Mary, I'm not taking you to a cheap motel, you need a hospi—

MARY: Motel 6 is fine...just—*(another contraction comes)* ooohh—get me there...fast.

CLERK: *(as* **MARY** *and* **JOSEPH** *hurry from the desk back outside)* I can arrange for an ambulance if you can wait a few minutes...

SCENE FOUR

(Long shot of the Motel 6. Move in through the door of one of the ground-floor rooms. A pile of clothes lies on the floor; the suitcase has obviously been emptied quickly. Camera moves to bed, on which sits **MARY** *and* **JOSEPH***, gazing at the opened suitcase on the bed. Close-up on the suitcase, which is found to be lined with blankets, in which is cradled a baby.)*

NARRATOR: And she gave birth to her first child, a son. She wrapped him in a blanket and laid him in an empty suitcase because they had no time to get to the general hospital.

MARY: What can we name him?

JOSEPH: We will name him Jesus, for he shall save his people from their sins.

SCENE FIVE

(A car pulls into a service station. While **NARRATOR** *reads, an* **ATTENDANT** *walks toward the car as the driver rolls down his window. There are three* **ASTROPHYSICISTS** *in the car. It is dusk.)*

NARRATOR: After Jesus was born in _________ in the state of ______________, during the time __________________ was president of the United States, astrophysicists came to the city of __________.

ATTENDANT: Unleaded, unleaded plus, or unleaded supreme?

ASTROPHYSICIST 1: Where is the one who has been born King of the Jews? We have seen his supernova in Virgo and have come all the way from ______________ to worship him.

ATTENDANT: Funny you should mention that. An old geezer came by a few weeks ago, talkin' crazy...said something about a supreme leader being born right here in _______________, and mumbled something about a star and Motel 6...or was it Best Western?

ASTROPHYSICIST 2: *(quick to pick up the*

clue, to **ATTENDANT***)* You got a Yellow Pages in there? *(cut quickly to next scene)*

SCENE SIX

(Back at the motel. As **NARRATOR** *reads,* **ASTROPHYSICISTS** *pull up in their car, get out holding objects, check the room number against what's apparently written on a scrap of paper in the hand of one of the* **ASTROPHYSICISTS**, *and knock.* **JOSEPH** *opens the door and lets them in. Camera follows them in.)*

NARRATOR: After they had heard this, they went on their way. As they followed the directions to the motel Joseph gave them over the phone, they could have sworn that the supernova they had first seen from their observatory in ________________ went ahead of them until it stopped right above the motel.

ASTROPHYSICIST 1: We have followed the supernova from ________________ and have come to worship the child.

ASTROPHYSICIST 2: We have brought our finest gifts for the child—

ASTROPHYSICIST 3: A ______________ *(popular video game title).*

ASTROPHYSICIST 1: A ______________ *(popular recording artist)* Christmas video.

ASTROPHYSICIST 2: And a ________________ *(the nearest college)* sweatshirt to keep the baby warm.

NARRATOR: And with this they left, because they had heard on Traffic Watch that a tomato truck had overturned on the ________________ freeway *(expressway, tollway, highway, boulevard, etc.).* There were five tons of tomatoes spread across every lane, and traffic was backed up all the way to ___________________ *(overpass, exit, a cross street, etc.).* So they went back to ______________ by a different route.

SCENE SEVEN

(Afternoon of the next day. As **NARRATOR** *reads,* **YOUTH MINISTER** *pulls up next to a park, gets out, and approaches a half dozen high schoolers playing an informal game of football.)*

NARRATOR: And there were in the same city some guys, playing football in a park after school. And lo, the messenger of the Lord appeared next to them.

YOUTH MINISTER: Hey, guys! Guess what? I've got the greatest news. Today, here in ___________, a Savior has been born to you; he is Christ the Lord. Let's go to the Motel 6 down on __________ Street *(Ave., Blvd., etc.)* and see him.

NARRATOR: *(Background Christmas music plays as they all pile into the car of the* **YOUTH MINISTER** *and pull away from the park into traffic.)* So they all left their game and went to visit the Christ child. As they were leaving, they heard Christmas music playing in the heavens. *(Increase volume of music as they pull away.)*

SCENE EIGHT

(Back at Motel 6. Inside are **MARY, THE BABY, YOUTH MINISTER,** *and* **HIGH SCHOOLERS.***)*

NARRATOR: They drove to the motel and found Mary, and the child lying in a suitcase.

HIGH SCHOOLER 1: Where's the father?

MARY: He ran down to 7-Eleven for some Pampers. He'll be back any minute…

HIGH SCHOOLER 2: *(to* **YOUTH MINISTER** *in a whisper)* She doesn't have a ring on…are they even married?

YOUTH MINISTER: *(also whispered)* Long story…tell you later.

NARRATOR: Next day at school, the high schoolers spread the word around campus about what they had seen. *(Camera begins to gradually back out of open motel room door. By the time NARRATOR finishes, camera has entire motel in view.)* It even made the newspapers—section B, page 8. Everyone who heard the story was amazed. Mary clipped the article and read it often, treasuring in her heart those things that had happened.

The next afternoon the high schoolers returned to the park for another hour of football, praising God for the messenger. Because they had seen the Christ child, their lives would never be the same again.

Children's Christmas Coloring Book

That's right—your teenagers can create homemade coloring books to distribute to children in your city's hospitals.

Ask each student to draw a couple of pictures on a Christmas theme. The drawings should be of bold lines (not too many) with lots of open space in which kids can color. Ask one of your artists to design a cover picture, and assign another youth to write up the Christmas story (Luke 2:8-14) for the back cover. Choose the most suitable drawings, run two or three hundred copies of each picture and the covers, then bind the sheets together (give your local quick printer a call for inexpensive binding methods).

Toward the beginning of the Christmas holidays, tour some of your hospitals and give the youngsters there coloring books as well as new boxes of crayons.

If you must cover your costs, you might sell the books to your church members to give as Christmas gifts. If you **don't** need to cover your costs, give the proceeds to a mission project that your group adopts. (Contributed by Timothy Wilkey, Dayton, Tenn.)

Christmas Daffynitions

Prepare a written list of Christmas items and provide one copy, along with a pencil, to each player. Explain that players are to create original definitions for each item on the sheet.

Beware! Some of the definitions you'll hear will be pretty wacky. We've heard "blizzard buns" (snowman), "a toilet decoration you don't want to sit on long" (wreath), and "Ivana Trump's lawyer" (Santa Claus). Award points or prizes for the most ludicrously appropriate definitions. (Contributed by Greg Fiebig, Maryville, Mo.)

Christmas Scattergories

Using Scattergories rules, have teams work from a homemade game sheet that lists Christmas categories—Christmas goody, Christmas character, Chrismas decoration, Christmas tradition, Christmas song, popular toy to give, etc.

Prepare enough sheets for several rounds of play. Give players one game sheet and a pencil. Per the rules of Scattergories, choose what letters of the alphabet you'll use by using a word—**Christmas**, **joy**, **noel**—or by a more random selection (be creative). The object of the game is to see which player or team can come up with the most answers that begin with the letter of the alphabet selected.

For example, if you choose to use the letters in the word "Stable" then the first round of answers could include **Santa Claus** (a Christmas character), **sugar cookies** (Christmas goody), **Silent Night** (Christmas song), **snowflake** (Christmas decoration), **stocking** (Christmas tradition), **sledding** (things to do at Christmas), and so on. For the next round, think of words in those categories that begin with T, etc.

Points are scored for every word that was not chosen by another player or team. In other words, if more than one player writes "Santa Claus," then no one gets any points for it. To earn points players must write down words or phrases that no one else has written down. (Contributed by Greg Fiebig, Maryville, Mo.)

Crazy Christmas Scavenger Hunt

This Christmas activity (see page 143) is a guaranteed hit for both small and large groups. Here are a few hints to make it more successful.

- Keep the details of the hunt secret.
- Send someone along to videotape the various groups out hunting. (Show the videos at a post-hunt social.)
- Send the groups to separate neighborhoods with well-defined boundaries.
- Depending upon the size of the group hunting, consider 30 to 45 minutes for the time limit.

(Contributed by Michael McKnight, Kingsport, Tenn.)

First-Century "Dear Abby"

Read the following letter to give students an up-to-date scenario for discussing the emotions and choices of Mary and Joseph as they faced Mary's unusual pregnancy. (Contributed by Greg Asimakoupoulos, Concord, Calif.)

Dear Abby,

I don't know where to begin. Only a few weeks ago everything seemed perfect. My life was fulfilling and full. I graduated from school with honors, my father made me a partner in his woodworking business, and after weeks of getting up enough courage I asked my steady girlfriend to marry me.

The day after my father made me a partner, she said yes. I was so elated and so in love. Life seemed complete. I was healthy, free from stress, and without a worry about the future responsibilities that my job and marriage would bring. Even my faith was at an all-time high. I have been a religious person all my life (I'm Jewish), but only recently has my personal awareness of God's love and power been so much a part of my consciousness. My rabbi often comments about my depth of belief, my moral convictions, my unswerving values. My reputation as a successful businessman who does not believe in sex before marriage has earned me many opportunities to speak to our Sabbath school students.

But Abby, my dream has become an unending nightmare. I feel like ending my life.

Last Friday my fiancée met me after work—our weekly routine. Her face told me something was on her mind. No matter how I pried at dinner, I couldn't get her to talk about it. Leaving the restaurant, we went to the synagogue. I couldn't concentrate on the service. My imagination ran wild with fantasies...she didn't love me any more...she wanted to call off the wedding...maybe she's dying...does she have cancer?...had her father abused her?...had she rejected her Jewish faith at the hands of some proselytizing gentile group?...

On the other hand, maybe it wasn't bad news at all. Maybe the year-long engagement we set was too long for her, and she simply wanted to shorten it, but was afraid of what I might say. But that didn't explain why she didn't talk to me over dinner.

The questions kept coming. I was a nervous wreck.

As we left the service, I was so preoccupied I didn't hear the Rabbi ask me if I was free to speak to the youth group the coming week. He had to grab my shoulder to get my attention. I told him I'd have to think about it.

I was determined to not take Mary Beth home until I succeeded in discovering her secret. We went out for dessert to one of our favorite spots. I took my time ordering, hoping she would volunteer the information. She didn't speak. Finally, looking down into her coffee, she started to cry. "I'm pregnant," she whispered.

Abby, I was numb with shock. I didn't speak the rest of the night. I paid the bill, walked her to the car, drove her home, and left.

I cried myself to sleep that night. I woke up early the next morning, drained of tears but filled with angry questions. How could she do this to me? Didn't she love me? Hadn't we promised to save ourselves for each other? Who was he? How long had they been sleeping together? Who initiated it? Did she? How could this person exist and I not even know about him? I was the only man in her life—or so I had thought. How could Mary Beth share such intimacy with someone else when things were so good between us? Didn't she believe in God's standards for successful relationships? Was she thumbing her nose at my faith?

I avoided her for a whole week, Abby. Didn't see her, didn't even call her. I just couldn't bring myself to talk to her. My heart ached. My stomach burned. I called in sick the first three days of work.

Then today she showed up just at I was closing up shop. "We need to talk," she said. "I can't stand this. I love you."

"If you loved me, you wouldn't be in the condition you're in." But I couldn't help seeing love in her eyes (for me) and that face I cherish. I knew I still loved her with all my heart. That's why I hurt so much. But Abby, how can I keep loving someone who sleeps around?

I finally forced myself to ask The Question, though even as I asked it I wondered if I really wanted to know the answer. "Who is he?"

She looked down. "I can't tell you. You wouldn't understand. I'm not sure I understand myself. Actually, I don't know who it is."

"You don't know who it is?" I nearly lost it right there. How many guys had she been with that she didn't know who the father was? "You mean you don't know who the father is because...because..." But the thought was too painful to say out loud. The words wouldn't come.

"No, love," she said. "It's not that at all. I just can't explain it to you now. But I want you to know I still love you and want to be your wife."

As she spoke I could see the innocence in her face...the look that had first attracted me to her.

"I've made arrangements to leave town for a while," she continued. "I think it's best for you and me and our families. I'll be staying at cousin Beth's home upstate. She's a special lady. I've always been close to her. In fact, I was named after her. I'll be in good hands.

"By the way, she's expecting a child, too." She reached into her pocket. "Here's where I'll be," she said, handing me a piece of paper with a phone number pencilled on it. Then she turned and walked away.

What should I do? I love Mary Beth so very much in spite of my anger and anxiety. Yet I can't go ahead with the engagement. She's destroyed my trust in her. Still, the thought of walking away from that girl leaves me empty inside. But the shame and embarrassment of being pregnant and not married in our small town is unbearable. She'd be the target of countless harassments. Her reputation would be ruined forever.

All the same, for me to stand by her and pretend that the child was mine would destroy *my* reputation. All my advice to young people about chastity and commitment...what a joke. And the integrity and credibility I've established in my shop with the guys would take years to rebuild.

Abby, is this the time to terminate a pregnancy? It would make everything more manageable. She doesn't show yet—Mary Beth would be spared the shame, I'd be spared my reputation...perhaps even our relationship could be spared.

Everything would be spared, that is, except that tiny life. What a sad joke...here I pride myself in morality and virtue, but I'm ready to justify abortion when it can benefit me. Besides, who knows who that baby will become someday?

I don't know, Abby. My gut feeling is to break off the engagement and try to forget what happened. I care too much for Mary Beth to make an ugly scene, though she deserves an ugly scene. I could tell everyone we called off the wedding...that it was my idea to break up, that she felt she had to get out of town to escape the pain of an unexpected jilting. Then everyone will think she got pregnant by some guy upstate. That would at least remove some of the stigma from her. I'd be the bad guy for calling off the wedding, but I wouldn't lose my reputation.

So what do I do, Abby? Stay with Mary Beth regardless of what others think? Urge her to an abortion? (I mean, she doesn't even know the father.) Break off the engagement and get on with my life?

—Devastated Boyfriend

Dear Devastated Boyfriend,

Your last idea is the best—drop her now and get on with your life. Your Mary Beth is a pathological liar, has a very vivid imagination, or is unbelievably naive. You deserve better. I know it's painful for you to think of life apart from her, but face it—there are more fish in the sea. She may seem special, but she's not the one for you.

For what Devastated Boyfriend finally decided to do, read Matthew 1:20–25.

Crazy Christmas Scavenger Hunt

Instructions:

1. The object is to attempt to collect the items below in the given time limit.
2. As you divide up to hunt, you must stay in groups of at least **three**.
3. You **cannot** get more than **one** item at any house.
4. Be careful out there—it's a **crazy** world.

GOT IT!	ITEMS TO BE COLLECTED
______	pine needle off a live Christmas tree
______	mail-order Christmas catalog
______	piece of fudge
______	candy cane
______	Christmas bow
______	Christmas card (used or new)
______	picture of a Christmas tree from a magazine
______	name tag (used on a present)
______	piece of mistletoe
______	hair off a Santa's beard
______	piece of green candle
______	Christmas sales ad from a newspaper
______	pine cone
______	ornament
______	recipe for egg nog
______	scrap piece of wrapping paper
______	Christmas-related postage stamp
______	recipe for fruitcake OR a piece of fruitcake

GOT IT!	ITEMS TO BE COLLECTED
______	sprig of holly
______	pecan (in the shell)
______	poinsettia leaf
______	piece of white tissue paper
______	piece of red candle
______	spare Christmas tree bulb (could be burned out)
______	piece of peppermint stick candy
______	picture of Santa
______	Christmas sticker
______	paper cup of water from a Christmas tree
______	Christmas cookie
______	Ask someone under five years of age what Santa is bringing them— Child's name: ____________ Age: ___ ____________________ ____________________ ____________________ ____________________

The Real Meaning of Christmas

This Bible study (see page 145) gets kids searching the Scriptures for the real meaning of Christmas. It lets the kids see the Christmas message in other places besides the traditional Christmas story.

Wheel of Fortune's Wacky Christmas Carols

Play this game as you would Wheel of Fortune or Hangman. The phrases the players uncover, however, are revised titles of favorite Christmas songs. Samples:

- Bleached Yuletide (White Christmas)
- Frigid the Flakey Dude (Frosty the Snowman)
- Sterling Dingers (Silver Bells)
- Minuscule Male Percussionist (Little Drummer Boy)

Award a point for the individual or team who first names the wacky title, and two points to the first individual or team who discerns the title of the real song behind the wacky title. (Contributed by Greg Fiebig, Maryville, Mo.)

ST. VALENTINE'S DAY

Kissing in the Dark

For this two-team relay, you'll need two identical bull's-eye targets 18 inches (or greater) in diameter. Mark the targets' concentric circles with values like -10, 10, 25, 50, and 100. You'll also need two blindfolds, two tubes of lipstick, two tubes of Chapstick, and one adult with a marker for each target. (For larger groups, make more

Continued on page 146

The Real Meaning of Christmas

Fill in the blanks by looking up the Scripture passages (from the NIV).

C ______________ came into the world to save sinners. (1 Timothy 1:15)

H The Word became flesh and made ______ dwelling among us. We have seen ______ glory, the glory of the One and Only, who came from the Father, full of grace and truth. (John 1:14)

R But when the time had fully come, God sent his Son, born of a woman, born under the law, to ________ those under law, that we might ________ the full ________ of sons. (Galatians 4:4)

I "The virgin will be with child and will give birth to a son, and they will call him __________"—which means, "God with us." (Matthew 1:23)

S For the grace of God that brings ___________ has appeared to all men. (Titus 2:11)

T __________ be to God for his indescribable gift! (2 Corinthians 9:15)

M And he will be called Wonderful Counselor, ________ God, Everlasting Father, Prince of Peace. (Isaiah 9:6)

A But the _______ said to them, "Do not be ________. I bring you good news of great joy that will be for all the people. Today in the town of David a Savior has been born to you; he is Christ the Lord." (Luke 2:10)

S This is how God showed his love among us: He ________ his one and only Son into the world that we might live through him. This is love: not that we loved God, but that he loved us and sent his Son as an atoning __________ for our ________. (1 John 4:9-10) teams, adding one of the above items for each team added.) Post the targets on a wall 15 feet away from the starting line. Line up the two teams single file at the starting line, facing their target across the room.

Now announce the title of the game: Kissing in the Dark. Explain that you will blindfold the first members of the teams, put Chapstick or lipstick (player's choice) on each one, and spin them around. Then, guided by their teammates shouts, the blindfolded players attempt to kiss the bull's-eye and then return to their own lines and blindfold the next player in line. Play continues until each player has had a chance to kiss in the dark.

It is helpful to have an adult circle each lip print immediately after it is made so that smearing from subsequent kisses doesn't confuse the scoring. For males who will put on the lipstick instead of the Chapstick, give their teams 10 bonus points. If play is too slow, add a time limit. (Contributed by Doug Thorne and David Tohlen, Batesville, Ark.)

Valentine Bingo Games

Read on for two ways to combine Cupid's day with a favorite living-room game.

Valentine Candy Bingo

Make up a bunch of bingo cards—but instead of putting numbers in the squares, fill the squares with phrases from those little valentine candy hearts ("kiss me," "too cute," "be mine").

Buy enough candy hearts for all players to fill up all their bingo cards. Give players equal quantities of randomly selected candy hearts. On "Go!" players don't wait for a caller, but immediately try to cover their "kiss me" squares with "kiss me" candy hearts, their "lover boy" squares with "lover boy" hearts, etc. If they have a surplus of one kind of candy heart, they can trade with other players for hearts with phrases they need in order to cover every square on their card (or achieve a "bingo"—you make house rules).

Players can eat the candy when the game is over.

Love Bingo

This is a suitable crowd breaker for a study on love—especially around St. Valentine's Day. Make up bingo cards like the sample on page 147, using phrases applicable to your group. Make sure everyone has a game sheet and pencil. The first person to get bingo wins a small prize.

(Contributed by Jeff Brown, Charleston, S.C.)

LOVE BINGO

Directions: Here is your Love Bingo card. Your mission: To be the first to get a bingo (across, down, or diagonal) by having persons sign the block that describes them.

Someone who was kissed today	A female friend	Someone who is 27 years old, 6'6", and 190 pounds	The person you want to date but never have	FREE FREE	Someone wearing red socks	Give someone a hug and have them sign here
The love of your life	The biggest female flirt	Your relative	Give someone a hug and have them sign here	The biggest male flirt	A close friend	FREE FREE
FREE FREE	A male with blue eyes	Your Sunday-school department director	Someone doing a lip sync tonight	Someone not wearing anything red	Someone kissed in 1991	"Sweet" describes this person
Give someone a hug and have them sign here	Someone wearing a red sweater	Someone with a charming personality	FREE FREE	Go up to some of the opposite sex, smile, and say, "Don't I know you from somewhere?" then have them sign	here Someone married	Your first boyfriend/girlfriend
Someone you want to get to know better	FREE FREE	A blonde	Someone who sleeps with a teddy bear	One of your closest friends	Give someone a hug and have them sign here	Someone wearing red shoes
The person you have a crush on	Your Sunday-school teacher	FREE FREE	Someone wearing red	A brunette	A former boyfriend/girlfriend with whom you are still friends	A female with blue eyes
Someone who often encourages you or compliments you	Anyone at the party	Give someone a hug and have them sign here	Someone you really admire	Someone who has it all together	FREE FREE	A male friend

ST. PATRICK'S DAY

Green Thangs

When folks arrive, pin or tape on their backs a 3 X 5 card with the name of a green object written on it (with a green marker, of course). Players may ask only yes-and-no questions of others in the group to determine what "green thang" they are. Players may only ask two questions of each person, then must move on to question a new person.

When a player thinks she knows what green thang she is, she tells her guess to a supervising sponsor. If the guess is correct, the sponsor removes the old card, gives it to the wearer, then attaches a new "green thang" card to her back. Players hold on to the cards they correctly guessed until a final count at the end of the game. The person holding the most cards at the end of the time limit wins the game.

Some green thangs are avocado, green onion, cucumber, leprechaun, four-leaf clover, turtle, frog, grass, tree, ivy, lima bean, green pea, green apple, lettuce, paper money, artichoke, lime, kiwi fruit, Green Bay Packers, Green Hornet, green Jell-o, pond scum, clover, spinach, pistachio ice cream, olive, mold, snot, pickle, parrot, green parakeet, emerald, green underwear, Greenpeace, envy.

Possible St. Patrick's Day prizes are Lucky Charms cereal, can of green beans, can of Slime, green jelly beans, a green apple, small plastic cup covered with gold foil holding candy in it (the pot of gold), green socks, green soda, green breath mints, green mouth wash. (Contributed by Jason Walker and Marcy Buford, Dallas, Tex.)

Leprechaun Mad-Lib

In this holiday mad-lib, assign 24 people at a banquet or meeting one of the assignments on the list below (simply photocopy the list on page 149, cut the 24 assignments apart on the dotted line, then hand them out at the event). After the 24 players write their words or phrases on their slips, they come to the front and line up in numerical order according to the numbers on their slips.

Now the narrator reads the story (see page 150). When the narrator gets to the appropriate place in the story, the person with the corresponding number reads his contribution into the story. Also, every time the word "leprechaun" is read, everyone in the audience stands up and loudly says, "Aye!" (Contributed by Gwyn E. Baker, Knoxville, Tenn.)

Word/phrase list for Leprechaun Mad-Lib:

1. Name one of your special treasures
2. Noun (a thing)
3. Adjective
4. Part of the body
5. Adjective
6. Adjective
7. Adjective
8. Name of man in this room
9. Name a place where you'd be afraid to walk (common noun)
10. Name what you were wearing the last time your spouse or mom complained about the way you looked
11. Name of person in the room
12. Past-tense verb
13. The most useless advice you've ever been given
14. A catchy phrase from a TV commercial you detest
15. Name of a living thing
16. Noun
17. A tool
18. Name or describe what you do when you get mad
19. Plural noun
20. Noun
21. Plural noun
22. Liquid
23. Part of the body
24. Part of the body

Story for Leprechaun Mad-Lib

As tradition has it, if you catch a leprechaun, he must take you to the pot of 1, at the end of the 2. But you must beware! If you take your eyes off of him, he will disappear. These tricky little fellas are 3. Their 4 are 5. They wear a tiny 6 cobbler apron because they are in charge of making shoes for the fairies.

Once upon a time there lived a 7 Irishman named 8. One day he was strolling down the 9 wearing his 10. Then suddenly he spotted a leprechaun named 11 and 12 him and said, "13," to which the leprechaun said, "14." The Irishman threatened the leprechaun with his life if he didn't show him where the pot of [same as 1] was.

So the leprechaun took the Irishman this way and that. Rough and hard ways they were, but the Irishman never took his eyes off the leprechaun. At long last they came to a place with large 15 trees. "Dig under the roots of this tree and you'll find your treasure," said the leprechaun.

The Irishman thanked the little leprechaun and tied a 16 around the tree so he could mark the spot. He ran back to get his 17 to dig with, and when he came back there were [same as 16] around every tree. So he 18.

The moral of this story is: Love of 19 is the root of all 20; too many 21 spoil the 22; and the way to a man's 23 is through his 24.

Leprechaun Softball

Groups of 12 to 30 are perfect for celebrating St. Patrick's Day with this indoor or outdoor baseball variation.

Using a bathroom plunger for a bat and a small, lightweight rubber ball (such as a Squish Ball), play Leprechaun softball on a makeshift diamond:

- At first base is a table with paper cups and a pitcher full of green water (use food coloring).
- At second base is a bag of green balloons.
- At third base are two tubes of green lipstick.
- At home plate is the plunger, two wide-rim cups, and a box of Lucky Charms breakfast cereal. Place two empty cups about four to six feet behind home plate, either on the floor or on a table.

In addition to a pitcher and catcher,

the fielding team has a baseman at each of the three bases. That's all—no shortstop or fielders. At each base is an umpire. Play is three to four innings.

Here's how to play:

- The batter tries to catch an underhand pitch in the plunger, with which he attempts to toss the ball back into the field.
- Only the pitcher is allowed to attempt to field a "hit" ball. The pitcher must catch the ball before it hits the ground in order to get the batter out on a hit. If the ball is immediately caught by the pitcher, the batter goes to the back of the batting line.
- If the pitcher cannot catch the ball, the batter runs to first base, where he races the first baseman in drinking a glass half-filled with green water. The first-base umpire calls the runner safe if he is the first one to set his empty glass upside down on the table. If the first baseman beats the runner at this drinking feat, the runner is called out.
- The next batter follows the same routine as the first batter, while the runner on first runs to second base, where he must again compete with the baseman—this time to blow up a small green balloon, tie it, and sit on it until it pops. The second-base umpire determines the winner; if the runner wins, he stays on second base. If the second baseman wins, the runner is out.
- A third batter follows the same routine as the earlier batters. At third base, the runner and third baseman must each pick up a tube of green lipstick, apply it to their lips, close the lipstick, and lay the tube down. The third-base ump calls the runner safe or out, depending on if the runner won or lost the contest.
- While the fourth batter follows the same routine, the runner going home must compete with the catcher by tossing a handful of Lucky Charms piece by piece from home base into the empty cup. The first person to get three pieces of cereal into the cup—with at least one piece being a marshmallow—wins. If the runner wins, his team scores 10 points. If the catcher wins, the runner is out.

The team with the highest score wins the game. More bases with activities at each one may be added if you wish. (Contributed by Jason Walker and Marcy Buford, Dallas, Tex.)

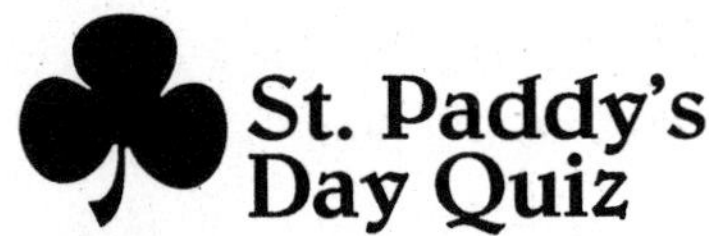

St. Paddy's Day Quiz

Celebrate a St. Patrick's Day festival by planning a green scavenger hunt, by making as many words as possible from the greeting, "Happy St. Patrick's Day," and finally by taking the quiz on page 153 (print it on green paper, of course). The questions are designed to lead students into a discussion of who St. Patrick was, what he did, and how God can use bad or difficult circumstances for good—such as Patrick's six years in slavery. (It was during those six years that he learned to pray and depend on God, that his faith matured and was strengthened.)

To take a different direction, discuss luck. What things are lucky? What brings good luck? Compare the idea of luck with the Christian concept of God's blessing or of providence. Conclude the festival with green cake and punch.

Here are the answers:

1. green
2. Ireland
3. A.D. 389
4. Blarney Stone
5. pot of gold
6. Roman Catholic
7. leprechauns
8. pop quizzes
9. Ireland
10. Ireland
11. Blarney (in Britain)
12. Blarney
13. True
14. Blarney (used by the Irish to symbolize the Trinity)
15. Blarney
16. Blarney
17. True
18. Blarney (a deacon and alderman)
19. Blarney
20. True

(Contributed by Dianne Deming, Ft. Morgan, Colo., and Gary McCluskey, Colorado Springs, Colo.)

LENT/EASTER

Easter Baskets for Shut-ins

Decorate those green plastic containers that strawberries come in, using yarn, ribbon, lace, and so on. Place Easter grass in the baskets and fill with homemade candy. Make chocolate candy from molds and buy jelly beans to add color. (Contributed by Deborah J. Nickel, Johnstown, Penn.)

St. Paddy's Day Quiz

Directions: Circle the correct answer to the question.

1. What color is associated with St. Paddy's Day?
   green   red   mauve
2. Of which country is St. Patrick the patron saint?
   Ireland   England   Afghanistan
3. About which year was St. Patrick born?
   450 B.C.   A.D. 389   A.D. 1956
4. Which stone do the Irish kiss?
   Barney Stone   Barry Stone   Blarney Stone
5. What is found at the end of the rainbow?
   winter storm warnings   a bucket of coal   a pot of gold
6. What was Patrick's religion?
   Presbyterian   Roman Catholic   Jewish
7. Whom do the Irish call "little people"?
   anyone under 5'3"   leprechauns   folks from Scotland
8. Which of the following are not associated with good luck?
   four-leaf clover   horseshoe   rabbit's foot   pop quizzes
9. Which country gives us the festival of St. Patrick?
   England   Ireland   Afghanistan
10. Patrick was called back into service in which country?
    England   Ireland   U.S.A.

Directions: Circle the correct answer for each statement, depending on whether it is truth or blarney.

True	Blarney	11.	St. Patrick was born in Ireland.
True	Blarney	12.	St. Patrick chased all of the snakes out of Ireland.
True	Blarney	13.	St. Patrick was poorly educated.
True	Blarney	14.	St. Patrick first used the shamrock.
True	Blarney	15.	Patrick's real name was Glockenspiel.
True	Blarney	16.	St. Patrick wrote "When Irish Eyes Are Smiling" after a visit with Tip O'Neil in Boston.
True	Blarney	17.	At a young age St. Patrick was a slave and received a divine call to work in the church.
True	Blarney	18.	St. Patrick's father was a pagan soldier.
True	Blarney	19.	St. Patrick drank green milkshakes at McDonald's.
True	Blarney	20.	St. Patrick was a bishop.

Scoring:		
	18-20 correct	You must be Irish.
	14-18 correct	Your grandmother was probably Irish.
	10-14 correct	You are full of blarney.
	below 14 correct	You must be English.

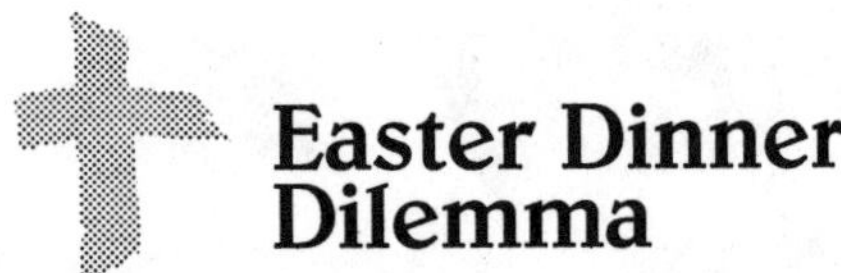

Easter Dinner Dilemma

On page 155 is a logic puzzle that's a perfect addition to an Easter-season get-together. Here is the solution:

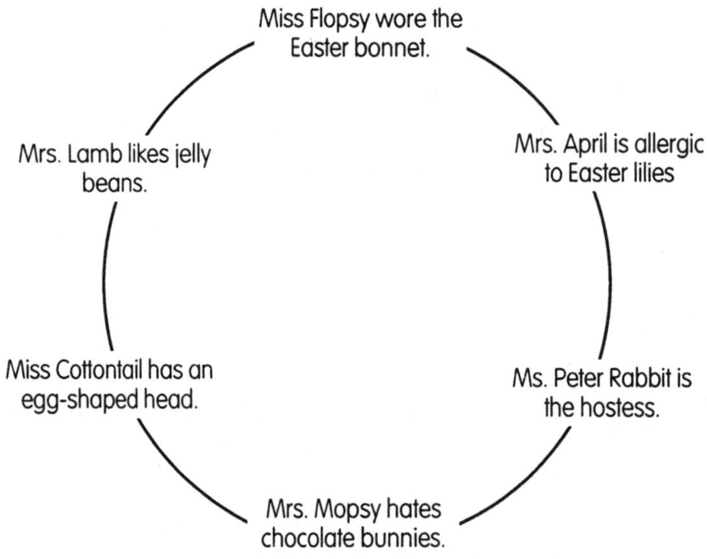

Miss Flopsy wore the Easter bonnet.
Mrs. April is allergic to Easter lilies
Ms. Peter Rabbit is the hostess.
Mrs. Mopsy hates chocolate bunnies.
Miss Cottontail has an egg-shaped head.
Mrs. Lamb likes jelly beans.

(Contributed by Lynne Hartke, Chandler, Ariz.)

Easter Scavenger Hunt II

In this scavenger hunt all the items on the list have to be living—a plant, pet, mold, someone (not on the scavenger hunt, that is), wild flower, palm leaf, and so on. Following the scavenger hunt, study Scripture about the living Christ. (Contributed by Bert Jones, Lancaster, Ohio)

EASTER DINNER DILEMMA

A woman invited five guests to her Easter dinner. The names of the six people who sat down at the round table were Mrs. April, Miss Flopsy, Ms. Peter Rabbit, Mrs. Mopsy, Miss Cottontail, and Mrs. Lamb. One of them liked jelly beans, one wore an Easter bonnet, one had a head like an egg, one simply hated chocolate bunnies, one was allergic to Easter lilies, and one was the hostess.

Can you identify each of these ladies, as well as determine where around the table each woman sat?

- The woman who hated chocolate bunnies sat directly opposite Miss Flopsy.
- The lady who liked jelly beans sat opposite Ms. Peter Rabbit, who sat between the woman who was allergic to Easter lilies and the woman who hated chocolate bunnies.
- The woman who had a head like an egg sat opposite Mrs. April, next to the lady who like jelly beans, and to the left of the woman who hated chocolate bunnies.
- The woman who was allergic to Easter lilies sat between Mrs. Peter Rabbit and the woman who sat opposite the woman who hated chocolate bunnies.
- Mrs. Lamb, who was a good friend to everyone, sat next to the egg-head-shaped lady and opposite the hostess.
- The woman who sat across from the one who wore a bonnet was not Miss Cottontail.

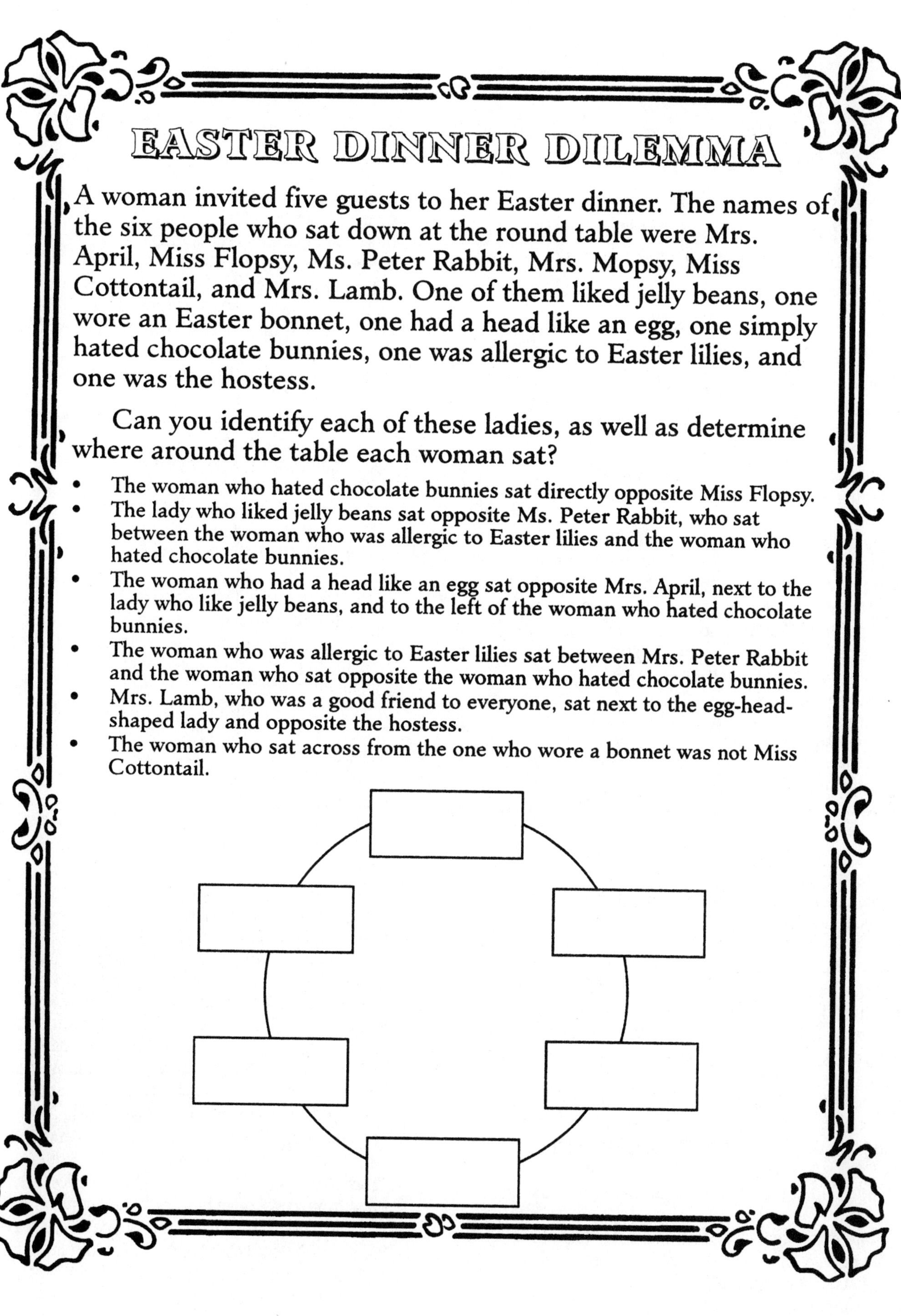

Last Supper Simulation

This creative worship service is best with senior high youths at the beginning of Lent (or even Advent, with some adjustments).

Leader Preparation

1. Become familiar with the general sequence of events of the Last Supper (study Matthew 26:17-35; Mark 14:12-31; Luke 22:7-34; and John 13:1 through 17:26).
2. Arrange to use a room (preferably an upstairs room) with little furniture and where you will not be disturbed.
3. In the center of the room place a long, low table where everyone can sit on the floor among cushions; light the room only by candles or kerosene lanterns.
4. Ask parents to make a simple, thin soup and round loaves of bread. Bring grape juice. Set the table with no utensils, but with only water glasses and bowls for each participant. Leave an empty space at the table for Jesus.
5. You dress in layered, loose-fitting garments—i.e., imitate Jesus' first-century attire. Prepare the students for the evening only by telling them to dress casually and come ready for a light meal.

Actual Reenactment

1. Before kids enter the room: All participants should remove their shoes; ask them to imagine themselves as Jesus' closest friends about to share in his last meal on earth before his crucifixion.
2. When they enter the room, welcome them to the Passover Feast and explain about the place reserved for Christ. Pray together that Jesus will bless this time and invite the Holy Spirit to empower and guide everyone's thoughts. Ask that God's gift of Jesus will be made real to all.
3. As you eat, let students tell what they already know about the Passover Feast (when and why it started) and fill in background from the Old Testament story (in Exodus 12). Read Luke 22:7-16 and discuss who was present at the Passover meal we call the Last Supper.
4. Explore with them what Jesus was about to suffer. What do they think was felt by those who heard Jesus' words? Create a vivid picture.
5. After supper rise, take off your outer shawl or cape, and wrap a large, dark towel around your waist. Fill a large basin with warm water, then wash the feet of at least several of the youths. (Drop whatever hints you must ahead of time so they won't feel too embarrassed. Cue one student to, like Peter, refuse to let you wash her feet until you finally insist.)

   Explore together Jesus' purpose in doing this and the significance of God's own Son choosing a lowly servant role.
6. Read aloud Luke 22:19-20 and Mark 14:22-24. Don't rush; let it sink in.
7. Take an unbroken, oval loaf of bread, wrap it in a rough cloth, and cradle it, reminding them of God's Son's coming to us. Roughly strip the loaf of the cloth, reviewing how the world refused the gift. While you hold the loaf up as if offering it as a sacrifice, break it in half and talk about how Jesus was willing to die, to be broken for us as a sacrifice for us.

   Then pour a few drops of the grape juice into a cup. While holding half the bread, drip a few drops of juice from the cup onto the bread, reminding participants that Jesus' life blood was poured out for us. Finally, share the Lord's Supper by passing the broken bread and grape juice around the table.
8. Review the main message of Jesus to the disciples—and to us—as found in John 13:31 to 17:26. Jesus said the following:
   - He would be glorified.
   - He was going away and couldn't be followed.
   - Our most important new commandment is to love one another.
   - We have a place in heaven.
   - He sends us the Holy Spirit.
   - We must be fruitful for God.
   - He did all of this so that we can have his full joy.

   Get the group to explore what all this means. Ask how they think his friends responded.
9. Point out how Jesus prayed for his dearest friends—to be kept safe, united and one with God, dedicated to God's purpose, and entitled to all the resources and power that God has already given to Jesus. Ask what Jesus guaranteed to us through this prayer.
10. Lead the group to explore their experiences of the Last Supper. Help them think about God's gift of Christ to us. Furthermore, explore what talents and opportunities we have been personally given from God. How do we give back gifts to God? Does reliving this poignant Last Supper with Jesus cause you to think differently about what or how you do or don't give back your gifts to God?
11. Close with prayer, asking the Holy Spirit to continue

to speak to each individual. Ask that the loving Lord Jesus' gifts be openly received by all and that we would be helped to discover new ways to give God's love outward to a needing world.

12. When your students leave the room, urge them to not speak in order to help the experience sink in deeply.

Follow-up

1. For several weeks following, pray for each participant by name. Ask that they will know the Holy Spirit's guidance and God's challenge from this experience.
2. Mail personal pledge cards to each youth, and follow-up with a personal call.
3. Reenact the Parable of the Talents.

(Contributed by Connie Hewett, Bakersfield, Calif.)

GRADUATION

Gallery of Graduates

A month in advance of graduation Sunday at your church, ask your seniors to bring in items that represent them, their school and community activities, and their accomplishments—for example, 5 x 7 senior portraits, graduation announcements, varsity letters, athletic equipment, photos, ribbons, awards, plaques, certificates, programs from plays and concerts, yearbooks, and anything with their school logo on it.

Make individual displays for each grad, using colored mat board as a background (available from art supply stores). Write the name of the honored graduate across the top in calligraphy. Use photo-mounting corners to mount photos, certificates, programs, and awards. Rubber cement or masking tape is fine for mounting letters, ribbons, and such. Place large items—yearbooks, athletic equipment, etc.—in front of each display.

On graduation Sunday, exhibit the individualized displays in the church lobby, then move them to where you'll hold the reception. (Contributed by Tom Lytle, Marion, Ohio)

Grad Place Mats

For next June's graduation banquet, adorn the place mats with your graduates' photos, names, alma mater, a poem, "senior wills," or your congratulatory comments.

Buy blank paper place mats at a party supply store. If you want to print their photos on the mats, you first must make a screen of each photo (also called a Velox, paper positive, etc. Call a nearby quick-print shop—if they don't screen photos, they can

GREG BENZINGER
Northfield H.S.

DANA CRANDALL
Northfield H.S.

JOHN MEMMER
North Miami H.S.

DESIREE' HARTMAN
Northfield H.S.

MAX MEYER
Northfield H.S.

JENNIFER RICHWINE
Wabash, H.S.

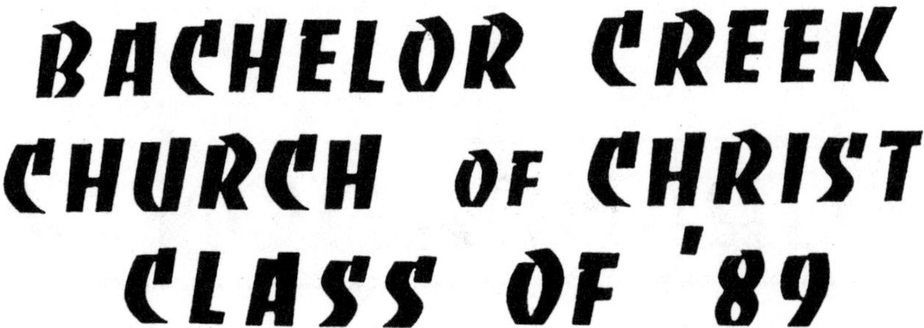

JAMI WALKER
Marion H.S.

KRIS McCOLLEY
Northfield H.S.

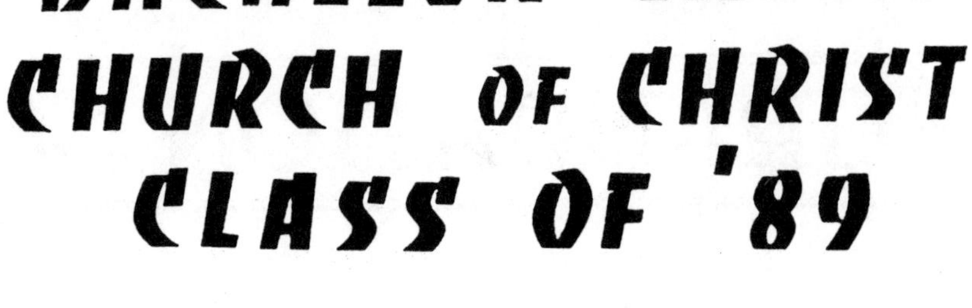

SCOTT KIRTLAN
Northfield H.S.

TAMI WALKER
Northfield H.S.

TODD ELLIOTT
Northfield H.S.

ANGIE CASTLE
Southwood H.S.

ERIN HUIRAS
Northfield H.S.

CAROLINA LORDUY
Northfield H.S.

refer you to someone who does). Lay out an original with text, art, and screened photos in place, and your photocopier can do the rest. If you're interested in a second or third (or more) color, call a quick-print or a color-photocopy shop. (Contributed by Mike Duggan, Wabash, Ind.)

Graduation Roast

When you announce this Sunday afternoon cookout and senior roast, explain that people only roast those they love, care for, and deeply respect.

In the weeks before graduation, dig up all the "dirt" you can on your seniors by talking to parents, brothers and sisters, other relatives, youth group members, and other friends. Gather moderately embarrassing photos, slides, and movies of the seniors when they were much younger. Plan some funny remarks about each senior and some transitional comments that keep up the momentum between roasts.

On a Sunday near graduation and in the worship service just prior to the roast, have your graduating seniors come to the front of the sanctuary. Briefly extol their virtues and recount their ministry in the life of the church. Present them with a Bible or helpful devotional book. Deliver a brief charge and pray for the grads.

That afternoon begin the fellowship activities with a cookout—followed by the roast. One at a time the seniors come forward and sit facing the group. Proceed to roast them—and watch the fun unfold. Give each of them a gag gift related to one or more of the anecdotes you tell on them. (Contributed by Vernon Edington, Manchester, Tenn.)

Not So Trivial

At your next graduation event, introduce your group's graduating seniors with year-of-birth trivia that is relevant to each student. For instance, introduce a musically inclined boy by playing snippets of the top 10 hits from his birth year. For a girl who lettered in softball, tell an anecdote about a baseball star from her birth year.

Find the trivia in encyclopedia year books, library files, back issues of **Rolling Stone** or other trendy magazines, or old almanacs purchased at a used bookstore. (Remember that an almanac dated 1973 will contain information from 1972.) If you want to personalize it further, dig up facts for their birth **month** and **day**. Or make life real easy by ordering from a card shop a mock-up newspaper for a student's actual birth date. (Contributed by Len Cuthbert, Hamilton, Ont. Canada)

Parting Shots

Your senior can have the parting shot with this idea. On audiocassette record their answers to various questions that deal with high school, youth group, favorite magazines, TV shows, teachers, musicians, etc.

Using a dual deck that has a microphone jack, edit bits and pieces of their answers to make a hilarious spoof interview. Build different stories around each youth's supposed experiences—dating a current rock star, stealing vital information from the space shuttle, advising the vice president of the United States.

Put all the interviews on one tape and play it for the whole group. With effort and creativity, this idea can be a smash. The tape is also an appreciated memento for the students to remember their classmates. (Contributed by David Flavin, N. Mankato, Minn.)

Senior Bless

Though high schoolers find it hard to say goodbye when seniors graduate, they yearn to tell each other how they feel. Give them a format for sharing their feelings by holding a "Senior Bless." Once you've had a Senior Bless, your freshmen and sophomores will look forward to their turn.

Invite your seniors by phone or written invitation to come to a special meeting to honor them. At the last meeting before the seniors graduate, bring them up front one at a time and invite the rest of the group to tell things they like about each senior. Then ask kids to tell blessings they hope will be in each senior's future. As each compliment and blessing is spoken, write it in a super-size card to be presented to that senior. Bless seniors in order by birth date.

Some actual blessings bestowed by teenagers on seniors:

- "I hope people are as good to you as you have been to me."
- "I hope you can always see God clearly no matter how murky things get."
- "I pray you'll build a marriage that brings strength and joy to both you and your spouse."
- "I hope your job is awesome."

After all seniors have received their blessings, invite them to say anything they'd like to the group. It's not uncommon for some seniors to be too moved to speak. Others will add comments like, "Thanks for my blessing," "I really appreciate this group because you've shown me that God is real and he makes the world beautiful," "I'll miss you," "I'm glad I'll always be welcomed here." (Contributed by Karen Dockrey, Hendersonville, Tenn.)

OTHER SPECIAL DAYS

Super Bowl Prophecies

No wagering here—just no-risk guessing at some of the innumerable details of pro football's climax. For next year's Super Bowl party, print up a quiz like the sample on page 161 and pass it out before the game. The point values are in parentheses. Tally points after the game and award creative or humorous prizes. (Contributed by Sam Vernon, Macon, Ga.)

Super Bowl Prophecies

1. Winner Bills (1) By how much 12 (2) Exact score 30-18 (3)

2. The first team to miss a field goal (circle one): (1)

   Bills   Redskins   No misses

3. The first team penalized in the fourth quarter (circle one): (1)

   Bills   Redskins   No penalties

4. Which player will score first? (1)

   Kelly   Lofton   Thomas   Reed   Norwood

   Rypien   Monk   Clark   Riggs   Lohmiller

5. How many commercials during halftime? (exact count 3; closest count 2) 7

6. First team to score: Redskins (1)

   Last team to score: Bills (1)

7. Total points (circle one): (1)

   More than 40   Less than 40

8. Who will have the ball at the first-half two-minute warning? (1) Skins

9. How many punts will there be in the game? (2) 9

10. Game length (circle one): (1)

    Less than three hours   Less than three-and-a-half hours

    Less than four hours   Overtime

11. Will there be any missed extra points? (1) yes

12. Which team will have the ball on last snap of game? (1) Bills

BILLS Forever!

BUFFALO RULES

Bills are Buff!!

April Fools

Here's a variation of "April Fools' Game" (**Ideas Combo 29-32**). As students enter the room, give them each a clear plastic clip-on badge cover. Inside each badge cover is the card on page 163 (photocopy and cut out enough for all attenders).

Give no verbal instructions to the kids—simply give them the badges as they enter. Throughout the allotted time, all who fool another player may take the losing player's badge(s) and attach them to their current string of badges. (Contributed by Jay Firebaugh, Blacklick, Ohio)

Living-Proof Moms

Honor mothers on their special day—or any day of the year—by asking your group members to answer two questions, and then printing the group's answers in a form letter of gratitude to their mothers.

Title a half-sheet of paper "Living Proof: Mother's Day Responses." Below the title write the following two sentence-starters with lines for the students to write on:

- "The thing I appreciate most about my mother is how she—"
- "If I could tell my mom one thing that I'm usually too embarrassed to say, it would be—"

When you've got all your kids' responses, then write the letter to moms by starting with something like this:

Dear Living-Proof Mom,

Mothering can be tiresome, unrewarding work. Since few mothers receive regular appreciation from their teenage sons and daughters, we asked them to say thanks anonymously this Mother's Day. Below is a bouquet of praises from the teens in First Church's youth group.

Here's what your kids have to say about you:

The thing I appreciate most about my mother is how she— (list all the quotes from the kids)

If I could tell my mom one thing that I'm usually too embarrassed to say, it would be— (list all the quotes from the kids)

You are appreciated—even though you rarely hear about it.

Then sign your name and send it off to all the moms. (Contributed by Jay Firebaugh, Blacklick, Ohio)

Wear this badge where everyone can easily see it. Your assignment is to pull an April Fools' trick on as many people as you can. (Tell someone his fly is open, there's a phone call for her, his shoe is untied, etc.). Players who fall for the trick (look down to check, go to the phone, and so on) must give you any badges they are wearing. AFTER YOU LOSE YOUR BADGE(S), YOU CAN'T PLAY ANY MORE. Whoever has the most badges at the conclusion of the time wins.

Wear this badge where everyone can easily see it. Your assignment is to pull an April Fools' trick on as many people as you can. (Tell someone his fly is open, there's a phone call for her, his shoe is untied, etc.). Players who fall for the trick (look down to check, go to the phone, and so on) must give you any badges they are wearing. AFTER YOU LOSE YOUR BADGE(S), YOU CAN'T PLAY ANY MORE. Whoever has the most badges at the conclusion of the time wins.

Wear this badge where everyone can easily see it. Your assignment is to pull an April Fools' trick on as many people as you can. (Tell someone his fly is open, there's a phone call for her, his shoe is untied, etc.). Players who fall for the trick (look down to check, go to the phone, and so on) must give you any badges they are wearing. AFTER YOU LOSE YOUR BADGE(S), YOU CAN'T PLAY ANY MORE. Whoever has the most badges at the conclusion of the time wins.

Wear this badge where everyone can easily see it. Your assignment is to pull an April Fools' trick on as many people as you can. (Tell someone his fly is open, there's a phone call for her, his shoe is untied, etc.). Players who fall for the trick (look down to check, go to the phone, and so on) must give you any badges they are wearing. AFTER YOU LOSE YOUR BADGE(S), YOU CAN'T PLAY ANY MORE. Whoever has the most badges at the conclusion of the time wins.

Wear this badge where everyone can easily see it. Your assignment is to pull an April Fools' trick on as many people as you can. (Tell someone his fly is open, there's a phone call for her, his shoe is untied, etc.). Players who fall for the trick (look down to check, go to the phone, and so on) must give you any badges they are wearing. AFTER YOU LOSE YOUR BADGE(S), YOU CAN'T PLAY ANY MORE. Whoever has the most badges at the conclusion of the time wins.

Wear this badge where everyone can easily see it. Your assignment is to pull an April Fools' trick on as many people as you can. (Tell someone his fly is open, there's a phone call for her, his shoe is untied, etc.). Players who fall for the trick (look down to check, go to the phone, and so on) must give you any badges they are wearing. AFTER YOU LOSE YOUR BADGE(S), YOU CAN'T PLAY ANY MORE. Whoever has the most badges at the conclusion of the time wins.

Father's Day Fun

Here are some ideas for a Father's Day or father/son event.

Necktie Tie

Fashion experts say that the tip of the properly tied necktie should come to the middle of one's belt buckle. Yet everyone knows how difficult it is to get a tie to do what you want it to do. Pick a few fathers and sons from the crowd and give each a necktie (if they don't already have one). Give them one (only one) chance to tie the thing around each other's neck, using the knot of their choice. The person whose tie tip comes closest to the belt buckle wins. Award prizes in different age categories.

Car Keys, Please?

Divide into teams of four or five people, and give each team five minutes to come up with snappy answers to the question, "May I borrow the car keys, Dad?" Have each team read their best answers to the crowd. Award prizes to the team with the most answers and the team with the one best answer.

Prairie Home Dad

Get a few of your better storytellers (dads as well as sons) to prepare a five-minute story (a la Garrison Keillor) about a lesson that they learned from their dad or a poignant memory of life with father. Intersperse these stories throughout the event.

(Contributed by David M. Shaw, Laurel, Md.)

Back to School Scavenger Hunt II

This will get 'em in the mood for a new school year. (See page 165.)

(Contributed by Todd Hinkie, Baton Rouge, La.)

Giving Thanks

The Thanksgiving holiday weekend is a natural time for teaching kids to be thankful for the spiritual blessings that God gives us. The worksheet on page 166 can open up good discussion on being thankful for the items or experiences suggested by the answers: (T) trials, (H) Holy Spirit, (A) all things, (N) news (as in Good News), (K) kingdom, (S) Son, (G) grace, (I) instruction of the Lord, (V) victory, (I) inheritance, (N) name of Jesus, (G) gift.
(Contributed by Bert Jones, Lancaster, Ohio)

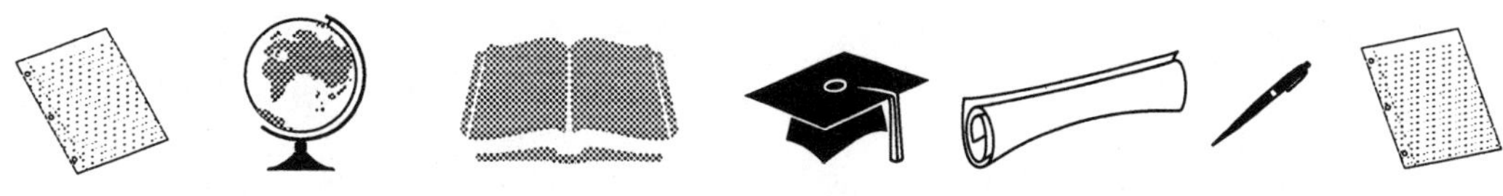

Back to School Scavenger Hunt

Rules:

1. You must travel by foot.
2. You may count each item only once.
3. You must be able to keep each item you get.
4. You must be back in the youth room by _______.

25 pts. ☐ something with a high school name imprinted on it

15 pts. ☐ old high school or college textbook

10 pts. ☐ exact change for lunch at your school

25 pts. ☐ combination lock

20 pts. ☐ piece of fruit that is one of your school's colors

30 pts. ☐ smelly, old tennis shoe

25 pts. ☐ note that was *actually* passed in class

100 pts. ☐ high school class ring (not your own)

50 pts. ☐ old research paper with a grade on it

40 pts. ☐ high school party or dance picture

50 pts. ☐ graduation tassel

35 pts. ☐ graduation announcement or name card

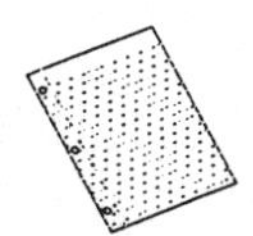

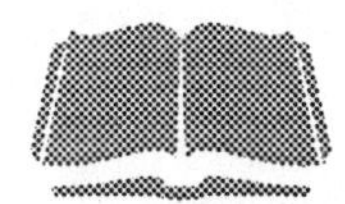

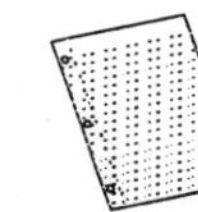

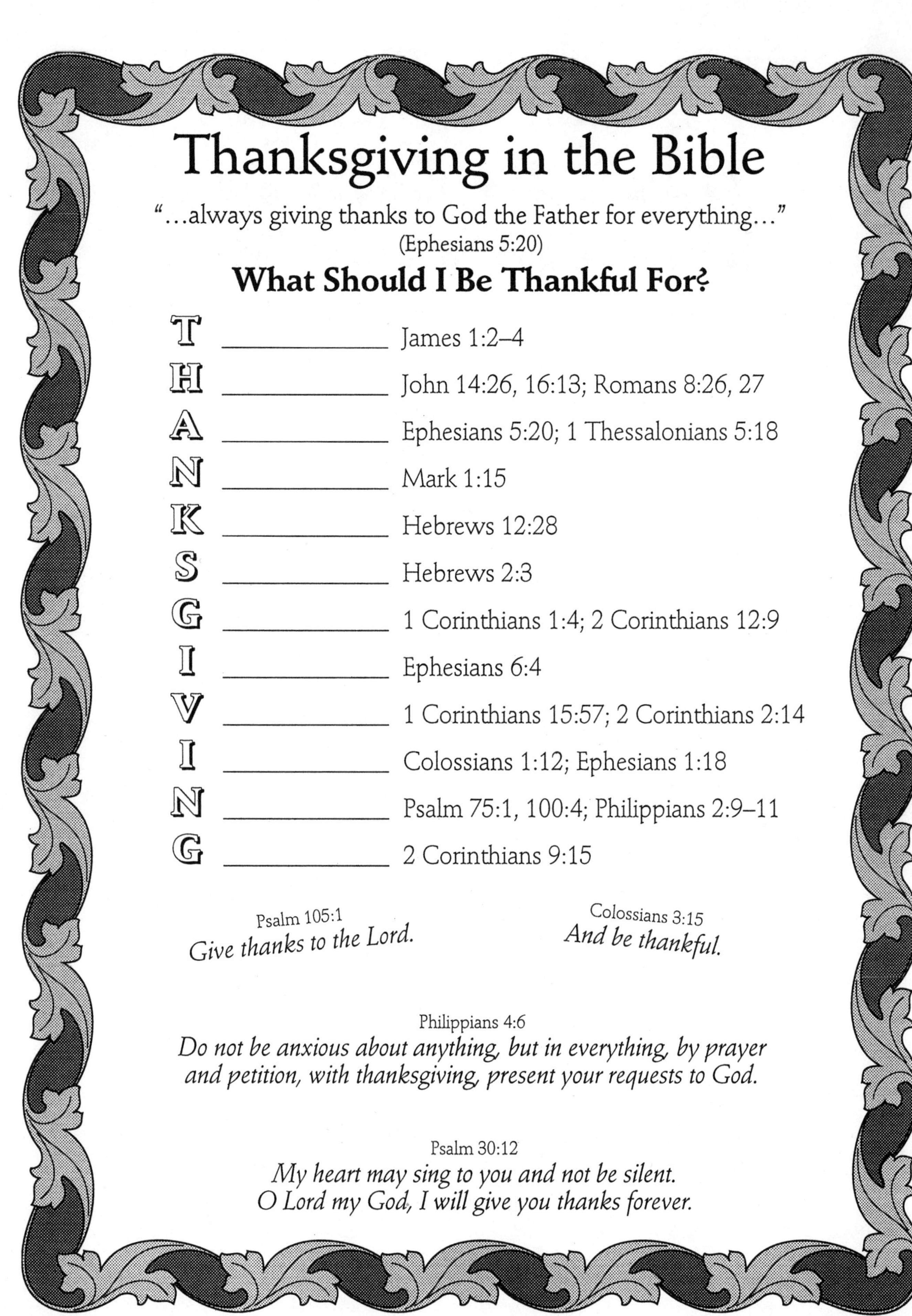

Thanksgiving in the Bible

"...always giving thanks to God the Father for everything..."
(Ephesians 5:20)

What Should I Be Thankful For?

T ____________ James 1:2–4

H ____________ John 14:26, 16:13; Romans 8:26, 27

A ____________ Ephesians 5:20; 1 Thessalonians 5:18

N ____________ Mark 1:15

K ____________ Hebrews 12:28

S ____________ Hebrews 2:3

G ____________ 1 Corinthians 1:4; 2 Corinthians 12:9

I ____________ Ephesians 6:4

V ____________ 1 Corinthians 15:57; 2 Corinthians 2:14

I ____________ Colossians 1:12; Ephesians 1:18

N ____________ Psalm 75:1, 100:4; Philippians 2:9–11

G ____________ 2 Corinthians 9:15

Psalm 105:1
Give thanks to the Lord.

Colossians 3:15
And be thankful.

Philippians 4:6
Do not be anxious about anything, but in everything, by prayer and petition, with thanksgiving, present your requests to God.

Psalm 30:12
My heart may sing to you and not be silent.
O Lord my God, I will give you thanks forever.

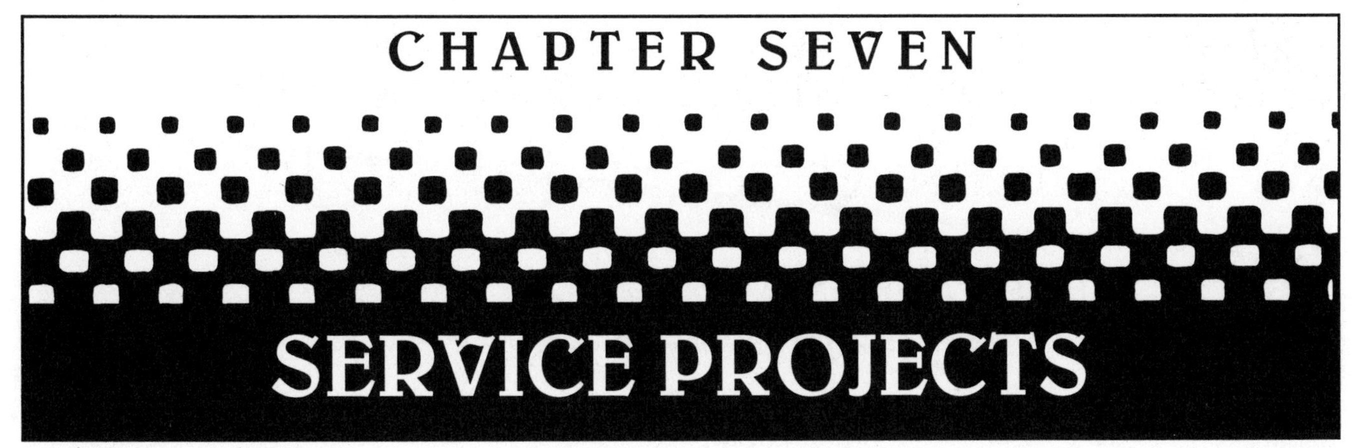

CHAPTER SEVEN

SERVICE PROJECTS

Church Who's Who

Looking for a way to increase the sensitivity of your kids to the rest of your church body? Consider a church-family information book. Using the church membership roll, assign the name of every individual and family in the church to a group of two or three youths who will make an appointment to visit them. Send with the youths a list of questions resembling those on a census: number of family members, ages, birth dates, place of birth, employment, school attending (or attended), degrees obtained, hobbies, interests.

The information the groups obtain can be stored on computer and updated annually. Students can also compile a booklet to distribute during a second visit to each family, thus insuring that each church family is visited twice a year. The youths become involved in visiting others (especially those that they don't know), relationships develop between the generations, and church members gain a valuable resource. (Contributed by Greg Miller, Knoxville, Tenn.)

Eco-Mug a House

The flier says it all. (Contributed by Kent Busman, Schenectady, N.Y.)

Get your house

Eco-Mugged

The Senior Youth Group, in keeping with its environmental concern, want to help you help us . . .

Save the Earth

HOW? By letting us "**Eco-Mug**" your house.
We will come in at a pre-determined time and . . .

- Get your name off junk-mail lists
- Install a toilet dam
- Check the air in your tires for proper inflation
- Install one faucet aerator
- Leave a hand-made Youth Group "Draft Dodger" to keep cold air from getting in under your door
- Leave a hand-painted Youth Group **Eco-Mug**
- Leave you with three beautiful note cards printed on recycled paper
- Take your unwanted clothing to an appropriate donation center

What better gift to give to a friend and our world!

Cost for getting Eco-Mugged is $30
All proceeds will go to our Youth Group
Spring Break "Give 'Em a Break"

We estimate that if 100 families get **Ego-Mugged** we could *each year . . .*

SAVE
150 trees to sit in the shade under
622,000 gallons of fresh water to swim in or enjoy
3,000 gallons of gas to enjoy cleaner air with
36,500 disposable cups

HAVE
100 more comfortable houses to wait out winter's cold in
300 more people told about saving God's earth through letters written
100 more people living with better clothes and dignity*

**based on research done in 50 Simple Things You Can Do to Save the Earth*

☐ **YES!** I want my house Eco-Mugged. Here is my $30 gift to help save the earth.

Name ____________________

Address ____________________

City __________ State ___ Zip ______

Phone (home) ____________________

(work) ____________________

Loafing Around

Bring your group out of the isolation that can characterize youth activities by baking bread for World Communion Sunday, for delivery to shut-in church members, or to sell at bake sales.

The Fleischmann's Yeast Company puts together bread-baking kits for kids to turn out 30 loaves of bread. Each kit provides 15 kids with aprons, mixing bowls, measuring cups, baking pans, and stir sticks. Also included in the kit are coupons for free flour and margarine, a demonstrator's guide, and take-home recipes. The cost of each kit is around $15 (including shipping and handling), which means that the cost per loaf can be as low as $.50.

For more information write to Fleischmann's Bread Kits, P.O. Box 44 Dayton, MD 21036. Phone 800/227-6202 (Mon.-Fri., 10 a.m. to 7 p.m. ET).

Sock Giveaway

This year don't bless the socks off the needy in your community. For a change, bless the needy **with** socks!

Decorate shoe boxes with a sock motif and place them throughout the church. By means of signs and fliers, ask those who attend church or Sunday school to donate money for the youth group to purchase socks to be given to needy children through an approved community agency. After three weeks, the group goes shopping for socks with the money collected.

The following week decorate the meeting room with socks—old socks, new socks, Christmas socks, huge socks, teeny socks—and display in some way the socks the group purchased to give away. Celebrate the collection effort with a sock hop (everyone must wear socks they decorated at home). Offer crazy prizes for the prettiest, ugliest, scariest, and funniest socks. Then turn up some oldies and dance the Limbo, the Twist, and the Pony.

The day after the sock hop, take the new socks to the agency. (Contributed by Mary Jo Mastin, Turlock, Calif.)

Thanksgiving Bingo Scavenger Hunt

Divide youths into carloads. Use the bingo card like the one below—it names foods to be collected within a certain time limit. Add your own specific instructions, time limits, etc. You may allow them to collect items door to door in a particular neighborhood, or limit them to only their own or other church members' homes. They can collect only one item per house visited.

The object is to collect items from the same row or diagonal to get a bingo. The first team back with a bingo wins. The collected items are donated to the needy. (Contributed by Cheryl Ehlers, East Point, Ga.)

THANKSGIVING BINGO SCAVENGER HUNT

can of green beans	box of light bulbs	can of refried beans	jar of peanut butter	can of fruit
box of Jell-O	can of soup	jar of jelly	cake mix	box of rice
box of crackers	box of hot cereal	can of hot chocolate mix	jar of applesauce	roll of toilet paper
can of evaporated milk	bar of soap	box of cereal	bag of sugar	jar of spaghetti sauce
bottle of shampoo	box of salt	package of spaghetti noodles	box of raisins	tube of toothpaste

Truck Troops

To help people with those project-sized chores that require a pick-up truck, schedule your group's teenage truck owners for Truck Troop missions. Divide the youth group into truck-troop teams that can haul and stack firewood, move furniture to storage, make a run to the city dump, deliver used furniture or appliances to the needy, etc. Advertise the service in your newsletter or church bulletin. You'll have plenty of takers and some unusual opportunities for ministry within your congregation and community. (Contributed by Bert Jones, Lancaster, Ohio)

VISION Team

Need a name for your youth group volunteers? How about "VISION Team"? It stands for Volunteers Investing Some (Time) In Others' Needs. Use Proverbs 29:18 as your motto: "Where there is no vision, the people perish." (Contributed by Bert and Cheryl Jones, Lancaster, Ohio)

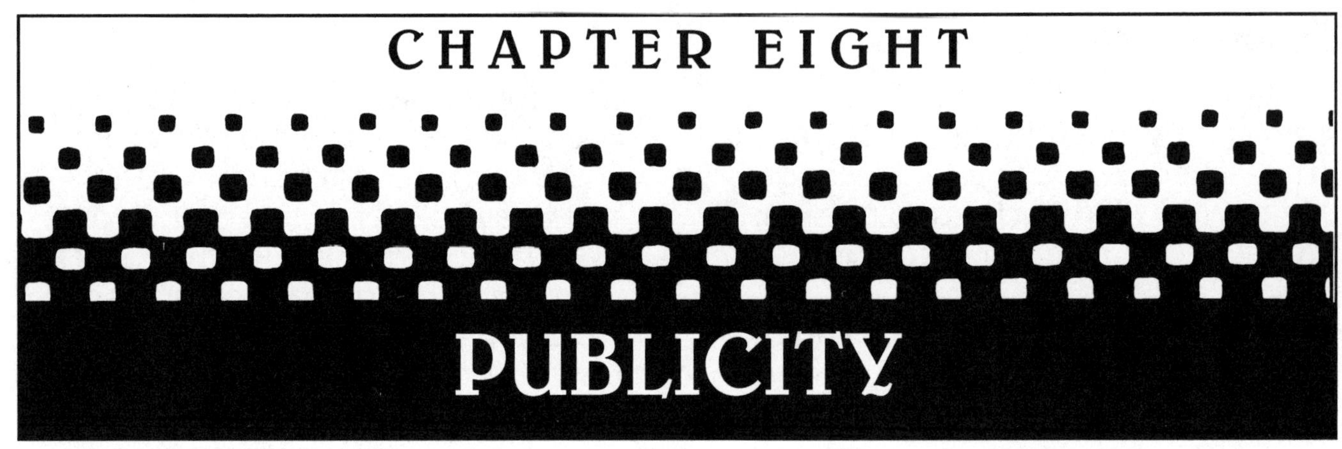

Advelopes

Every week or so you glance at the pile of old magazines in the corner of your office. You never use them, but you're loath to toss them because—well, you never know when they might come in handy.

Here's an immediate use for at least the colorful page ads—especially the ones in Christian music magazines. Carefully tear them out and fold them into envelopes in which to mail announcements for special activities. All your group will get an eye-grabbing, customized, one-of-a-kind envelope.

Simply fold the ad twice, then tape the sides and later the flap. The address will probably get lost in the design unless you use a white self-adhesive label. (Contributed by Len Cuthbert, Winona, Ont., Canada)

Air Mail

Want to remind kids of commitments they made at the last retreat? Of a big upcoming event? Look no further for an enthralling way to send short, quick notes to your kids. Inflate a light-colored balloon and tie it off with a paper clip or rubber band (so you can deflate it easily). With a fine-point, permanent-ink pen or marker (to prevent smudging), write your note on the balloon. (You may want to use phrases like "pumped up," "air mail," "lot of hot air," etc. Deflate the balloon and mail it in an envelope.

When your kids receive their balloon-notes, they'll either need a magnifying glass to read it—or have to blow it up. Chances are, they won't forget the message. (Contributed by John Blackman, Sault Ste. Marie, Ont., Canada)

Calendar Water Bottle

Quench your kids' thirst for summertime activity by printing your summer calendar on water bottles (or sport bottles) for distribution or sale among your group members.

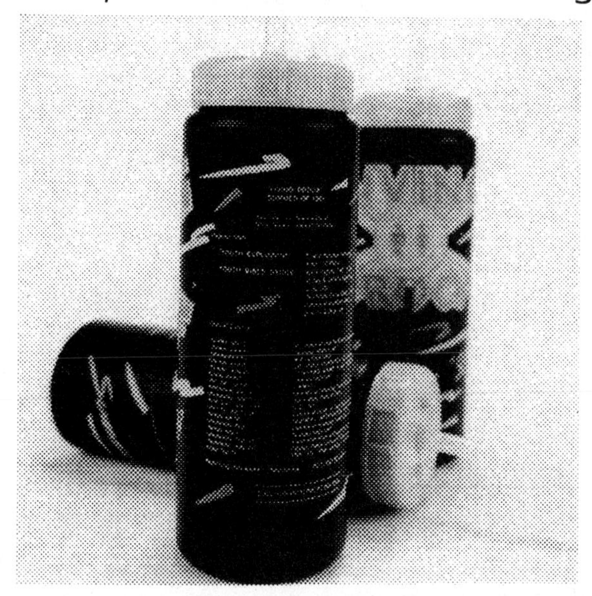

Whatever you usually print on a calendar sheet—names and times of programs, parties, retreats, studies—simply have printed on the bottles. Throw in some colorful graphics (coordinated with the colors of the bottle and screw-on lid), include a special youth group name—then make the bottles available to visitors as well as regulars at the beginning of your summer program.

A few phone calls to screen printers in your area will get you started. Otherwise, call Countryside Products (Pickerington, OH 43147) at 614/861-6116. (Contributed by Jay Firebaugh, Blacklick, Ohio)

Calling Cards

Think up humorous or just plain weird business or organizational names to precede your return or forwarding address. The smiles you'll generate just might increase your readership. Like this:

Anointed Worm Ministries, Inc.
1217 S. Carrier Pkwy
Grand Prairie, TX 75051
"If God can use a worm, he can use you."
Jonah 4:7

Here are some more examples:

- Elvis Is Alive International Headquarters (use this for your Elvis lovers)
- Mozart Is Alive International Headquarters (use this for your classical-music lovers)

Or, instead of being comical, you can add to the envelope an affirming touch:

> Maker of Marvelous Melodies
> Jill Reynolds
> Box 111
> Littleton, IN 68071

More examples of affirming address additions:

Wonderful Grandparents
Pat "The Patient" Pickleseed
Harry "Helpful" Hines
Gene "Gentle" Smith

It goes without saying to avoid comments about a person's physical appearance, behavior, habits, family or cultural background, etc. (Mark "Meathead" Dormer) that are even anything close to derogatory, negative, or uncomplimentary comments. Nor should you flatter; be sure the statements are truthful and accurate. Choose only those phrases you can back up with reasons—because the kids themselves will inevitably ask for evidence of the virtues you assign them. (Contributed by Roger Haas, Grand Prairie, Tex.)

Dinner Theatre

This three-skit series was used to promote a St. Valentine's Day youth group dinner theater. You can adapt it to fit your own February special occasion. (Contributed by Doug Mathers, Rochester, Minn.)

Student Ministries Present

The Calvary Dinner Theatre

6:45-9:30 on the evenings of
February 14 and 16
Tickets: $9.50 per person

Please join us for an evening of culinary delight and theatrical merriment. An impeccable evening to venerate your Valentine sentiments.

Le Menu

Poulet grillé
Riz mélange
(sauvage et domestique)
Haricots verts aux champignons
Cerises suprême
Lait
Café

For reservations: Please call 282-4612, or put a check in the offering plate (please note the event in the memo for the convenience of our ushers).

Dress Code: Please dress as ostentatiously and gaudily as possible. Put on those ties, prom dresses, and costume jewelry. Sequins are encouraged.

Ticket Reservations

Name of party: ____________________

Number in party: ____________________

Date of reservations: ____________________

Phone number: ____________________

All proceeds will be used to support our summer mission trip to the Dominican Republic.

Promo Skit One

A couple who not only talk loudly but also dress loudly, Mr. and Mrs. Loud are each dressed in clashing polyester clothing. Mr. Loud's hair is slicked down, and Mrs. Loud wears a flowered hat and cat-eye glasses. They remind you of how the Beverly Hillbillies might dress for a fancy occasion. Both speak in a very loud drawl. The couple enter the sanctuary late, walking down the center aisle until they get to the front. They then turn to face the congregation and continue talking very loudly to each other.

He: *(yelling)* Let's sit back here in case the preacher sprays when he preaches—I forgot my handkerchief today.

She: *(in an equally loud voice)* Iam Loud, how many times do I have to tell you that I like being up front? I want to hear the choir. If they aren't too good, maybe we'll join. I can sing in one of them purty robes. If he's a sprayer, I'il give you some Kleenex. *(pulls out her Kleenex and, blowing her nose loudly, fills the Kleenex—which she hands to Iam)*

He: This shur is a big fancy church. *(fumbling with the bulletin, inserts flying)* Look how much stuff is in their bulletin. I like this church. Now I'll always have paper to doodle on during the preachin'!

She: Let me see that. Wow, they even got colored paper in here! Look at this. *(reading slowly and with difficulty)* "Student ministries present"—that must be a fancy name for a youth group—"Student ministries present the Calvary Dinner Theatre, 6:45 to 9:30, February 14 and 16." That's on Valentine's Day and the Saturday after, ain't it? "Tickets, $9.50 per person."

He: I spend more than that at Baker's Square!

She: Yeah, but you eat half a pie for dessert.

He: Well, you eat the other half.

She: *(continuing to read, loudly and laboriously)* "Please join us for an evening of cul...culi...culiflower...no, that ain't it...cul-i-na-ry delight and theehatrical merriment."

He: What does that mean?

She: It means there'll be skits and stuff after the dinner. *(slowly, feeling her way through the syllables)* "An impeccable evening to venerate your Valentine sentiments."

He: They gonna venerate their Valentine sentiments right here at *church*?!

She: *(hitting him with her purse)* I'll venerate *my* Valentine sentiments!

He: Does it say what they're gonna eat?

She: *(reading)* "Le Menu, Poulet Grillé."

He: That must be the cook—Paulet Griller.

She: "Rits me-lanj, harry cots verts ox champ...champ-pig-nons."

He: What is that stuff?

She: I don't know what this hairy cots is, but I think they're gonna serve the champion pig.

He: Oh, boy!

She: "For reservations, please call 282-2612, or put a check into the offering plate."

He: They always want a check in the offering plate.

She: Honey, can we go to this-here dinner theater?

He: Why sure, Sugar Lumpkins.

She: Oh, there's even sumthin' here about what to wear. *(reading)* "Dress code: please dress as ostentashuslee and gawdlely—as possible. Put on those ties, prom dresses, and costume jewelry. Sequins are a welcome sight."

He: *(leaving with his wife)* I just hope we have something to wear. It's so hard to be ostentashus.

Promo Skit Two

Mr. and Mrs. Megabucks are richly dressed, Mr. Megabucks perhaps with a hat and cane and unlit pipe in his mouth, and Mrs. Megabucks with a sequinned purse, a fur, hat, white gloves, lots of costume jewelry. Their speech should be slow, loud, and haughty (think of Mr. and Mrs. Thurston Howell the Third from "Gilligan's Island"). Ham it up. They enter talking and walk down the center aisle until they reach the front of the sanctuary behind the microphone.

She: It's really so difficult to find a church worthy of our attendance.

He: I know exactly what you mean, my dear. Not a single BMW or Porsche in the parking lot. But there were certainly a lot of those...

He & She: *(disdainfully, in unison)*...minivans!

She: I was furthermore disappointed with the doorman. Far too friendly. I like my help to be seen, not heard. They really should purchase uniforms for those men. Those little badges they wear that say "Greeter" on them—they give me a dreadful feeling of *equality* with the doormen.

He: The absence of a valet service certainly strikes two points against us coming here.

She: Yes, it was appalling to have to *walk* in from the parking lot.

He: *(perusing the bulletin and inserts)* As I examine this newsletter, I fail to notice any mention of a men's polo club or even a racquetball club.

She: Darling, you don't play racquetball, and you're allergic to horses.

He: Not the point, my dear. The lack of these two very fine forms of entertainment only emphasizes the absence of elegance—an absence that violates our sense of refinement. Not to mention that attending this church would certainly diminish our social status.

She: There does appear to be one exception, Darling. Hand me that colored insert. *(reading)* "Student ministries present the Calvary Dinner Theatre."

He: Now, *there's* a prestigious group.

She: Yes, and it appears that they're sponsoring a truly cultural event. Listen to this..."The dinner is to be on the evenings of February 14 and 16. Tickets are only $9.50."

He: Excellent planning. We can justify the expenditure as an investment in our love.

She: How romantic! *(continues reading)* "Please join us for an evening of culinary delight and theatrical merriment."

He: By Jove, I could use some culinary delight—and I certainly enjoy the theatre. I wonder if they'll be doing Shakespeare?

She: Oh, wouldn't that be grand? "An impeccable evening to venerate your Valentine sentiments."

He: The very words I was thinking, my dear.

She: Oh, the food sounds absolutely divine.

He: Read the menu, my dear.

She: I can't. It's in French.

He: In French! Simply elegant!

She: And look, they've even put in a dress code for the commoners.

He: Very open minded of that Student Ministries group. I find myself actually eager to mix some with the lower classes.

She: This church may keep us from the horrible arrogance that is *sooo* prevalent in our world today.

He: Thank God we're not snobs, my dear. *(both exit)*

Promo Skit Three

Iam Lonely, an unsuccessful dating specialist, is a nerd and looks it, complete with taped glasses, white shirt (half untucked), mussed hair, a plethora of pens in his pockets, flood pants, etc. The leader or a student introduces Iam with words to this effect: "This morning we have a special announcement from dating specialist Iam Lonely."

Iam: *(awkwardly, nervously approaches the microphone, stumbling as he reaches it and almost knocking it over)* One, two, three...testing...one, two three...is this thing working? It is? Oh, good...My name is Iam Lonely, the world's foremost authority on first dates. I have had more first dates than anyone on earth. Unfortunately, I haven't had any second dates yet.

Many of you think going to a movie is a good first date. Incorrect. First of all, the popcorn is far too expensive. Secondly, your date may compare you with the actors on the screen and drop you like a hot potato. *(defensively)* Now don't think that this has ever happened to me, *personally,* but, uh, it *has* happened to some of my closest friends.

Others prefer to go bowling on their first date. The bowling alley, however, is not a good place to strike the match of love either. Reason number one: you may embarrass yourself with a low score. (This has not been my problem; I have a 68-pin average.) Reason number two: your date may be embarrassed. I believe this to be the case with many of my dates. For some reason, they never want to be seen in public. I've concluded this is because of their poor bowling skills. Reason number three: your thumb may become lodged in the ball and you may find yourself sliding down the alley right into the pins. This sporting moment is not a pleasant one; although when this very event transpired on a recent first date, me and my ball scored a strike. Nevertheless, I contend that those who go bowling for a first date are headed straight for the gutter.

"So," you ask, "what is a good first date?" I'm glad you asked. Please locate the pink insert in your bulletin. It gives you the details of not only the best first date, but (speaking to those who have already articulated your nuptial vows) the best evening to rekindle the romance in your marriages.

Please read this carefully with me.

"Student ministries present the Calvary Dinner Theater." A dinner theater is an appropriate dating environment. It provides one with ample opportunity for conversation, as well as entertaining diversions for those times when one lacks subject matter for discussion.

"6:45 p.m. to 9:30 p.m., February 14 and 16." That is this Thursday and Saturday. Another reason to commend the dinner theater for your first date is that I have found that it's always a good idea to have a second alternative to your initial request. By the time your potential date thinks of an excuse not to go with you on Thursday, you can spring *Saturday* on her. Because it is difficult to think of *two* legitimate excuses within 30 seconds, you'll probably snag your potential date for one of those evenings.

"Tickets are $9.50 per person." This is a genuine bargain. A movie and McDonalds (a terrible first date, by the way), approaches $10 per person, if you go dutch (which I recommend for first dates. No sense investing in a possibly dead-end relationship). The dinner theatre price of $9.50 per ticket is far less than I had to pay for repair of the bowling-alley lane.

I trust you will read on in this insert about the food and entertainment yourself.

Note especially the bottom of the insert, which explains how to make reservations: *"For reservations please call 828-4261."* That's the church number. And when you call, a very pleasant secretary will ask you for the information that you see on the bottom of your insert. Please do not ask the secretary out. She is married (an startling fact, in view of her ignoring my first-date advice).

Another method of registering is to simply fill out the form you are now looking at and turn it in to the office, or place it in the offering plate.

Finally, I would like to say a word about blind dates. I have found that blind dates are one of the most effective ways to get a date. I myself am nearsighted, an impairment that helps conversation inestimably. Just be careful not to step on your date's cat.

That's all the advice for today. Make your reservations soon, and happy dating.

A Head for the Summer Calendar

One youth group put their heads together about how to publicize their summer program—and decided that their heads were the very place for it! Call the same screen printers that print T-shirts and ask if they also print on painters caps. (Most will. If no one locally does, call American Mills in Minneapolis for prices and a catalogue—800/876-4287.)

After you get a reasonable quote, use a laser printer to print out your

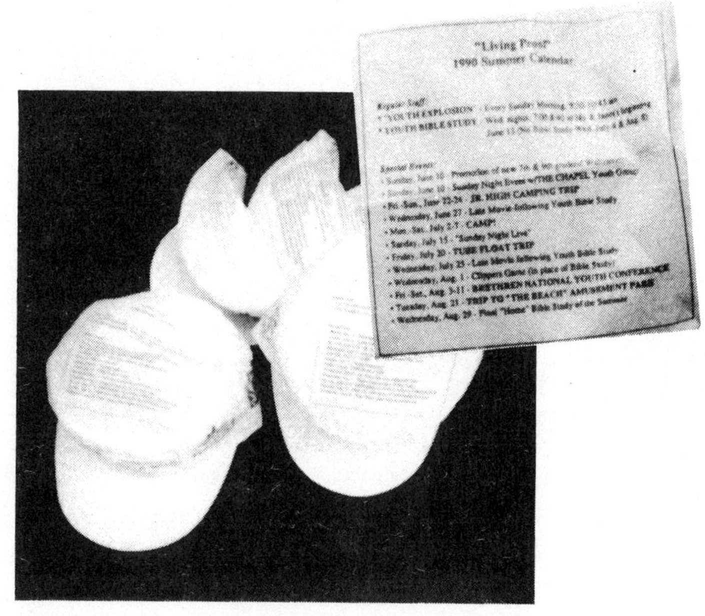

summer schedule, then take the printout—plus your youth group's logo and some clip art—to the screen printer. The painters caps imprinted with your group's logo and summer schedule make great publicity—and kids love wearing them during the summer, too. (Contributed by Jay Firebaugh, Blacklick, Ohio)

How to Evade a Date

Announce your next youth event with the skit on page 179. Irwin the nerd calls Susan for a date. He is nervous and awkward during the conversation, but he's determined to get a date. Susan, desperate for reasons to refuse, uses the youth group calendar for convenient excuses—each excuse, of course, being an announcement of an actual upcoming event for your group. Just replace Susan's excuses with your own group's upcoming events. As usual, hamming it up adds to the fun. (Contributed by Doug Mathers, Rochester, Minn.)

Photo Endorsements

Do you routinely photograph your students at various get-togethers? If you don't, start the habit now. When you have something of an inventory of photos, use them for publicity purposes this way: When you need to publicize an event, select and mount some pictures of teens in your group.

Next, think up entertaining and informative dialogue about the upcoming events to place inside comic strip-type dialogue bubbles attributed to the teens in the photos. Make them fun without embarrassing anyone. If you feel the photos might be torn down, mount them inside a large glass poster frame.

Your kids will watch for these from week to week. (Contributed by Bill Swedberg, Renton, Wash.)

Smile Postcards

One way to make the mirror-image announcement cards on page 180 is to type the message normally, make an overhead transparency of it, then lay the transparency in the photocopier so that it copies the message in reverse. Get your kids to color the lips bright red, and mail off the cards! (Contributed by Rick Jenkins, Cleveland, Tenn.)

Spiral Calendar

The shape isn't the only curiosity about this monthly or quarterly activity calendar. Take a closer look at it (see page 181): between the events are whimsical one-liners that mention the names of the kids in your group.

As you can see from the diagram, start with 15 or so concentric circles; when you fill the outermost circle with words, erase a segment of the

How to Evade a Date

Cast: Narrator, Irwin, Susan

Scene: *Irwin, stage left, is dressed in the latest nerd look. Susan, chewing gum and wearing a cheerleading outfit, stands with her back to the audience at stage right.*

Narrator: February has begun, and within this auspicious month lurks a holiday that puts us all in the mood for love. Yes, I'm talking about President's Day—I mean St. Valentine's Day. While we all enjoy the thought of romance, you probably don't go out with just anyone who calls. As a service to those of you who must plot ways of getting out of a date, we now present to you a brief educational drama called "How to Evade a Date."

Irwin: ***(nervously rubbing his palms together as he works up courage to make a phone call)*** Eight-three-one-four-five-seven-eight. One ring, two ri—Hello? This is Irwin. Do you want to go out with me this Friday night? Oh...sorry, Mr. Vanity...uh, is Irwin there? I mean, is Miss Susan Vanity there?...Yes sir, I'll hold.

Susan: ***(enters calling over her shoulder in a sickeningly sweet voice)*** Okay, Daddy. I'll get it on my own phone. ***(picks up receiver)*** Hello?

Irwin: Hello. Is this Susan Vanity?

Susan: Yes.

Irwin: Hi, Susan. This is Irwin Testube. I'm in your biology class.

Susan: ***(obviously not recognizing who Irwin is)*** Yes?

Irwin: I sit right in front of you...***(awkward pause)***...you copy my answers during tests.

Susan: ***(nervously clearing her throat)*** Yes, I know who you are now.

Irwin: Well, I was wondering, Susan, if you'd like to go to a movie with me this Friday night? *Return of the Nerds* is showing at Cinemax for only a dollar.

Susan: Oh, I'd love to, Irwin, but I have to...to...***(looks frantically around her room, sees the trash can, reaches in and pulls out a crumpled youth group calendar)***...I have to go to a junior high progressive dinner with my church. It starts at six and goes until almost midnight. But it would have really been fun. Sorry, but—

Irwin: But you're in senior high.

Susan: I know, Irwin, but I promised to...uh...help with the dishes.

Irwin: How about joining me on Saturday, February 24? There's a really swell exhibit at the science museum on the reproductive rituals of African elephants.

Susan: Well, that does sound interesting, but I...***(still flipping through calendar)***...I'll be gone that whole weekend on a retreat up in northern Minnesota with my senior high youth group—you know, skiing, horseback riding, playing broomball, cheering the snow-football players.

Irwin: Well, what about Wednesday, the 14th? I hear there's an Elvis look-alike contest at the mall.

Susan: Sorry. Gotta go to church and make sure I pay my deposit for the retreat by that night. And every Wednesday I have youth group.

Irwin: How about Tuesday?

Susan: Uh, Tuesdays...no, I use Tuesdays to wash my hair so I look my best for youth group.

Irwin: Sunday night?

Susan: No good. Small groups at—

Susan and **Irwin:** ***(in unison)*** church.

Irwin: How does March look?

Susan: Well, I don't have that calendar yet, but I know that there is a junior high retreat I'll need to pray for and a senior high progressive dinner on the seventeenth. Boy, I'm afraid I'm pretty booked up.

Irwin: You know, all that stuff is beginning to sound fun. Maybe I can come with you for some of them...?

Susan: Sorry, Irwin, I've got to go...I hear your mother calling. 'Bye, and thanks for calling. ***(hangs up)***

Irwin: ***(looking at phone)*** Boy, is she ever religious. And I wonder why my mother was calling her?

THE END ***(massive applause)***

Youth Ministry
First Baptist Church
340 Church Street, N.E.
Clovington, MO 37311

This card is guaranteed to
put a smile on your face!

NON-PROFIT ORG.
U. S. POSTAGE
PAID
PERMIT No.276
CLOV. MO.

**Important things that you need to
know to keep you smiling . . .**

"Do You Know the Way?"

- **Sunday Morning Bible Study at 9:35—"Do You Know the Way?"**
- **Big Huddle—Wed. at 7:30 a.m.**
- **Prime Time—Wed. at 6:30 in the Youth Building**
- **School Spirit/FCA Breakfast—Sun. Oct. 22**
- **Grow For It—Sat. Oct. 28. Cost: $12**

To read this very important message, you need to—
1. Stand in front of a mirror.
2. For best effect, place this card under your nose.
3. Read it!

circle in order to form a "door" to the next circle; etc. The effect is dizzying, yet kids will read it to the end if for no other reason than to catch all the quips and see if **their** names are mentioned. And with some clever scissor work, kids can make unique mobiles to hang in their rooms. (Contributed by Marty Young, Atascadero, Calif.)

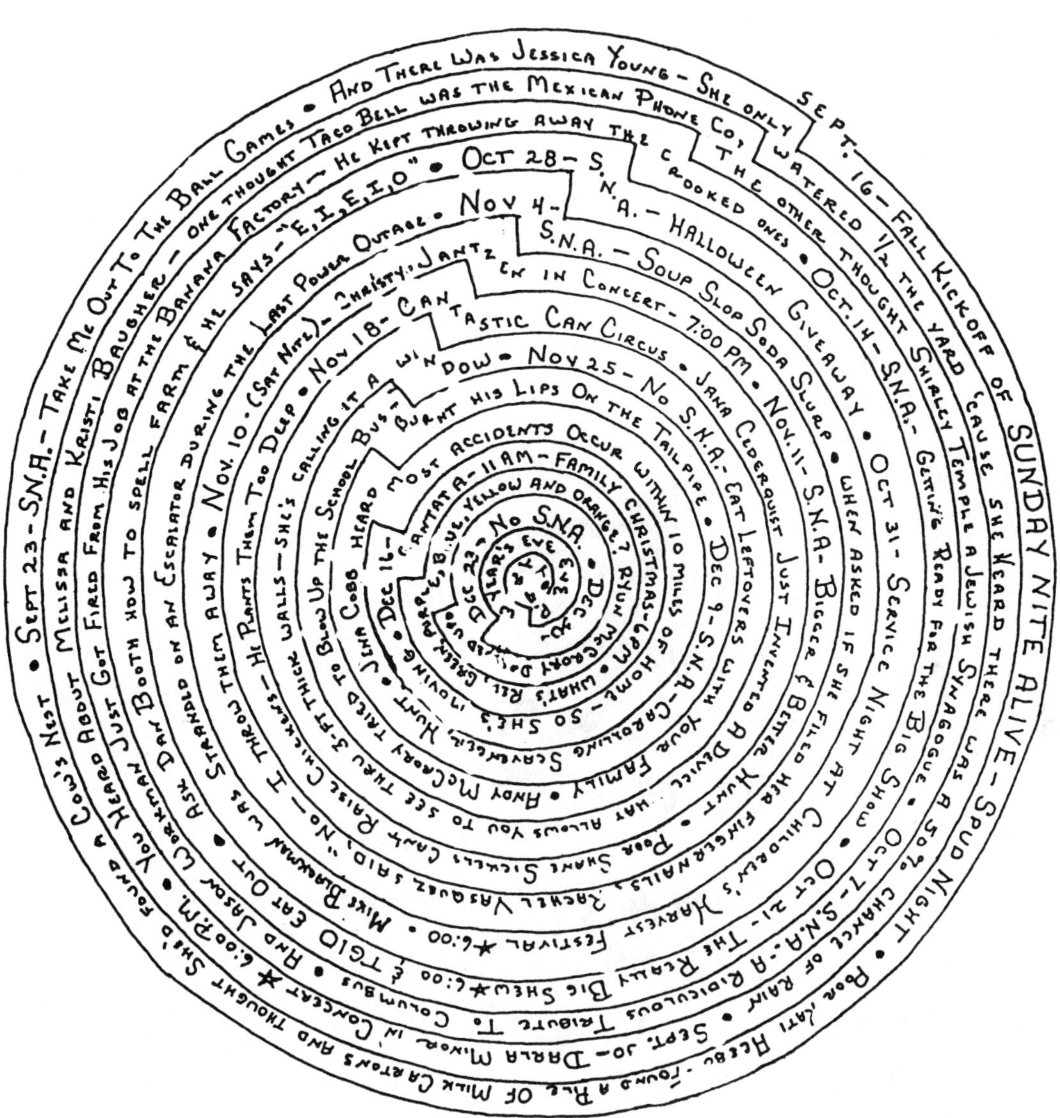

Sponsor Sweepstakes

In a day of ten-million-dollar sweepstakes, methods of recruiting sponsors for retreats, camps, and lock-ins may need an update. (Contributed by Tom Daniel, Starkville, Miss.)

Congratulations
You may be a winner!!

You have been chosen to be a possible winner in the First Baptist Youth Ministry

DiscipleNow Weekend
Host home contest

To determine if you'd like to be a winner, simply call (toll free) Tom Daniel at the church office (212-3635).

Prizes for the lucky Grand Prize Winners include:

- **Two luxurious nights** with young people from our church!
- **Cash** for any meal purchases!
- **Excellent cuisine** prepared and provided by youth parents and youth workers!
- **Quality leadership** from New Orleans Baptist Theological Seminary and Mississippi State University!

Call Today!!
No purchase necessary
Void in all states except Mississippi

We need your help! If you are interested in serving as a host home for our Youth DiscipleNow Weekend March 1-3, or if you have any questions about DiscipleNow, give Tom a call.

Tabletop Publicity Boards

Short of bulletin-board space? No bulletin boards period? Lean one or two six- or eight-foot folding tables up against the wall. You can tape announcements or whatever to the tabletops (avoiding the damage that tape does to most walls) and add streamers, balloons, etc., to a creatively arranged couple or three tables. And with a little muscle power, these publicity boards are even portable. (Contributed by Russ Porter, Rosenberg, Tex.)

Titanic Advertising

Want to make a quality banner or huge poster but feel you can't draw? Using clip art, rub-on letters, and other graphic helps, create your poster on unlined, white notebook-sized paper. Then use a photocopier to transfer your creation to an overhead transparency.

Place the sheet on an overhead projector and focus the image onto butcher or table-top paper taped to a large wall. Outline the images using black water paint and a medium-sized brush that allows you to keep detail. When the outline is complete, turn off the projector and fill in the giant letters and figures with water paints of whatever colors suit your design. The process works as well for creating theatrical backdrops. (Contributed by Len Cuthbert, Hamilton, Ont., Canada)

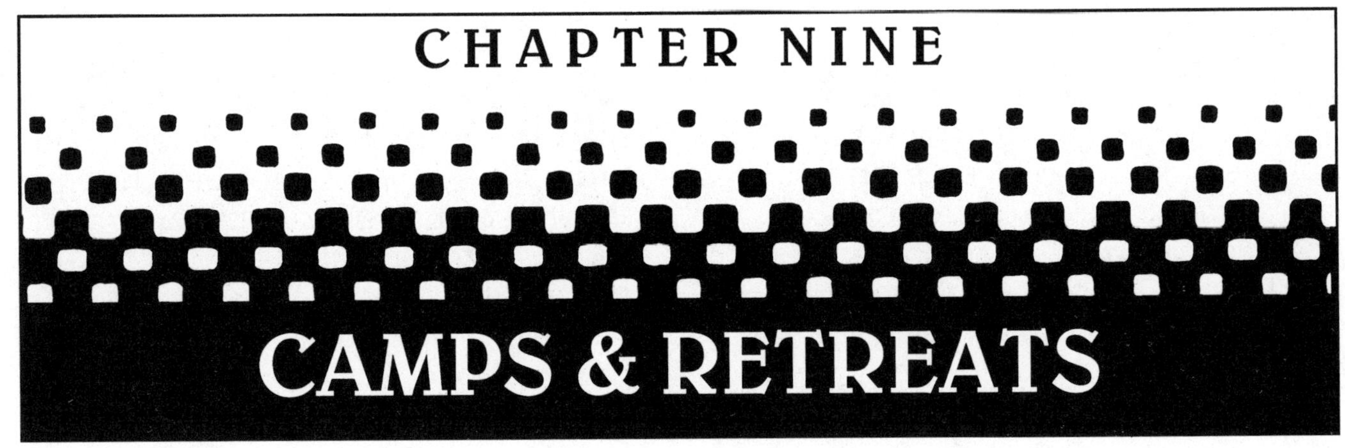

Convict Community

Kids learn the definition of teamwork in a hurry with this exercise in togetherness. At your next retreat pair up kids by "handcuffing" them together with two-foot lengths of soft poly rope. Tie a bowline knot at each end. Members of each pair place one of their hands into the knot to become secured to their partners (a bowline knot neither slips off nor restricts circulation). As kids play games, eat meals, attend meetings, and go through their daily routines, ask them to consider their experience a parable about living one's life with others in mind.

Before the kids are tied together, explain safety precautions—move more slowly than normal, give advance warning about changes of direction, don't yank at each other, always be aware of your partner. Set ground rules about bathroom breaks and privacy. Stress safety over and over whenever the groups meets together. (Contributed by Pat McGlone, Savannah, Ga.)

Interest-Earning Sign-ups

With a little advance planning you can cut student costs for retreats, while at the same time making it easier for you to spend more money on improving events.

About 6 to 12 months before a retreat, request registration payments from your students. At that time offer registrants a monthly payment plan that concludes the month **prior** to the retreat. It's easier for the kids to come up with small amounts at intervals—plus it builds anticipation for the retreat.

As soon as you receive advance registration, invest the money to receive interest to be used to cover the cost of the retreat (or other events). For example, if you charge $100 per student for a retreat and you expect 15 youths to attend, you could expect the following return:

- $20 down multiplied by 15 students equals $300.
- $10 per student in monthly payments for eight months equals $1200.
- Deposited in a savings account that calculates monthly at 5%, the investment would produce an extra $28.
- The return increases with more money down, longer-term savings, more frequent payments, a higher interest rate, and a larger group.

Do one better—show your students the numbers and let them designate the resulting interest money to world relief or missions. (Contributed by Len Cuthbert, Hamilton, Ontario, Canada)

Winding Down at Night

Settling down a cabin full of junior highers for the night doesn't have to stump you any more. It's a fact that listening to stories actually decreases the heart and respiration rates in people, allowing them to relax.

So make the traditional cabin bedtime story do double time for your campers: tell stories from your own life. Since part of the camping experience is the melding together of the campers' lives with their counselor, retelling humorous personal anecdotes about yourself lets kids know who you are and what you are about. With a little bit of advance planning, you can make an easy transition to the more serious side of your life and finally drift off to sleep after praying together. (Contributed by Kevin Turner, Tacoma, Wash.)

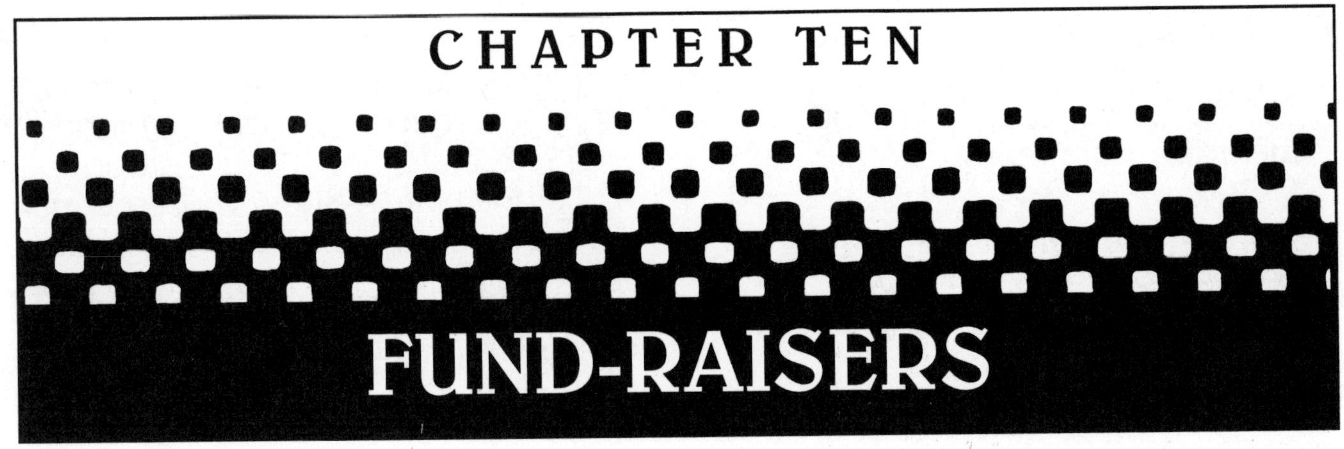

Bagel Breakfast Fund-Raising

Preparing and delivering pre-sold bagel breakfasts requires some legwork, but the fun and profit to your youth group make it worthwhile.

Choose a Sunday for delivering the breakfasts. Well ahead of the event, get the kids together to plan a breakfast menu. An easy meal could include one quart of milk, one quart of orange juice, four croissants and four bagels, and a copy of the Sunday paper of your choice. (Try asking the supervisor of a paper boy in your group for free copies for the day of your event.) Together create a logo expressing the purpose of the fund-raiser to be duplicated and glued on the grocery sacks that will be filled with the breakfast being delivered. Plan the promotion for the fund-raiser. Schedule announcement dates and opportunities to sell the breakfast to members of the congregation, as well as to friends and neighbors.

Set a cost for the meal—the cost for the above meal, for example, could be $15. Assign to several kids and a sponsor the task of approaching local grocery stores to request a price break on the purchase of the milk and juice and to seek out a bakery that might do the same for the breads. When merchants discover you are attempting to raise money for specific needs of neighborhood youths (i.e., your youth group), they are often willing to help. The profit margin can be as high as 100% to 200%. Finally, make a plan for distribution of the breakfasts on the proposed Sunday.

On the Saturday before you plan to deliver the breakfasts, meet with the kids to purchase or pick up the needed products, to decorate the delivery bags with the logo, and to assign delivery teams for the next day. On that Sunday after church, the kids can distribute as many of the breakfasts as possible to members of the congregation who have come to the service and deliver the remainder to the homes in the afternoon. A group of three to five kids will make delivery to a defined geographical area both fun and efficient.

The event may be worth repeating annually, in which case the legwork becomes less as people know what to expect and have already helped you in the past. (Contributed by Bradley Bergfalk, Bedford, N.H.)

Buck-a-Roo Club

To raise money for an upcoming camp, retreat, or other activity, sign up members of the congregation to join the Buck-a-Roo Club. Members donate $1 for each youth participating in a given event. For example, if 15 young people are going to the youth convention, each Buck-a-Roo Clubber would donate $15. It's simple and relatively inexpensive for each donor.

Adjust the rules if your youth group is large. If 70 kids sign up for a retreat, for example, Buck-a-Roo Clubbers can together pool $70. Be sure to acknowledge the givers with Buck-a-Roo Club Membership Cards. (Contributed by Sean Smith, Alta Loma, Calif.)

Ironman Contest

Select some willing church board and staff members (male variety) or dads to compete in this hilarious fund-raiser. The contestants—armed with their own iron, ironing board, and shirts—will iron as many shirts as possible in a given amount of time. Each shirt is judged for quality and detail while people in the audience pledge money to any or all of the Ironmen for each shirt completed. A trophy is presented to the best overall Ironman (though all contestants receive certificates—see page 189). Collect people's pledge money at a designated table before the event ends.

Promotion

A few weeks before the contest, perform a skit for the congregation, playing off the idea of the Ironman Triathlon (see Ironman Promotional Dialogue on page 189). Another Sunday invite to the front one of the contestants who's claiming to be the shoo-in winner and have him show off a shirt he has been "practicing" on. It should be burned clear through in places and scorched in others. Line up several of the best cooks to make their favorite dessert bar to bring the night of the contest. The youth group can provide drinks for everyone.

The Trophy

Make an Ironman trophy. At any trophy shop purchase a marble base ($3–$6) with an undated brass plate engraved with the words "Ironman Champion." Then find an old travel iron at a thrift shop, spray it with gold paint, and mount it on the base. You can circulate the trophy in subsequent Ironman fund-raisers.

The Pledges

You can receive pledges the night of the contest, which saves time and requires less planning. Or you can display pictures of the contestants in a high-traffic area of your church and let your youths collect pledges like other "a-thons" for any or all of the Ironmen (see Ironman Pledge Sheet on page 190).

The Big Day

Set up the contest like a TV game show. Ask someone to keep a hilarious running commentary on the contestants during the action. Use a portable scoreboard clock or videotape a scoreboard/swimming clock and play the tape to show the time elapsed. Play some fast-paced game show music to intensify the contest. Contestants' wives can act as personal trainers and coaches. Give them water bottles and sweat rags and let them play their part to the hilt.

Judging

Make copies of the Ironman Contest Judging Form on page 191 for judges to use in determining the winner of the contest. Check for things like creases on the sleeves, wrinkles in the collar, smooth around the buttons, pleated in the back, overall crispness of the shirt, whether an apron was worn, whether the wife helped. Each area is rated from 1 to 10.

The Conspiracy

Midway through the contest, draw the audience's attention to the fact that the trophy is missing and accuse one of the contestants of stealing the trophy and selling it. Then, on a TV in the room, play a hidden-camera video (like FBI footage) of two unidentified people in a motel room exchanging the trophy for a large sum of money.

Presentation is everything for the Ironman Contest to be successful. Make it fun for the audience as well for as the contestants. Have plenty of pledge sheets on hand so that everyone present can get in on the fun. (Contributed by Martin Barker, Bradenton, Fla.)

Ironman Promotional Dialogue

Perform this promotional skit to your congregation a week or two before the Ironman Contest. Equip someone with a ridiculous amount of athletic gear—bike, biker's helmet, running shoes, Lycra tights, stopwatch, etc. Throw in a snorkel, mask, and backpack.

PERSON *is already in the auditorium.* **IRONMAN** *enters.*

PERSON: *(as if Ironman is interrupting)* Excuse me!

IRONMAN: Huh?

PERSON: Who are you?

IRONMAN: Biff.

PERSON: What are you doing, Biff?

IRONMAN: Radical mind twister, dude. I'm training.

PERSON: Training for what?

IRONMAN: The greatest test of man's endurance, agility, and strength.

PERSON: And what might that be?

IRONMAN: The Ironman Contest, man. See my equipment?

PERSON: Yeah...that's, uh, impressive...but isn't the Ironman Triathlon in Hawaii?

IRONMAN: No, man. I just saw posters up everywhere saying there's gonna be an Ironman Contest here.

PERSON: Well, yes. We are having an Ironman Contest, but it's not the same kind of Ironman Contest.

IRONMAN: Huh?

PERSON: Want to see the trophy? ***(holds up trophy of an iron—as in "ironing board")***

IRONMAN: Dude! That's an iron!

PERSON: Very perceptive! Our Ironman Contest will decide which of our Ironmen from our church board are the best at "pressing" toward their goal of being the best at handling an iron. It's to help raise money for the youth department here at ***(name of your church)***.

IRONMAN: Totally excellent! But what about food? I'm not coming unless there's food.

PERSON: We'll have some of the best desserts that you'll find anywhere. It all happens here ***(date and time)***, so don't miss it.

IRONMAN CONTEST

This is to certify that

____

participated in the

19__ IRONMAN Contest

and has received the

____

award on this

______ day of ________________, 19__

IRONMAN PLEDGE SHEET

Name ____

Address ____

City ____

Zip ______________ Phone (____) ________________

Please fill out your pledge by indicating which Ironman you would like to pledge towards.

1) Write in the amount you want to pledge per shirt.
2) When the contest is finished, calculate what the total is for each Ironman.
3) Add up your total for all pledges taken.
4) When you have completed your form, take it to the designated table where you can arrange for payment.
5) The stub at the bottom of this form can be used as a receipt.

Ironmen	Pledges per shirt	Total pledged
____________________	\$_____ per shirt (x ____ shirts)	= \$___________
____________________	\$_____ per shirt (x ____ shirts)	= \$___________
____________________	\$_____ per shirt (x ____ shirts)	= \$___________
____________________	\$_____ per shirt (x ____ shirts)	= \$___________
____________________	\$_____ per shirt (x ____ shirts)	= \$___________
____________________	\$_____ per shirt (x ____ shirts)	= \$___________

GRAND TOTAL \$___________

Thank you for your continuing support for the youth department.

IRONMAN CONTEST

____

(date)

Thank you for your support! Total \$________

Ironman Contest Judging Form

for ______________________________
(contestant's name)

Rate each category on a scale from 1-10

___	Completed shirt	10 points
___	Wore apron	10 points
___	Creases on sleeves	10 points
___	Collar	10 points
___	Button front	10 points
___	Overall crispness of shirt	10 points
___	No help from wife	10 points

__________ total

Ironman Contest Judging Form

for ______________________________
(contestant's name)

Rate each category on a scale from 1-10

___	Completed shirt	10 points
___	Wore apron	10 points
___	Creases on sleeves	10 points
___	Collar	10 points
___	Button front	10 points
___	Overall crispness of shirt	10 points
___	No help from wife	10 points

__________ total

Spud Night Fund-Raiser

A lavish baked-potato bar makes a great fund-raiser. Request a per-person donation, or charge a certain amount per potato. Invite the entire church to come.

The following skit works great for publicity. Perform it during announcements in the worship service or another appropriate time when the congregation is assembled. (Contributed by Don Orange, Chino, Calif.)

SPUD NITE FUND-RAISER COMMERCIAL

CHARACTERS

Youth group sponsor, Youth group student

SPONSOR: Say, *(name of youth group member)*, I heard about your cool fund-raiser called Spud Nite. When is it?

STUDENT: *(with no enthusiasm)* Oh, it's *(date)* on *(day of the week)* night, from *(beginning time)* to *(ending time)* at *(location)*.

SPONSOR: You sure don't sound very excited about it. What's the problem?

STUDENT: Well, you know we've put up with lots of our youth worker's crazy ideas, but this one is the worst. "Spud Nite." That sounds like something they do in Idaho. I don't think many *(the term for citizens of your state)* are going to come to something called "Spud Nite."

SPONSOR: What?! Nobody come to Spud Nite? These just aren't your ordinary potatoes, bud. These baked beauties will be covered with your choice of delicious toppings—nacho cheese, cheddar cheese, chili, salsa, ham, broccoli, mushrooms, sour cream, butter, bacon, hamburger, onions. These are no common tators, I can guarantee that. Trust me—this spud's for you. Besides, a lot of people in this church love potatoes. Why, they grew up with potatoes at every meal. In fact, most of these people are part potato.

STUDENT: What do you mean they're part potato?

SPONSOR: Well, when I look over this crowd, I see all sorts of potatoes.

STUDENT: Like where?

SPONSOR: Look at the guy back there. See him? His name is DICK TATOR. He'll **command** his wife to take a night off and go to Spud Nite.

STUDENT: Really?

SPONSOR: Yeah. And look over there. That guy's name is COMMON TATOR. He's always got something to explain to you. He'll be there because he'll want something to talk about next Sunday morning after church.

STUDENT: Okay, I think I see a tator out there.

SPONSOR: Good! You're catching on quick. Where's your tator?

STUDENT: Right...there. She's HESI TATOR. She's not sure she wants to come. What did you say would be on those potatoes at Spud Nite?

SPONSOR: *(loudly)* I said, "These baked beauties will be covered with your choice of delicious toppings—nacho cheese, cheddar cheese, chili, salsa, ham, broccoli, mushrooms, sour cream, butter, bacon, hambur—"

STUDENT: Not so loud!

SPONSOR: Why not?

STUDENT: You'll wake up MEDI TATOR here in the front row.

SPONSOR: Sorry.

STUDENT: You know, *(name of sponsor)*, the more I think about Spud Nite and the more I look at this great group of people here, the more I really think we **will** have a great turnout.

TOGETHER: *(to the audience)* Come out and support the *(youth group name)* fund-raiser next week. Don't crash in front of the TV and veg out. Don't sit out in the parking lot, like SPEC TATOR there. Instead, be like IMMY TATOR and follow everyone else to the *(place, date, time)* for a night your taste spuds will never forget!